THE VANISHED ARMY

TIM CAREW

THE
VANISHED
ARMY

WILLIAM KIMBER
46 WILTON PLACE, LONDON S.W.1

Published by
WILLIAM KIMBER AND CO. LIMITED
46 Wilton Place, London, S.W.1

First impression July 1964
Second impression August 1964

MADE AND PRINTED IN GREAT BRITAIN BY PURNELL AND SONS, LTD.
PAULTON (SOMERSET) AND LONDON

They shall grow not old, as we that are left grow old;
Age shall not weary them, nor the years condemn.
At the going down of the sun, and in the morning,
We will remember them.

From *For The Fallen* by LAURENCE BINYON.

DEDICATION

To my old friend, Major A. N. S. Roberts, O.B.E.,
late of the 2nd Battalion the Queen's Royal Regiment, who was there, so he'll know.

INTRODUCTION

This is the story of the Old Contemptibles, the men of the British Expeditionary Force who fought in France and Belgium from August 1914 up to the end of that year; the story of the old 'Regular Army'.

It is possible that surviving members of the territorials—the London Scottish, the Queen's Westminsters, the Hertfords and all those magnificent regiments of yeomanry—may feel that this story has failed to do justice to their fine achievements during the fighting in 1914. The Indian Corps, too, may rightly feel that they have been left out. These two omissions, grave as they may seem, are intentional.

They—the British territorials and the Indians—are given little space in this book, not because they don't deserve it, but because this is essentially the story of Britain's minute standing regular army, the 'shilling a day' men—who were sent to France to fight the Germans.

These are the Old Contemptibles—the most exclusive people in Britain today. No one else, in this year of 1964, must be allowed to edge them out of the limelight.

*   *   *   *   *

A medal, in the grey words of the *Pocket Oxford Dictionary*, is a 'coin-like metal disc with device etc. made in commemoration of an occasion and given to those associated with it by presence, service, special distinction etc.'. To the millions of holders of decorations and assorted campaign stars it seems to be as good a description as any.

Immediately after a war or campaign they seemed enormously important; they were assiduously polished and furtively admired in private. But as the memory of the battles receded they shrank in significance; the ribbons became faded and frayed; the 'coin-like metal disc' tarnished. They now lie, if they can be found at all, with the pipe cleaners, knitting needles, unpaid bills, income tax demands and dog-eared photographs. Occasionally they are taken out for an airing. On Armistice Sunday old and middle-aged men of extraordinarily unwarlike appearance march to church in a blaze of colour, making a loud tinkling noise.

vii

Introduction

Not a great deal of ribbon was handed out in the war of 1914–18. In this holocaust of death only three medals were issued: the 1914 Star; the General Service Medal; and the Victory Medal—known colloquially as *Pip, Squeak* and *Wilfred*—or, in the case of the last two awarded to the later arrivals to the slaughter, *Mutt* and *Jeff*. They are not seen often on uniforms in 1964—a few of the more vintage commissionaires, some veteran hall porters, bank messengers and allied trades.

A sharp eye will discern on the red, white and blue watered ribbon of the 1914 Star a small silver rosette. This is the Mons Star for service in France between 5th August, 1914 and 22nd November, 1914. They are old now, the men with the Silver Rosette—the 'Old Contemptibles'—and each passing year sees a new thinning in their ranks. The survivors are short of sight and hard of hearing; a trifle rheumy; somewhat stiff in the joints. Their hair, what little remains of it, is white, as are their carefully trimmed moustaches. They talk little of those three months which changed the course of history; they are more concerned with the paucity of old-age pensions measured against the cost of living in an age which is sometimes a little hard to understand.

This is the story—the long and true story—of a battle and the men who fought it; the septuagenarians, the octogenarians and even the nonagenarians who wear the Silver Rosette.

TIM CAREW

Binfield, Berkshire.
April, 1964.

ACKNOWLEDGEMENTS

To MAKE acknowledgements to everyone who has helped me in the writing of this book would require a volume similar in size and content to a Classified Army List. I can therefore only do my best to include all those who generously gave me the benefit of their experiences.

Firstly, the officers: with a few exceptions they were subalterns in 1914, and it is the subaltern who sees most of the game in war because he has no choice in the matter. All of the names listed here experienced the fighting during the first three months of the Great War: some of them were both wounded and decorated; some were wounded but not decorated, and some were decorated but not wounded. A few, but only a very few, were neither wounded nor decorated. It matters not, for they were all there.

The British Army has always listed everyone alphabetically, so let us stick to that time-honoured method: Brigadier E. Backhouse, C.B.E., 2nd Suffolks; Lieutenant-Colonel K. Bruce, 2nd Gordon Highlanders; Captain Sir Roger Chance, M.C., 4th Dragoon Guards; Major E. Carr, 1st Cheshires; Lieutenant-Colonel A. Chitty, D.S.O., 1st Royal West Kents; Lieutenant-Colonel R. Churchill-Longman, 1st Royal Sussex; Brigadier J. Kingstone, C.B.E., D.S.O., M.C., The Queen's Bays; Colonel H. Lloyd, D.S.O., 1st Northamptons; Lieutenant-Colonel K. Oliphant, M.C., 1st Wiltshires; Lieutenant-Colonel H. Rose, M.C., 1st Wiltshires; Major A. N. S. Roberts, O.B.E., 2nd Queens; Brigadier G. Roupell, V.C., C.B., 1st East Surreys; Colonel G. Wright, D.S.O., M.C., 1st Royal Irish Fusiliers.

I cannot thank these gentlemen enough. Many of them lent me books and diaries, which I was an unconscionable time returning. For this I apologise most humbly.

And the Other Ranks, the Rank and File, the 'squaddies'—there seems to be some doubt about their proper nomenclature these days, so I will call them soldiers—I think it is the title they would like best; Sergeant J. Bishop, M.M., 1st Warwicks; Sergeant W. Carvell, Royal Engineers; Trooper J. Christie, M.M., 9th Lancers; Trooper A. Comber, 9th Lancers; Trooper J. Crow, 9th Lancers; Sergeant R. Casely, 1st Devons; Private G. Criddle, 2nd Queens; Drummer

C. Downham, 2nd Grenadier Guards; Trooper C. Darley-Pyne, Queen's Bays; Driver W. Dobson, A.S.C.; Bombardier A. Deering, Royal Field Artillery; Private B. Ellis, A.S.C.; Sergeant T. Fish, D.C.M., 1st Bedfords; Gunner W. Fry, Royal Field Artillery; Sergeant V. Fletcher, Royal Engineers; Sergeant G. Gilkes, A.S.C.; Private A. Dugdale, 1st King's Liverpool Regiment; Private J. Haley, 1st King's Own Scottish Borderers; Trooper P. Hefferman, 5th Lancers; Sergeant G. King, D.C.M., Royal Engineers; Sergeant P. Key, Royal Garrison Artillery; Sergeant S. McCrea, Royal Irish Rifles; Private J. Masters, 1st Royal Scots Fusiliers; Bombardier H. Philpott, Royal Field Artillery; Corporal F. Rozee, 3rd Rifle Brigade; Private V. Rogers, 4th Middlesex; Private P. Smyth, 3rd Coldstream Guards; Private J. Spooner, 20th Hussars; Sergeant G. White, 1st Duke of Cornwall's Light Infantry; Sergeant G. Wills, D.C.M., M.M., Royal Engineers.

It is a long list, and it deserves to be longer. They are the salt of the earth, and I am proud to have met every one of them. I hope this story is worthy of them.

I have a special word of thanks to Brigadier P. Cuddon, C.B.E., M.C., Adjutant of the Royal Hospital, who arranged a number of interviews with those peerless old gentlemen, the Chelsea Pensioners —they deserve to live for ever and, indeed, show every sign of doing so.

I am indebted to those patient and agile ladies of the Reference Section of the War Office Library, who raced in search of unobtainable books with a cheerfulness and alacrity worthy of the men of the B.E.F. themselves. My thanks are also due to Mrs. George Bambridge, Messrs Methuen & Co. Ltd. and the Macmillan Company of Canada Ltd. for permission to quote from several of Rudyard Kipling's poems.

Finally, I would add that much of the material for this book was gleaned from the men who were there, and their average age is seventy-five. Perhaps I can excuse any inaccuracies—and in a book of this sort a certain amount must be inevitable—by quoting the title of a book written by the late Right Honourable Sir Alfred Duff Cooper, P.C., G.C.M.G., D.S.O., former Secretary of State for War and First Lord of the Admiralty, and officer of the Grenadier Guards. The title of the book is *Old Men Forget*.

CONTENTS

ILLUSTRATIONS

   *All photographs, unless otherwise stated, are reproduced by courtesy
   of the Imperial War Museum*

MAPS

PART ONE

THE CONTEMPTIBLE LITTLE ARMY

We took our chanst among the Khyber 'ills
The Boers knocked us silly at a mile
The Burmans give us Irrawaddy chills
An' a Zulu *impi* dished us up in style
But all we ever got from such as they
Was pop to what the Fuzzy made us swaller;
We 'eld our bloomin' own, the papers say
But man for man the Fuzzy knocked us 'oller. . . .

RUDYARD KIPLING in *Fuzzy-Wuzzy*

CHAPTER I

Iᴺ the eight lines of verse reproduced overleaf, Rudyard Kipling, the invariable champion of the British soldier, summarised the activities of Queen Victoria's regular army during the latter part of the nineteenth century. To the young officer studying for the Staff College it is a good enough introduction to the weightier volumes that he will later have to study; to the young private, who knows little and cares less about military history, it is as good a summing up of Army life in his great-grandfather's day as he is ever likely to read. And a bare dozen pensioners at the Royal Hospital at Chelsea—they must be aged eighty or more to remember those days —will take long pulls at their tankards and affirm that it was just like that, for no old soldier of whatever vintage has ever underestimated his enemy.

Kabul 1879, Kandahar 1880, Tel-el-Kebir 1882, Nile 1884–85, Suakim 1885, Burma 1885–87, Khartoum, Atbara, Tirah, Relief of Ladysmith, Modder River, Paardeborg—these were some of the hard-won battle honours added to regimental colours already illustrious with forgotten battles against the French.

The men who made these victories against the French possible were charitably described by the Duke of Wellington as 'scum'; 'They may not frighten the French,' observed the Iron Duke, 'but by God they frighten me.' Wellington's assessment of British soldiers did not appreciably change in the ensuing years, although after 1870 it began to dawn on the generals that soldiers were human beings who were capable of thought—though they got little enough opportunity to think. In 1881 the British Army, ever slow to institute reforms, abolished flogging.

In those days, as now, a private soldier's excuse for some dereliction of duty inevitably began: 'I thought——' and the inevitable interruption from an unsympathetic N.C.O. was: 'DON'T THINK! Know what thought did? Thought shit its breeches!' And to this improbable theory, the private soldier wisely gave no answer.

The soldiers of the 'eighties and 'nineties were despatched to subdue the enemies of the Queen Empress in Burma, India, Egypt and South Africa. Clad in khaki drill uniforms and wearing helmets designed for almost any purpose except protection from the tropical sun, they were hastened on their way by cheering crowds waving patriotic union jacks.

As the trains steamed out of the sidings the populace sang 'Soldiers of the Queen' and, for the benefit of the Scottish regiments, 'Will ye no' come back again?' The troopships, asthmatic tubs with a maximum speed of twelve knots and accommodation reminiscent of cattle boats, sailed away to the vocal accompaniment of 'Auld Lang Syne'.

In exchange for these stirring and martial send-offs, Her Majesty's Government banished its soldiers to the outposts of the Empire for six years or more and forgot about them. Young men were cheap enough at a shilling a day. If it was adventure they wanted, then service in Her Majesty's Forces would provide it in plenty.

The British soldier of the period enlisted in the Regular Army for economic, alcoholic or amatory reasons, but rarely from patriotism. It is sometimes said that soldiers are born and not made, but this was not strictly true; for every man who joined because he wanted to, there were ten who joined because they could find nothing better to do. There were many, indeed, who accepted the Queen's shilling because the problem of the next square meal was becoming embarrassingly pressing. A few young romantics enlisted because they were fascinated by tales of the mystic East. Others, again, used the British Army as a refuge from determined young women with matrimonial intent. The Army demanded no references and if the recruit was physically fit he was in for seven years and liked it or lumped it.

The British Army speedily set about converting an eighteen year old youngster into a man. It fed him adequately, if austerely; it pulled out bad teeth and cut hair to a Spartan brevity; it took flesh off suety bodies and put it on skinny ones. It taught a young man pride in person and regiment. And it was a hard and merciless taskmaster to the recalcitrant or rebel: 'Never try to beat it, son,' the old soldiers counselled the recruits. 'The Army always wins in the end.'

Satisfied with its end product, the Army sent its young men overseas and the British Empire flourished; with income tax at one and sixpence in the pound, the tax-payer had a good bargain. On arrival in the East, so Kipling tells us, the young soldiers acted like babes and drank like beasts. They also won new battle honours for their regiments. They were chased and reviled in scathing terms by sergeants who, recalling with masochistic nostalgia the bad old days of the 'seventies and 'eighties, compared them variously to old whores at virgins' meetings and Egyptian washerwomen. The recruits of today, they informed their wilting charges, needed nursemaids not sergeants—'like wrecks of the bleedin' 'esperus, you are—when I says fix you don't fix; when I says *BAYNITS*! the right 'and file . . .'

They were led into action by pink-faced and expensively educated young gentlemen with clipped moustaches and voices. These young gentlemen, in their turn, were terrorized and shorn of any individuality—initiative in a young officer was frequently interpreted as insubordination in those days—by grizzled and grim-faced colonels, liverish majors, irascible captains and sadistic senior subalterns.

In the winning of these new battle honours they marched or rode incalculable distances in murderous heat on a diet of bully beef, biscuits of a toothbreaking hardness and a nauseating tinned confection universally known as 'Knock-me-down' stew.

The infantry fought with rifle and bayonet, to the call of the bugle; the cavalry, armed with sabre and lance, charged knee to knee in column of squadrons to the sweet notes of the trumpet; the gunners hurtled across deserts and up and down ravines with their artillery pieces.

Thomas Atkins marched, fought, groused and swore for a shilling a day. Accoutred with spine pad, cholera belt and long, sweaty puttees—items of equipment unheard of today—and shod in heavy-nailed ammunition boots, he formed square, bivouacked, skirmished, picqueted, went on guard, proceeded in column. He was inspected, went on fatigue and polished endlessly. He was admonished frequently; congratulated occasionally and sparingly.

Victoria Crosses and Distinguished Conduct Medals were won; gaily coloured ribbons were awarded for campaigns in India, Egypt, the Sudan, South Africa. . . .

And as he did all these things he swore roundly and continuously, prefixing every third word with the standard copulative British Army adjective. His blasphemous utterances embraced the climate, the local inhabitants, the officers, the sergeants, the generals, the staff—he had a *very* special repertoire for them—the paucity of mail and leave. And, of course, the iniquitous ingredients that went into the making of 'Knock-me-down' stew.

The British soldier speedily formed the conviction that he was an accomplished Oriental linguist and intermingled with the conventional obscenities of speech were words in bastard Hindi and Arabic.

His conversation was rarely suitable for mixed company, but on India's North West frontier in a temperature of 110° nothing was.

He thought of the home he was unlikely to see for six years—if ever again. It was probably a mean and leaking slum, but better than a tent smelling of other soldiers' feet inside and the smell of cooking fires and camel dung outside.

He thought, inevitably, of women: the recruiting sergeants had painted rosy pictures of dusky maidens who would be his for the taking:

> By the old Moulmein Pagoda, lookin' lazy at the sea,
> There's a Burma girl a-settin', and I know she thinks o' me . . .
> 'Er petticoat was yaller an' 'er little cap was green . . .'[1]

It rarely worked out like that in real life. The private soldier's romantic attachments more likely consisted of perilous liaisons with diseased women at wildly inflated rates.

He thought of beer—the powerful and heady solace of the lower classes—which cost a penny a pint in the wet canteen and twopence a pint in the pubs. Instead, they made do on gut-rotting concoctions, distilled by God knew what unmentionable processes, in the grog-shops—'drinks that 'ud eat the live steel from your butts . . .' He talked frequently of gin and beer, but when it came to slaughter (as it often did) he did his work on water—brackish and filthy liquid which brought cholera, typhoid and enteric in its foul wake.

And, of course, he sometimes died—from spear, assegai, knife, double-handed sword, Pathan and Boer bullet; enteric, cholera, rabies, heatstroke, malaria, dysentery, scrub typhus.

So did the nineteenth century soldier fight and swear and die— as he formed square to repel the suicidal charges of the fuzzy-wuzzies and dervishes; as he went on column with the Malakand Field Force; as successive attempts to relieve Mafeking failed.

Poor bloody Tommy.

Then home service came round again and it was back to Aldershot, Tidworth, Crownhill, Portsmouth and the Curragh. Back to schapska and plume, lance pennons, sabretaches and busbies and embroidered saddle-cloths for the cavalry; scarlet, blue and green for the infantry. Khaki field service kit was put in store, as if it were some shameful prison garb. 'Now,' said tight-lipped colonels and adjutants, 'we must teach the men to be soldiers again.'

Thus was the British Army at the turn of the century—after 'the last of the gentlemen's wars'.

[1] Rudyar Kipling in *Mandalay*.

CHAPTER II

I

WITH the end of the Boer War came the end of the romantic conception of war. The British Army, indeed, took the view that it was the end of war altogether and concentrated on the intricate business of 'getting back to peacetime'. War, in truth, became a dirty word.

It was back to ceremonial parades and 'sham-fights', as manoeuvres were then called; back to barracks, audit boards, stables, inventories, kit inspections, peacetime accounting, firing on the range, boxing, football, route marches, summer camp; back to doing everything by numbers to the music of the band and to the accompaniment of crashing iron-clad heels. And always discipline, today known by the homelier expression 'bull', was the keynote.

Regiments proceeded on foreign service: to India, South Africa, Egypt, Gibraltar, Mauritius, Malta, Jamaica, Ceylon, China and Malaya. A grim reminder that a soldier's life was not all beer, skittles, nursemaids and regimental hops was to be found on India's turbulent North West Frontier, where Afridis and Mahsuds had no intention of 'getting back to peacetime' and placed every obstacle in the way of the British Army's doing so. Even in the spacious year of 1908 there was the ever present threat of a sniper's bullet or a gory hand-to-hand struggle in the interests of British prestige. On the North West Frontier a twenty-year-old became an old soldier overnight.

Royal Warwicks, Seaforth Highlanders, Munster Fusiliers and Northumberland Fusiliers, fighting shoulder to shoulder with Gurkhas, Sikhs, Punjabis and Bengal Lancers took part in the Mohmand Expedition and felt better men for it. It was certainly better than forming fours and pipeclaying equipment in Aldershot. The astringent atmosphere of the North West Frontier brought out all the best qualities of the British soldier: his endurance, his patience, his wry sense of humour. He learned, after a long and stultifying tour of duty on the plains that not all Indians were shiftless, idle, thieving 'wogs', but courageous fighting men like himself. And, better still, he found that on his return to England he could wear a half inch of green and black ribbon. This put the young soldier on the same footing as the veterans who sported the Egyptian medal and the South African medals.

In England, too, the civilian population were beginning, albeit grudgingly at first, to appreciate the soldiers. No longer was it 'Tommy this an' Tommy that, an' chuck him out the brute. . . .'

Reforms for the welfare of the soldier were going ahead apace, and for this much of the credit belongs to General Sir Horace Smith-Dorrien, then General Officer Commanding at Aldershot. By 1907 little trace of the bad old days remained. Food, good and plentiful, was high on the list of Smith-Dorrien's improvements. In the nineteenth century army cooks had been selected largely for their military incompetence, unsoldierlike appearance and insanitary habits. In 1907 a new army cook came into being: a man of impeccable appearance, who well knew that a speck of dirt under his fingernails would bring the direst consequences, and a man of professional culinary skill.

Few soldiers who enlisted in the early twentieth century had been extensively educated; many, indeed, had not been educated at all. But Smith-Dorrien was determined that soldiers should be taught to think.

It was sternly impressed upon the officers that soldiers were human beings and must be treated as such. Before the Boer War an officer rarely spoke to a soldier by name; indeed, he rarely spoke to one at all unless he happened to be his servant or groom. Under Smith-Dorrien's tutelage, regimental officers at all levels learned that soldiers were not work-shy riff-raff, who thought only of women and beer. Inevitably, a large proportion of the rank and file of Britain's army thought of little else; but women and beer, like cigarettes and mail from home, have always been essential adjuncts to the well-being of the British soldier, though they have also contributed on occasion to his downfall.

2

From the officer's standpoint, the pre-1914 Regular Army was, as a number of unreflective young men phrased it, the best club in the world. It called for little sustained mental effort, and physical endeavour was largely reserved for the polo field. In the days when only a small proportion of upper-class young men worked, it was regarded as an alternative to the Church. It was also generally considered that in matters of intelligence the clergy had the slight edge over the soldiers.

'Same old faces, not a single gleam of intelligence on one of them. . . .''

'He was so stupid that some of his brother officers noticed it. . . .'

'Sort of chap who sticks a telescope up your backside to see if your hat's on straight. . . .'

These were some of the verdicts passed by civilians on their Regular Army officer friends and relatives. They were cruel and unfair, but there was a certain element of truth in them.

In the days before and after the Boer War, the phrase 'officer and gentleman' meant exactly what it said; it was only during the war, when strange and heterogeneous units came out to South Africa, that it became apparent that, in the strictly pedigree sense, many of the wartime officers were certainly not gentlemen.

There were Yeomanry regiments, mounted infantry and irregular horse: the irregularities of some of these units of horse often caused the War Office as much if not more concern than did Kruger. Many of these temporary gentlemen were apparently mere adventurers, who knew little about discipline and tradition and cared a great deal less: they got drunk in Bloemfontein, chased the women in Pretoria, sang bawdy songs and rode like cowboys. Some of them—final heresy—had even served in the ranks.

The day was not so very far off when platoons would be commanded by shipping clerks, companies by stockbrokers and battalions by university dons. But if anyone had made such a prophecy in an officers' mess, he would have been considered guilty of uttering near blasphemy. In the early part of the twentieth century officers of Britain's tiny Regular Army lived in watertight social and financial compartments. At the top were then, as now, the Household Brigade: the Royal Horse Guards (the Blues), the Life Guards, Grenadiers, Coldstream, Scots and Irish (the Welsh Guards did not come into being until 1915). The Household Brigade has changed but little in the past century because, as is fiercely argued by guardsmen, there is nothing about them that needs to be changed.

The Household Brigade subjected its would-be officers to searching inquiries about their social and financial status: failure to satisfy these exacting requirements frequently resulted in social extinction in one of a score of regiments, classified contemptuously as 'The Feet'. They were never allowed to travel on public transport, carry cigarettes in a packet or refer to London as 'Town'.

The officers of the Household Brigade have always behaved in a manner which, to the outsider, seems strange. It is not done to express enthusiasm about military matters at any time; they give the impression that they are slightly sorry for anyone who is *not* an officer in the Brigade of Guards; they are parochial to a degree which may seem insufferable to the casual observer. More specifically they heap derision on the other regiments of the Brigade. Thus, in the Grenadiers the Coldstream are the last word; the Scots are the end; the Irish are beyond the pale; the Welsh are the Foreign Legion; and the Household Cavalry merely laughable. It goes without saying that the other Guards regiments dispose of the Grenadiers with the same degree of cordial malice. Other regiments, like seedy and impoverished relatives, are seldom mentioned at all. Unaccountably, officers of the Foot Guards wear their forbiddingly-peaked caps in the mess, whether drinking sherry before lunch or eating scrambled eggs for breakfast. Ask them why this is so and they will produce the unanswerable rejoinder: 'But, my dear fellow, why not?'

It is no good trying to understand them. One can call them 'debs' delights', 'chinless wonders', 'scarlet-tunicked popinjays' and all the other things that spring easily to the minds of their more rabid critics; all these appellations are a matter of supreme indifference to the officers of the Household Brigade.

They have always given and will continue to give the impression that they know little and care less for the job that they have at heart. Nevertheless, beneath this degagé façade is the simple desire to prosper in their chosen profession and a cold professional efficiency. It was precisely this same rarefied attitude which led the Commanding Officer of a Guards battalion who had been ordered to surrender to reply that the regiment had not practised such a manoeuvre in peace and was therefore unable to carry it out in war.

Today, of course, the Household Brigade are an ever-present target for a side-swipe from Labour Members of Parliament and the more bile-ridden newspapers. Sadly bereft of past achievement and tradition themselves, they take a spiteful delight in sniping at a body of men rich in both.

It was certainly difficult to imagine them at war. But students of military history and others with longer memories recall that where the fighting was most deadly in South Africa and Egypt at the turn of the century, there would be found a company of guards and many a hard-pressed commander in the field was grateful for their presence. And their smartness, even in the vilest conditions, always excited the admiration—tinged, perhaps, with envy—of other regiments.

Their uniform and kit were always that little bit neater than their neighbours; their bivouacs or camp lines were that much straighter and better ordered; their movements on parade were that much more impeccable.

And as it was on ceremonial parade, so was it in battle.

Next in the social scale were the Cavalry of the Line: the Dragoons, Hussars and Lancers. Nudging them in matters of birth and wealth were the Horse Gunners.

The cavalry were, like the Guards, a law unto themselves. They, too, condescended with elegant patronage to all other arms of the service, except the Household Brigade. Cavalry officers, too, needed considerable private means: indeed, an income of £750 per annum was on the small side for a gentleman who owned at least three horses and was expected to ride in steeplechases and play polo as a matter of course. Conversation in a cavalry officers' mess centred exclusively round the horse, although care had to be taken to avoid talking 'shop': polo and the military meeting at Sandown did not come into the conversational pitfall of 'shop'; an argument about the relative efficacy of charging with lance or sabre did.

The convention which prohibited the discussion of professional matters in officers' messes had its origin in the days of duelling. Women came into the same category. With these two subjects forbidden in the mess, it is hardly surprising that conversation in a cavalry mess was severely equine and virtually limited to polo and racing.

In the twelve years between the wars nothing happened to disturb the even tenor of life in the Dragoons, the Hussars and the Lancers. Regiments, in rotation, went to India. There the officers shot tiger, snipe, gaur, ibex, snow leopard and giel; they stuck pigs; they charged, all four squadrons in line, on manoeuvres. The sabres and lances flashed, the trumpets sounded the 'rally'; the sweating horses were groomed until their coats shone silky in the sun, while the officers sat on verandas with burra pegs and discussed the day's sport, but never manoeuvres. And on polo fields there were the white topees, the thunder of hooves, the whirling sticks, the leaping white ball between goals. There were race meetings at Lahore, Poonah and Bombay.

It was a spacious and unreflective life that these cavalrymen led on infinitesimal pay. And the subject of the paucity of that pay earned many a young officer a crushing rebuke from grizzled colonels and majors who had charged at Omdurman. 'You can't have it both ways, young man,' these colonels would grate at the complaints; 'either we're privileged people and must pay for it, or we're ordinary public servants. And if we're public servants, then the tax-payer is entitled to wonder why we don't do a damn' sight more work—and that applies to *you* too.' At which the young officer with financial grievances fell abruptly silent.

Then it was home service again: Aldershot and Tidworth; manoeuvres and reviews and tattoos; point to points and the Grand Military at Sandown Park. And, of course, polo. The possibility of war—a European War, as supposed to a 'bit of a skirmish with the savages'—was heavily discounted: it could happen, but it never would. And the cavalry would be out of date by the time it did . . .

Thus the unimaginative, limited and unreflective life of the Dragoon, Hussar or Lancer officer between the wars—it was the pattern of the *arme blanche*. If a revolutionary young man thought about aeroplanes, armoured vehicles or machine guns as an alternative to the horse, then he was well advised to keep such thoughts to himself. And how could any cavalryman bring himself to think, let alone talk of such things when it looked as if some *infantry* show or other might lift the polo cup . . .?

Stupid . . . stolid . . . narrow-minded . . . bigoted . . . unimaginative . . . reactionary—these were adjectives beloved of pacifists and intellectuals when describing the more conventional type of cavalryman of the period, and the cavalryman of the period was conventional because he had no choice in the matter.

Our greatest Englishman—Winston Churchill—experienced this mode of life in all its spacious luxury at the end of the nineteenth century. He has described a cavalry officer's day in all its casual glory: the awakening just before dawn, followed by 'a dusky figure with a clammy hand adroitly lifting one's chin and applying a gleaming razor to a lathered and defenceless throat'. By six o'clock the regiment was on parade and rode to a wide plain. There it drilled and manoeuvred for an hour and a half. Next came baths in the bungalow and then breakfast in the mess. Stables and orderly-room followed until 10.30 a.m.; then a leisurely hack back to the mess for a prolonged luncheon, followed by sybaritic oblivion in sleep until 5 p.m. Then the station began to live again, for it was the hour of polo—the time for which the cavalry officer had been living all day long. Drill, manoeuvres, orderly-room, stables—these were tiresome chores to be got through as quickly as possible. Dinner at 8.30 p.m., to the strains of the regimental band and the clinking of ice in generously filled glasses; cheroots and still more cold drinks until 11 p.m. And then came the end of the 'long, long Indian day'.

'And not such a bad day either,'' wrote Winston Churchill some sixty years later.[1]

Sybaritic and unreflective it may have been; expensive and unashamedly snobbish it undoubtedly was. But the young Winston Churchill was not found wanting in the sterner business of charging the Khalifa's dervishes at Omdurman, any more than his lancer, hussar and dragoon contemporaries were found wanting during those desperate first three months in France. The proof of the pudding is, after all, in the eating.

On approximately the same social level as the cavalry of the line were the officers of the Royal Regiment of Artillery. And the two arms of the service were further bound together by the horse. The gunners, conceded the cavalry grudgingly, rode almost as well as they did; their steeplechasing achievements were almost as good and they gave them a fair run for their money on the polo field. Of course, gunners were noisy and clumsy and uncouth at times—many of them seemed unable to hold their liquor like gentlemen and the Royal Regiment as a whole had an unwarrantedly good opinion of itself, but then it was obviously absurd to attempt any sensible comparison between a cavalryman and a gunner. It goes without saying that artillerymen had precisely this same attitude to the cavalrymen. The gunner officers, more serious-minded and professionally dedicated, regarded themselves as practical soldiers as opposed to polo players and socialites subsidised by a niggardly government: in India, for instance, they sometimes worked during the murderous heat of the afternoon. And when the hour of polo came, then let these Dragoons, Hussars and Lancers put their best men into the field. As to steeplechasing—any reasonably well-mounted gunner could make a cavalryman look like a ploughboy.

The Infantry of the Line—the despised 'Line' or 'Feet'—were sub-divided into still more social compartments.

The Rifle regiments—the Greenjackets—hardly counted as infantrymen; they wore green instead of scarlet; their buttons were black (for which many a rifleman and soldier servant was piously thankful); they marched at a theatrical quickstep and spoke of bayonets as swords; some of them could even ride a horse and the majority of officers in Rifle regiments were rich.

Riflemen apart, let us start in Scotland. At the top, geographically and socially, were the kilted Highland regiments: the Argylls;

[1] Winston Churchill in *My Early Life* (Cassell).

Camerons; Seaforths; Gordons; and Black Watch. Officers of these regiments, who had stormed Tirah and Atbara to the accompaniment of the wail of bagpipes, bore the great and ancient names of Scotland: Gordon, Cameron, Grant, Campbell, Drummond, Buchanan, Blair, Colquhoun, and a half-hundred and more beginning with Mac. The Highland regiments were exclusive and therefore wealthy.

Thence to the poorer relations in the Lowlands: the Highland Light Infantry (Glasgow's own regiment, with its fierce and touchy esprit de corps); the Royal Scots Fusiliers; the Royal Scots—First of Foot and by the same token senior regiment of the Line; the Cameronians (Scottish Rifles), known as the 'Covenanters'; the King's Own Scottish Borderers.

Over the border into England: the Northumberland Fusiliers; the Durham Light Infantry; and the Border Regiment. These were known collectively as the 'Geordie' regiments.

Farther south to the vast tracts of Yorkshire and Lancashire, ever generous with their gifts of manpower to the British Army: the East and South Lancashire Regiments; the York and Lancaster Regiment; the Lancashire Fusiliers; the King's Own Regiment; the East and West Yorkshire Regiments; the Green Howards and the Duke of Wellington's Regiment; and the Loyal Regiment (North Lancashire); the King's Own Yorkshire Light Infantry.

The huge and thickly populated cities of Manchester and Liverpool, each with its own regiment—the King's Regiment (Liverpool) and the Manchester Regiment: socially unambitious both, but invariably close at hand in all theatres of war where the fighting was most bloody and the climatic conditions most vile. Down still farther to the Midlands—the bleak, industrial wilderness of the Black Country and the Potteries: the North and South Staffords; the Royal Warwicks; the Sherwood Foresters; and the Leicesters.

And Birmingham itself, with its huge population and the ugly accent peculiar to itself—'Brum', ever a prolific breeding ground for soldiers. Name any regiment, be it cavalry, artillery, guards, infantry of the line or one of the ancillary services and there will be 'Brummies' in its ranks—as often as not they joined a regiment before setting foot for the first time in its county of origin: the Devons inevitably collected a nucleus of 'Brums', as did the Duke of Cornwall's Light Infantry and the Gordon Highlanders.

From the Mercian counties come the Cheshires, famed for machine gunners; the Worcesters; and the Lincolns.

Go eastwards and here are Norfolks; Suffolks; Northamptons;

Bedfords (later to become the Bedfordshire and Hertfordshire Regiment); and the Essex.

Strike westwards again to the King's Shropshire Light Infantry; adjoining another regiment of Light Infantry, the 52nd—the Oxfordshire and Buckinghamshire. And into the Principality of Wales for the stubborn fighting men of the Royal Welch Fusiliers; the Welch Regiment; and the South Wales Borderers.

London, like Birmingham, produced her sons—the permanent, indestructible and virile Cockneys—for every regiment and corps, but those who were given any choice opted for the Royal Fusiliers and the Middlesex. The Home Counties found the Queen's Royal West Surrey Regiment; the East Surreys; the Royal Sussex; the Buffs; the Royal West Kents; and the Royal Berkshire.

Then to the West Country, home of many a stubborn and indefatigable fighting soldier: the Devons; the Duke of Cornwall's Light Infantry; the Dorsets; Gloucesters; Wiltshires; Hampshires; and the Somerset Light Infantry.

And as no battle, be it global warfare or bar brawl, is complete without a sprinkling of 'neutral' Irishmen, we must never forget the Munster and Dublin Fusiliers; the Connaught Rangers; the Royal Irish Regiment; the Royal Irish Rifles; the Royal Irish Fusiliers; the Royal Inniskilling Fusiliers.

But a commission in a regiment of Infantry of the Line did not necessarily free an officer from social distinction—far from it. From the purely social standpoint, regiments of the line were divided into three financial categories: those requiring its officers to have 'comfortable' private means; those that cautiously explained 'one must have a little money of one's own'; and those claiming that, in theory anyway, an officer could exist in it on his pay.

All these regiments had their share of tradition and past glory; some carried them off with casual modesty, others with a degree of snobbery which to a visiting officer from a less illustrious regiment seemed insufferable. Possibly because poverty and unemployment has always been more prevalent in the North than in the South, officers in the regiments from Yorkshire and Lancashire had to make their meagre pay go the farthest. In some regiments a private income of a thousand pounds a year was considered desirable; in others six hundred and fifty pounds per annum permitted a degree of gracious living. In others, again, one could just manage on four hundred; officers with less were apt to find themselves in perpetual and painful debt. The young officer with no private means at all soon found soldiering in England impracticable. He was, in fact,

in the vexatious position of trying to insert a quart into a pint pot.
The hypothetical second-lieutenant newly joined from Sandhurst
had a daily rate of pay and emoluments (many officers have, without
success, tried to discover the difference between the two) of five
shillings and threepence per day. He was not unnaturally discom-
fited to find that his mess bill, without even the most modest alcoholic
extras, came to seven shillings and sixpence per day. Such young
men found themselves closeted with tight-lipped, albeit sympathetic
(although not on the surface) adjutants who said that they knew it
was difficult, but . . . ending with a gesture which might have con-
veyed something to a Frenchman, but had little significance in the
British Army. There were alternatives. Many a young man, finding
himself in such a position, sought social banishment but a degree of
financial solvency in regiments which achieved no sort of social
category whatsoever: the King's African Rifles; the Royal West
African Frontier Force; or the Sudan Defence Force. It was damned
hard luck on a chap, especially if he had an elder brother in the
cavalry.

That left the Royal Engineers, the Army Service Corps (known
derisively as 'Ally Sloper's Cavalry') and the Royal Army Medical
Corps (R.A.M.C. meant then, as now, Rob All My Comrades).
Officers of these formations were regarded very much as the present-
day expense account executive in Surrey regards the proprietor of
his local garage: he would be helpless without him, but does not feel
called upon to entertain him in his own house.

The Sappers were, it was universally agreed, slightly mad—they
were absent-minded characters, of serious mien, who carried slide-
rules and gun cotton whilst they muttered darkly to themselves.
They had no money, studied at universities before going to 'the
Shop' and took the Army and themselves abnormally seriously. A
strange breed, indeed.

The R.A.M.C. were doctors and a shade higher in the social
scheme of things than the veterinary services (although in the cavalry
this was a debatable social distinction). The A.S.C. were . . . well,
they were just the A.S.C.

Occasionally, deeply tanned and hawk-eyed men appeared in
England and were immediately identifiable as British officers of the
Indian Army on long leave. They shivered in the unaccustomed
cold and blinked about them in a bewildered fashion—it was often
their first sight of England for seven years—and, like schoolboys long
deprived of tuck, laid violent siege to Ascot, Henley, Goodwood,
Lords, Wimbledon and as many restaurants and night clubs as

possible. To them England was like a gigantic hors d'oeuvres, difficult to take in all at once. So they grabbed haphazard and found it good, for all too soon another seven years of exile awaited them.

The Indian cavalry were tolerable—one had, of course, heard of the Bengal Lancers, Skinners' Horse, Probyn's Horse and the Guides, when it came to polo, some of them could even teach the 9th Lancers a thing or two. The Gurkhas, too, were invested with a certain glamour: their soldiers were small, grinning Mongolian men who struck terror into their enemies with curved knives called kukris. The Sikhs, too, sounded mildly interesting because it seemed that they had some strange religion which forbade them to cut their hair or shave their faces. But the British officers of the rest, Baluchis, Punjabis, Pathans, Rajputs, Dogras, Mahrattas, Garhwalis, were lumped together under the heading of 'black infantry'— people to be regarded with tolerant pity.

3

And what of the rank and file—the 'squaddies'—the swearing, grousing individual, so seldom credited with individuality, who was known affectionately and collectively as 'Thomas Atkins'?

In the years prior to 1914 why did he become a soldier? Was he motivated by patriotism, adventure or ambition? In nine cases out of ten the answer was none of these things.

Great Britain had done little enough for him to make him a blazing patriot; with the Boers vanquished and the Sudan won, there seemed little prospect of adventure; there were few field marshals' batons in haversacks during the early twentieth century.

The recruit of the period joined the Army at a time when there was no Welfare State; indeed, he would probably have wholeheartedly disapproved if there had been. There was no generous overtime; there was, in fact, little ordinary time to be had—in the strictly trade union sense of the word. There were unemployment, overcrowded slums and poverty in plenty. And one of these, or a combination of all three, sent many a young man to the recruiting centre.

Ask a vintage old soldier of the period *circa* 1906 why he joined the Army; he will nearly always attribute his enlistment to a woman or hunger. He may even add a grimly humorous rider to the effect that the Army got him before the police did.

Often called a spacious era, the years between the end of the Boer War and the outbreak of the Great War were far from spacious for the people from what is known as the working class. A young man who could only count with certainty on one square meal a day found that the British Army guaranteed three; in exchange, it demanded unquestioning obedience and unfailing loyalty to regiment, King and country. It got all three.

Successive generations of young men are accused by their elders of a lack of the spirit of adventure. No such accusation could be levelled at John Christie, sixteen-year-old Dundee telegraph boy. Dressed in a tight blue uniform of drab serge, he tore round Dundee with his messages. But his mind was obsessed with a very different type of uniform: the pill box cap, spurs, gleaming Wellingtons and skin-tight overalls with the double yellow stripe down the sides, of the Lancers. Only the week before, Hamish MacBride, trooper of the 9th Lancers, had been home on furlough. He was a fine figure of a man as he swaggered through Dundee's streets and he set many a feminine heart-a-flutter. Unfortunately for a number of Dundee's citizens who were destined to receive urgent telegrams, he was seen by John Christie.

The sight of Trooper MacBride convinced John Christie that a cavalryman's life was the life for him. In the temporary privacy of the room which he shared with his five brothers, he examined his face in a cracked piece of glass which did duty as a mirror. He looked, he told himself, every day of eighteen—the minimum age for enlistment. He had no need to shave, but presumably there were many young soldiers who had no use for a razor as yet.

The recruiting sergeant had had a slack morning and was glad to have a customer: the new arrival looked a likely enough lad. If John Christie said he was aged eighteen years and three months, then that was all right with him. What regiment was the young shaver thinking of joining?

'The 9th Lancers,' declared John Christie without hesitation.

'You'll never regret it, lad,' said the recruiting sergeant.

John Christie took the oath with Caledonian vigour and was attested trooper. Now he was a soldier and ready to die the sorest of deaths. But Christie *père* took a less exalted view. A man of un-militant nature—he had never considered the Boer War to be creditable or necessary and had barely heard of Kitchener or Khartoum—he descended on Maryhill Barracks with hard-breathing parental authority. He took with him John Christie's birth certificate which contained the damning proof that the newly-joined Trooper Christie was aged sixteen years and one week. Near to unmanly tears, young John pleaded with his father, but only collected a comprehensive hiding for his pains.

But exactly one year and fifty-one weeks later, on a brilliantly sunlit morning in 1905, John Christie was back. . . .

There were two young men, Walter Dobson and Richard Gilkes, who were as fiercely determined to join the cavalry of the line as John Christie had been.

Ten years separate their dates of enlistment and they have never met.

Today, Walter Dobson, seventy years old, ribald and indomitably humorous as he was in 1914, does a full day's work as a labourer in Berkshire and challenges any man half a century younger to do it better. Richard Gilkes, a sprightly seventy-seven, spends the evening of his life with John Christie, winner of the Military Medal and late (as they say of distinguished soldiers) of the 9th Lancers, at the Royal Hospital.

John Christie joined the cavalry. Dobson and Gilkes, although large of heart, were both short of stature: they fell short of the prescribed five feet three inches demanded of cavalrymen. They stood on tip-toe, inflated their chests to an impossible extent and incurred the risk of partial paralysis in their efforts to satisfy conditions of height which seemed cruel and unreasonable. Recruiting sergeants, for all their forbidding exteriors, were kindly men with a sense of humour—although it sometimes bordered on the macabre. These two small men, who have since achieved greatness, were told that they could join the cavalry after all—Ally Sloper's Cavalry. Dobson and Gilkes were both accepted for the A.S.C.

The early lives of both Dobson and Gilkes had been ruled by that essential mode of transport of the period, the horse and cart. A boy who spent nearly all his waking hours with a horse formed a strong attachment to the animal, just as a teenager today, who is fortunate enough to own one, loves his 'ton-up' motor cycle somewhat more than his current 'bird'.

In 1913 Walter Dobson, then aged eighteen, was, in butchery circles, reckoned to be a man with an illustrious future. His employer was Percy Colebrook, butcher and wholesale purveyor of meat in the Berkshire town of Bracknell. At the reins of his horse and cart Walter Dobson covered an incalculable number of miles, delivering meat, prime cuts of beef and mutton and pork, for in 1913 half a crown of anyone's money purchased a Sunday dinner of majestic proportions for a family of six. Walter's pony was his pride and joy: at the end of each day Walter groomed him with loving care, watered him, fed him—indeed, the pony frequently acquired a generous share of his midday meal—and bedded him down for the night. Walter did not only deliver, he also sold meat on his round at a commission of one shilling in the pound to augment his basic wage of six shillings per week.

Percy Colebrook knew a good lad when he saw one and was incensed almost to the point of apoplexy when he learned that his star employee had failed to report for work one morning. Scarcely less exercised were a number of Berkshire housewives, who encountered a bleak and meatless Sunday.

For some weeks past Walter Dobson had been seriously wondering if butchery was his true métier. And the spectacle of a horse gunner on leave in Wokingham—a superb figure in the walking-out uniform of the Royal Regiment—had finally turned the scale against Percy Colebrook: Walter Dobson rose early, patted his horse affectionately on the neck and set off on the fifteen-mile walk to Reading. Walter had long been fascinated by the Royal Horse Artillery—the guns and limbers in line, galloping into action; the hard-riding men, intent only on the destruction of the King's enemies.

In hot pursuit followed Percy Colebrook. In the recruiting office he tried frantically to persuade Walter to change his mind, drawing on past statistics of unwilling soldiers: there was the case of Arthur Walsh who had cried like a baby all through his first week and his dad had had to buy him out with his twelve years' savings. But Recruiting Sergeant Lanesborough's eloquence far outstripped Percy Colebrook's when it came to weighing army life against butchery. And even if Lanesborough could not stretch Walter Dobson to the prescribed five feet and three inches, he had still procured a recruit for Ally Sloper's Cavalry.

Richard Gilkes was recruited to the A.S.C. with comparable ease, although Walter Dobson's hours of work, wages and privileges in 1913 might have moved him to righteous scorn. For Gilkes' working life had started in 1898, at the tender age of eleven, at a commencing wage of two shillings per week. Gilkes, too, drove a horse and cart, and the commodity retailed was an equally essential one—milk. For seven days a week, in fair weather or foul, he maintained a cow-to-consumer service. At 3.30 a.m. he was milking six cows; 6 a.m., his churns full to the brim, found him clip-clopping round the streets of Chatham selling his wares in penny and half-penny measures.

34

Such was the austere pattern of life for Richard Gilkes until his seventeenth birthday. It struck him as being in no way strange that he should be doing a full day's work at such a tender age; at the turn of the century, indeed, it was the rule rather than the exception. The Army was in young Richard's blood. His father, a battered veteran of a dozen fearful battles, had served in the old 76th Foot in the Crimea. But Richard Gilkes, like Walter Dobson, could only measure feet five two inches in his stockinged feet which effectively prevented him from joining the 17th Lancers, the regiment of his choice. In 1904 Richard Gilkes joined the A.S.C.

The lack of an inch of stature was a bitter disappointment to Richard, and his father was roughly sympathetic. But—'Someone's got to take the food and ammunition up to the front,' declared ex-Sergeant Gilkes who was ever ready with harrowing military reminiscence, 'and it might as well be you. No one brought any food up for *us* at Sevastopol.' Mr. Gilkes was secretly aware of a feeling of relief; the departure of Richard meant that there were now only ten mouths in the family to feed. His mother instructed him to remember her in his prayers, pressed upon him a warm parcel containing a home-made pie and an apple for the journey, and wept in private.

Peter Key will tell you that he joined the British Army just seventy years ago; a brief calculation puts his age at eighty-seven. But he is surely younger than that: his hearing and eye-sight are good; he fills his Chelsea Pensioner's uniform as an apple fills its skin; his hair, although snow white, is plentiful; he walks with the aid of a stick, but only because the Army has issued him with a stick—like all good soldiers he makes the fullest possible use of Government property. But eighty-seven, or even seventy-seven? Surely not.

When Peter Kay says that he joined the Army in 1893, he speaks the literal truth. For in that year he entered the Duke of York's School at the age of nine; at fourteen years and three months he was serving as a boy trumpeter in the Royal Horse Artillery in Bangalore. At an age when his modern counterpart is thinking in terms of the G.C.E. and attendant puberty, Peter Key was half-way to manhood.

Apart from enemy shells and bullets, the artilleryman and cavalryman knows no more dreadful sound than the insistent peal of a trumpet sounding Reveille at 5 a.m. in the morning.

> Rise, soldiers, RISE!   (*the last G was always sounded with un-
> necessarily truculent clarity*).
> Get the muck out of your eyes . . . !

35

Unhappily, this shattering music did not end there. A positive fanfare of violent sound followed these opening two bars, a ghastly reminder that only sick parade, with its inevitable unsympathetic accompaniment, represented escape from the impossibly early start to the mounted soldier's day. The infantry were wont to say that the horsed soldier had a 'cushy' life; the artilleryman and cavalryman, aroused from sleep a full hour earlier than the foot soldier, gave the lie to this unwarranted theory with terrible oaths and curses.

Urging the sleep-drugged troopers and gunners from slumber at the turn of the century were two pink-cheeked and beardless boys, under the baleful eyes of Regimental-Sergeant Majors, who administered corrective cuffs at the merest suspicion of a wrong note: Boy Trumpeter Peter Key, Royal Horse Artillery, and Boy Trumpeter Patrick Hefferman, 5th Lancers.

Later in the day, punctual to the second, they pursed their hairless lips apprehensively and blew 'Boots and saddles', 'Water and feed', 'Orderly room', the 'Last Post' and 'Lights Out'. For these martial chores Key and Hefferman drew the princely sum of sixpence per week—'fivepence of it went on cleaning kit'.

Today, sweated labour is a loosely used term. But there are men still living who experienced sweated labour in its most daunting sense and fled from it into the iron discipline of the old Regular Army. The choice lay between the frying pan and the fire, of which the fire seemed most congenial.

George White was one of these. For five years he worked an eleven-hour day for eight shillings per week. His field of endeavour was a sweet factory in Peckham and in winter he saw no daylight except on Sundays. The scene in the factory was almost Dickensian: approximately one hundred young men laboured in a sub-tropical atmosphere to produce sticky confectionery for the gluttonous enjoyment of children at a halfpenny per packet. In the year 1900 George White, then aged seventeen, decided that he had had enough and took himself to St. George's Barracks in Orange Street.

The Boer War was dragging to a close and George White found that joining the Army was like joining an exclusive club. The regiment of his choice—London's own regiment, the Royal Fusiliers, had no vacancies. Nor had the Middlesex, the East Surreys, the Buffs, the Queen's Own Royal West Surrey Regiment or the Queen's Own Royal West Kent Regiment.

But the Duke of Cornwall's Light Infantry—ah, sighed the recruiting sergeant, there was something like a *real* regiment. (The recruiting sergeant had himself served in the old 32nd Foot, and was something of an authority on the subject.)

In 1777, said the recruiting sergeant to a highly impressionable George White, who only desired escape from the Peckham sweet factory, the 32nd had fought the Americans and would do so again if he had any say in the matter. They had held the residency at Lucknow in the Indian Mutiny and fought in Egypt at Tel-el-Kebir in 1882—the year of George White's birth.

The recruiting sergeant adjusted steel-rimmed spectacles, noisily rustled a sheaf of papers on his desk and gazed at George White with paternal concern. There were, he said, in the manner of a monarch conferring knighthood on a peasant, vacancies in the D.C.L.I. George White, in his considered opinion, should waste no more time in making up his mind. But, protested George White, he had barely heard of the county, much less ever been there—what possible link could a labourer in a Peckham sweet factory have with Cornwall?

The recruiting sergeant dismissed the Duchy with a comprehensive wave of his hand. The D.C.L.I., for some incomprehensible reason, recruited most of its men from London, Bristol and Birmingham.

It was good enough for George White and it seemed that George White satisfied the exacting requirements of the Duke of Cornwall's Light Infantry. A week later George set off on his longest journey to date—the 252 miles from London to Bodmin. It was the first of many long journeys, which were to take him to Ceylon, South Africa, the Curragh—and to France. . . .

In the spring of 1906 Frank Sims clashed with his employer: not for the first, but, as it turned out, for the last time. He had only recently celebrated his sixteenth birthday. Frank stood a wiry six feet and two inches in his stockinged feet. He had outgrown his strength a little, although this was not immediately apparent. But the thin wrists protruding from a jacket several sizes too small for him—the jacket had been handed down from two of his elder brothers—were indicative of insufficient nourishment. Sixteen-year-old boys are inevitably hungry and never seem to be able to get quite enough to eat: in the year 1906 the feeding of eight mouths—the daily ration strength of the Sims family—would have taxed the ingenuity of the most resourceful housewife.

But it was not hunger that drove Frank Sims from the security of a twelve shillings per week job with a leather manufacturer; rather was it the soul-destroying sameness of each working day. There could be no foreseeable future outside of the endless stitching of suitcases, portmanteaux and trunks. Every morning he rose at 5 a.m. and faced a long and uncomfortable train journey to work. He did not see his home again until 8 p.m. Of his twelve shillings a week, two were swallowed up in fares and he gave eight to his mother. It was, decided Frank Sims, no way for a man to live.

He told his employer this, on a morning in April, 1906. The proprietor of the leather goods shop, a sour little man with a squint and dyspepsia, expressed horrified surprise that Frank should want to leave his employ. Although there was little love lost between them, the proprietor was bound to admit that Frank Sims was admirably skilled at his trade. He was still more horrified to learn that Frank expected more money for his 78-hour week: if he objected to his conditions of employment, then he would have to have the sack. Perhaps Frank would care to think it over. Frank thought it over—for a full sixty seconds. He then drew the balance of wages due to him—four shillings and threepence—and walked out, never to return.

His first encounter with the British Army was not a happy or a distinguished one. The recruiting sergeant asked him his age and Frank, who had been brought up in a strict home where the telling of lies was statutorily punished, told the truth. The recruiting sergeant eyed him without friendship and told him to go and join the Navy.

But the next recruiting sergeant was infinitely more sympathetic. Frank Sims may not have looked like promising military material at first sight, but he'd seen many worse. A recruiting sergeant got two gold sovereigns for each recruit obtained for the Household Cavalry and times were hard.

'The Royal Horse Guards is the regiment for a fine upstanding young feller like you,' said the recruiting sergeant with relish. 'Think of sitting on a horse, spick and span, guarding the body of your King. The Royal Horse Guards—the senior regiment of the British Army— the Blues. Now, let the doctor have a look at you—you'd pay a twenty sovereign fee for the sort of free medical examination you're going to get—and all you've got to do is take the oath. Now then, what's your age?'

'Eighteen, sir,' said Frank Sims without hesitation. Years later he was to recall that he had represented the easiest two pounds that the recruiting sergeant had ever earned. . . .

Tedious, backbreaking and futureless jobs sent young men into the British Army in the first decade of the twentieth century:

William Masters, bespoke saddler's apprentice in Reading, left home with five shillings and was a Scots Fusilier in Ayr four days later; Victor Fletcher, whose working life started as an eleven-year-old trapper in a Derbyshire colliery in 1898, joined the Royal Engineers; in 1907 George Criddle, seven-and-sixpence-a-week gardener's boy in the Surrey village of Churt, walked the twelve miles to Guildford and enlisted in the Queen's Royal West Surrey Regiment; George Wills took his five feet and five inches of Cockney self-assurance to the recruiting officer in 1903 and asked for the Life Guards: when the recruiting sergeant, who had had a trying morning, instructed him to grow another seven inches within the next twelve hours or go to hell—George settled instead for the Royal Engineers (a decision which, fifteen years later, was to win him the Distinguished Conduct Medal and the Military Medal); Albert Deering, stable-lad in a Kent racing stables, found that he was becoming too heavy to be a jockey and departed to Gravesend and the Royal Field Artillery.

And so hunger, boredom, niggardly employers, overcrowding and a total absence of what is known today as a welfare state sent young men into an army which was to make history and save England.

Chapter III

I

ROBERTS of Kandahar, Pretoria and Waterford, 1st Earl (cr. 1892), P.C., K.P., G.C.B., G.C.S.I., G.C.I.E., V.C., K.G., D.C.L., LL.D.; Order of Merit; Field Marshal; Colonel-in-Chief Overseas and Indian Forces in Europe during European War, 1914.

So reads an entry in *Who's Who* for Lord Roberts; British soldiers to whom *Who's Who* was as remote as Somerset Maugham's '*Schiffbruchig*', knew him as 'Bobs'. To the Indian troops, who knew a good fighting man when they saw one, he was 'Bobs Bahadur'.

Lord Roberts was a man of action rather than words: scarcely surprising in a soldier who had been a subaltern of Bengal Artillery in 1851, had seen active service, in its goriest sense, in the Indian Mutiny; had commanded the Kabul Field Force and the British Army in Burma; had won the Victoria Cross and been mentioned in despatches no fewer than twenty-three times.

Although he had written two books, he was reckoned to be more skilled with cavalry, artillery and infantry than with pen; his only two publications—neither of them particularly wide sellers—had been *The Rise of Wellington* and *Forty-one Years in India*; although they were both prescribed reading for Staff College candidates, their utterances scarcely seemed to entitle him to dictate future European military policy. Nor had he made a lasting impression as an orator.

In 1908 he was seventy-six and already part of Britain's history, but he accurately enough summed up British unpreparedness in the face of a war that he considered inevitable.

He was in Quebec, trying to rid Canada of her complacent inertia:

> They refuse to believe me and we sleep under a false security. I do not hesitate to affirm that we shall have a frightful war in Europe, and that England and France will have the hardest experience of their existence. *They will, in fact, see defeat very near. . . .*[1]

[1] From *How Dear Is Life* by Henry Williamson (Macdonald).

But in 1908, a year in which income tax at one and sixpence in the pound, cigarettes at five for a penny, a speed limit for motor vehicles of twenty miles per hour and nights out at the Tivoli for a pound were supposed, separately and collectively, to make sense, it was difficult to take anything too seriously. And the suggestion that Britain might become involved in a major European war in the foreseeable future seemed like an excursion into the realms of a fire-eater's or visionary's dream. One might just as reasonably put forward the theory that the income tax was going up again.

Consequently, Lord Robert's words fell on deaf or disbelieving ears. Politicians conceded that it was conceivable, but added that it was very far from being inevitable. The comforting theory that 'the Germans have got a damn' sight too much sense' was held by many.

It goes without saying that no one consulted Britain's soldiers about what they thought—the men in barracks in Aldershot, Tidworth, Portsmouth and on the Curragh; the men sweltering in Belgaum, Cairo, Bareilly and Peshawar. Reasoning not why, they continued to march and counter-march, present, slope and order arms, swear, contract venereal disease, gamble and drink beer.

It seemed, in truth, impossible that Britain could ever fight a major war with her infinitesimal army: indeed, the Kaiser's original assessment of it as General French's 'contemptible little army' seemed reasonable enough. No single unit, whether cavalry, artillery or infantry, was up to strength, although the hundred or more senior officers at the War Office seemed to indicate a degree of round-the-clock preparedness. Of this Field Marshal William Robertson, who had enlisted as a trooper in the 16th Lancers in 1877, remarked scathingly:

> We have two armies . . . the War Office army and the Aldershot army. The first is always up to strength, and is organised, reorganised and disorganised almost daily. The second is never up to strength, knows nothing whatever about the first, and remains unaffected by any of these organising activities. It just cleans its rifles and falls in on parade.[1]

And so the British soldiers at home continued to practise manoeuvres, which none of them was to live to see employed in action: in September, 1908, on the Downs near Winchester, a cavalry brigade was 'captured' by an infantry company and accused the foot soldiers of unsportsmanlike conduct; in 1909 the 1st Division

[1] *From Private to Field Marshal* by Field Marshal Sir William Robertson (Constable).

carried out a practice mobilisation at Aldershot—the first occasion on which a division had ever been seen at full strength, and the last until August, 1914; King Edward VII paid an annual visit to his soldiers at Aldershot and on one unforgettable afternoon found himself 'attacked' by his own foot guards; aeroplanes, kites and dirigible balloons put in their first appearance; Indian frontier warfare was practised in the Welsh mountains and desert warfare on Chobham Ridges.

Staff officers were encouraged to cultivate friendly relations with regimental officers; a prominent peer declined to allow the use of his land for training purposes; Henry Asquith said that war with Germany was unthinkable; to the horror of the cavalry, an infantry regiment won the Inter-Regimental Polo cup and a naval officer won a steeplechase at the military meeting at Sandown Park; Lord Roberts pressed for conscription and a captain was removed from the Staff College for refusing to grow a moustache (seven years later, presumably still clean-shaven, he won the Distinguished Service Order and was killed on the Somme).

All too soon it was 1914. . . .

2

The year 1914 had been a troubled one from the beginning, although there has probably never been a time in the history of Great Britain when its inhabitants were less concerned with the affairs of Europe than in the spring and early summer of 1914. They had troubles enough of their own.

There had been a recrudescence of the unrest in Ireland, that distressful island, which seemed to be getting steadily worse. There was a very real threat of civil war in that country; the possible result seemed to be that the British Army might be called in to redress the balance between the Orangemen and the Southern Irish. The trouble was largely religious: the Protestant North was in a ferment at the prospect of being ruled by the Catholic majority in the South. But there were also military complications which became known as the 'Curragh Incident': as a result of an alarmist speech by General Sir Arthur Paget to his senior officers—among Paget's many virtues tact was not the most prominent—Brigadier-General Hubert Gough and the officers of the 16th Lancers, the 5th Lancers and the 4th Hussars issued an unprecedented ultimatum—rather than take part in the 'coercion' of Ulster, they would send in their papers.

The Curragh Incident was in March; in April there were Anglo-Russian naval talks; in June Germany widened the Kiel Canal, thus permitting her battleships uninterrupted passage from the North Sea to the Baltic. 'And why shouldn't she?' demanded anyone who happened to know about it; 'it's her canal, isn't it?'

There was a move to abolish the baggy red trousers of the French Army, which drew scandalised howls from the veterans of Sedan: '*Jamais! Le pantalon rouge, c'est La France!*' On the subject of trousers all was peace and tranquillity in Britain, for a pair of grey flannels cost only five shillings.

On the Home Front there were alarms in plenty: the *Daily Mail*, taking its cue from Lord Roberts, insisted with mournful and persistent truculence, that a major war in Europe was inevitable, while Mr. Asquith intoned 'wait and see' whenever the air grew military.

Lord Lonsdale's income was assessed at £100,000 per year from coal alone and it was estimated that the homeless in Britain numbered three million. Suffragettes were forcibly fed with tubes and the price of bed and breakfast in a Cyclists' Touring Club had gone up from 1s. 3d. to 1s. 6d.

The Royal Navy, on which so much of the tax-payers' money had been lavished, seemed serene and everlasting: the warships, like sleek and well-nourished whales, lay casually watchful around Britain's shores. In the Mediterranean, on the China Station, in the Indies and the Persian Gulf they were symbols of security and quiet strength.

The Army, too, seemed reassuringly splendid and never more so than on 22nd June, 1914, the day of the Full-Dress Review at Aldershot. On that day of brilliant sunshine there seemed nothing small about Britain's Army. King George V, splendidly mounted on a dark bay, flanked by General Douglas Haig, took the salute. The bands played stirring music as the regiments marched past: the Coldstream and Scots Guards, the lines of scarlet tunics and bearskins a miracle of disciplined perfection; the Queen's Bays, the 15th Hussars, the 5th Inniskilling Dragoons, the 11th Hussars—hoofs padding gently, curb chains jingling musically, as troop followed troop and squadron followed squadron; batteries of Horse Gunners, magnificent and invincible looking; company after company of infantry—kilted Black Watch, Highland Light Infantry in their trews, green-clad riflemen, Connaught Rangers, Munster Fusiliers, Royal Sussex, Loyals, Northamptons, Queens, South Wales Borderers, Gloucesters, Welch, Worcesters, Oxfordshire and Buckinghamshire Light Infantry, Royal Berkshires, King's Liverpool and South Staffords; Royal Engineers and Army Service Corps.

It was a spectacle to gladden the heart of the most recalcitrant tax-payer.

And then on 28th June occurred the 'damned foolish thing in the Balkans', as Bismarck phrased it, that was to ignite the Great War: the Austrian heir-apparent, the Archduke Franz Ferdinand was assassinated by Serbian nationalists.

The event, initially, made little impression in England: 'Where the devil *is* Sarajevo?'—and assassinations in Europe were common enough, one more could scarcely make any difference.

Chapter IV

I

THE men of the last peacetime church parade for five years made a brave show as they marched down Aldershot's Wellington Avenue on that scorching Sunday, the 2nd of August, 1914. They made a brave noise, too, as they roared out *'Fight the good fight'*; tell a British soldier to sing, and he will do so right lustily. Some of the more irreverent old soldiers actually enjoyed church services because the singing of hymns was an unrivalled method of raising a thirst. But the next morning their scarlet, blue and green jackets went into store and they paraded in khaki—the half-length trousers, tunics, long puttees and heavy ammunition boots. And that night in officers' messes the officers, clad for the last time in abbreviated mess jackets, tight overalls and spurred Wellingtons, heard their colonels proclaim from the fireplace that they were, presumably, at war. For now there could be no room for doubt: Germany, France, Russia and Austria had mobilised. Even Turkey, whose future role in a European war was uncertain as yet, was mobilising.

And at 8 a.m. on the morning of August the 4th the Kaiser, ignoring Britain's ultimatum, ignoring the might of France and Russia, ignoring the advice of some of his generals—ignoring everything save his own ruthless ambition—launched the forward elements of three armies, commanded by Generals von Kluck, von Bülow and von Hauen, over the Belgian frontier.

In launching the three armies into Belgium, the Kaiser was following the plan drawn up by Count Alfred von Schlieffen, Chief of the German General Staff from 1891 until 1906. The Schlieffen Plan was brilliant in concept, terrifyingly simple in its arrogant and confident theory: six weeks and seven-eighths of the German forces, reasoned Schlieffen, would ensure the smashing of France; the remaining one eighth of his troops would hold the Eastern front against Russia.

Schlieffen was a slavish disciple of Clausewitz, who contended that 'the heart of France lay between Brussels and Paris.' His plan, finally brought to perfection in 1905, was to hurl almost the entire

45

land forces of Germany against France: it had worked at Sedan and, with skill and boldness, it could work again.

To achieve his object and fold up the French Army, it would be essential to by-pass the fortress system which France had built up, and he planned to launch almost all his force in a massive right-flanking movement through neutral Belgium, avoiding France's main defences.

To the Kaiser Belgian neutrality represented a trifling obstacle, but it was his violation of it which was to bring Great Britain into the war.

2

Between fighting soldiers and the gilded staff, there has always existed a cordial dislike. In the Second World War men in desert, waterlogged trench and jungle, loudly and profanely contrasted their lot with the staff to whom the most exacting military crisis was lack of champagne or a defective refrigerator. It goes without saying that they blamed the staff for everything.

But in August, 1914, the days were still far off when men, driven to the limits of human endurance, were to curse impotently the exalted beings at Divisional, Corps or Army Headquarters who occasionally put in a token appearance near the front line in gleaming motor cars. Moreover, in the first week of the Great War even the most rabid critics of the Staff officers at the War Office grudgingly conceded that they had done their job well. And if they were cursed —well, everyone always cursed the Staff on principle. It was a monumental task. Scarcely a battalion of infantry or a regiment of artillery or cavalry had its full complement of men; many were as much as sixty per cent under strength. They had perforce to call upon that widely scattered and variegated host, the Reservists. Many a harassed Staff officer in the Adjutant-General's branch at the War Office would have been only too happy to return to regimental duty in those hectic days.

The Reservists poured into depots from Inverness to Bodmin, having been peremptorily summoned by letter and telegram. They came on bicycles, by train and on foot. The unquenchable sense of humour of the British soldier has been put to almost impossible tests over the centuries, but never to a sterner one than that which faced them in the first week of August, 1914. For the 'seven year men', whose reserve liability extended for a further five years, it was back to the Army at the double.

There were men who had soldiered soberly and inconspicuously in Egypt, China and Malaya; there were men who had been shot at on India's North West Frontier; there were many others who had never left England or heard a shot fired in anger and had begun to think that they never would. There were men who had been promoted and as speedily demoted; there were men with character 'excellent' on discharge and men with 'indifferent' or 'bad'. There were men with conduct sheets of vast dimensions, covering insubordination, alcoholic indiscretions and all possible variations of conduct to the prejudice of good order and military discipline. There were men who had clearly prospered in civilian life and men who, equally clearly, had not. There were men who cursed the day they enlisted and others, to whom industry had been less than kind, who were glad to be back—they could be sure of three square meals a day in the Army, if nothing else. . . .

Old friendships were renewed and in some cases old enmities. Men whom the reservists had known as privates had become company sergeant-majors; sergeants had been reduced to corporals. On all sides, in over-crowded barrack rooms and canteens, the reservists joshed one another:

'Blimey, when did they let you out?'
'War won't last long now ole Nobby's back.'
'Wait until old Chalkey gets busy with them madamerzelles . . .'
'We'll be home again for Christmas.'
'My ole woman reckons this war's done one good thing for 'er—she's got rid of me for a bit.'

Thus, the old sweats . . . Field Marshal Sir Gerald Templer, who served his apprenticeship in that toughest of regiments, the Royal Irish Fusiliers, has mourned their passing from the contemporary military scene:

> The old sweat has always been a problem, frequently a damned nuisance but an irreplaceable loss to the British Army.

They are the men who 'know it all', but in their own way they are fierce upholders of military discipline. They have, of course, done much overseas service—with and without distinction. Each sojourn abroad is commemorated by a lurid tattoo mark: from chest to ankle they are covered with Red Indian chiefs, snakes, tigers, unclothed women, pagodas, clasped hands, ships in full sail, tombstones and altruistic declarations that death is preferable to dishonour.

There were many men like this who, in August 1914, arrived at Woolwich, Preston, Glencorse Barracks, Exeter, Bodmin, Bury St.

Edmunds and half a hundred garrison towns the length and breadth of Britain.

There were married men, who could give their tearful wives no explanation except that 'it was back to the Army again and orders is orders'; they could tell them nothing about the vexed questions of separation allowance and, as was sombrely confirmed, there was pathetically little to tell. Of men engaged to be married, some rushed hastily to clergymen and demanded that the banns be read without further ado; less enthusiastic swains saw their recall as a merciful release and the parents of the girls comforted them as best they could with the assurance that the young man was no good to her anyway. There were bachelors of the devil-may-care variety, who got uproariously drunk as civilians for the last time and were delivered to their regimental depots by indulgent policemen; there were more serious-minded men, the sole support of aged parents, who stared dumbly uncomprehending at their telegrams.

Sergeant-majors and company commanders conferred together with mournful relish: 'Smith—Smith 96, sir, you remember 'im—well 'e's back for a start—as if we 'adn't got trouble enough . . .'

'Hawkins, sir—the bloke who threw a tin of stew at the post corporal in '07 . . .'

'Parker, sir—urinated on the *chowkidar's* prayer mat in Poonah—nearly started a riot . . .'

'All right, sarn't major—spare me the details . . .'

In this manner some 30,000 men went to war. And as many women—married and single; young and old; pregnant and virgin; nagging, resigned and resentful—wept for them, prayed for them or were glad to see the back of them.

A reservist of any nationality, his service behind him and civilian life in front of him, must inevitably be something of an unwilling warrior; he has lost some of his cutting edge as a fighting man. And it must be remembered that many of these reservists of 1914, for all their impressive length of service, had seen no fighting as yet; there had been nothing about their well-ordered existence in peacetime garrison towns to indicate that they ever would.

Jack Lamb, farm labourer in the little Berkshire village of Hurst, had put his army service far behind him. He had joined the Royal Berkshire Regiment in 1904 and spent all but one of his seven years' colour service in India. On the North West Frontier he had heard the spiteful whine of a Pathan bullet and had learned a healthy respect for these cruel and elusive warriors who waged ceaseless war against the British Army and seemed to regard it as a perfectly legitimate sport.

He had gazed, unimpressed, at the Taj Mahal; he had visited fly-blown bazaars in Bareilly, Barrackpore and Jhansi; under the influence of heady local beer, he had a snake tattooed on his right forearm—he remembered how it had throbbed painfully the next morning and the total lack of sympathy evinced by the platoon sergeant.

Army life hadn't been too bad on the whole, reflected Jack Lamb, as he strode off to milk the cows on a bright morning in the first week of August, 1914. But give him the farm any time: the pigs, the cows, the rolling fields; twelve bob a week and all found. Jack Lamb asked very little of life and got little enough in return; he was in that enviable state of mind that few men achieve today—perfect contentment. On this morning, as on all mornings, Jack Lamb was looking forward to his breakfast. The farmer's wife was generous with food and Jack thought nothing of eating five eggs at a sitting.

A postman was something of a rarity at the farm: neither the farmer nor his wife indulged in lavish correspondence—a fact for which the postman was profoundly thankful, for the delivery of letters meant a walk of three miles. Jack Lamb neither wrote nor received letters. But there was one for him this morning, in an official envelope bearing the letters O.H.M.S. It was brief and to the point: it instructed Private Lamb, J. to report to the depot of the Royal Berkshire Regiment in Reading by the fastest possible means.

Jack Lamb had been uprooted from a tranquil and well-ordered life on the farm. But for Fred Holmes, civilian life had ended almost before it had begun. He had completed his colour service just one week before and civilian life stretched before him, challenging and exciting. Holmes, more fortunate than most of his comrades, had a family business to step into: a prosperous building and decorating concern which his father had slaved for forty years to create. Now Holmes senior was old and tired, happy to hand over the responsibilities of the business to his energetic and ambitious son. Already some of the girls in Harrogate were interested: young Fred Holmes, it was whispered, was coming back from the Army; he was clearly a man with a future.

But Fred had scarcely got the feel of his new thirty-five shilling suit and civilian boots when a telegram summoned him to the depot of the King's Own Yorkshire Light Infantry at Pontefract. . . .

George Wilson, Edinburgh newsvendor, had also had his telegram and accepted it with Caledonian phlegm. He, too, had done his seven with the Highland Light Infantry; he had enlisted at seventeen, giving his civilian occupation as paper boy; seven years later he returned to Edinburgh in the same capacity—the only civilian trade he knew.

Maryhill Barracks had changed but little, he reflected, as he trudged towards the main gate with the loose sole of his cracked right boot flapping rhythmically. It had been winter when he had first joined in 1904 and there had been snow on the top of the forbidding high grey wall. It still looked like 'a bluidy prison'; so far as George Wilson could recall, it had not been unlike one inside. He wondered whether the H.L.I. still had his conduct sheet, which had been about to enter its third page; he wondered if the provost corporal, who had run him in for calling him a 'dirty wee ticket' was still there. . . .

Two years earlier he had stood sentry outside Buckingham Palace; he stood exactly as if he had grown out of the concrete—'properly at ease', heels twelve inches apart, the butt of his rifle in line with his right toe-cap. From the top of his bearskin to his shining boots he stood but a fraction under seven feet tall—the epitome of military perfection.

And then had come the day when he finished his seven years with the Colours and he had gone to the place called 'Civvy Street'—the place where you can eat fish and chips in the street if you wish; where no one cares whether your boots are dirty or down at heel or whether the peak of your cap is broken—or, indeed, if you wear a cap at all.

On this August day of 1914 his suit had seen many better days and his boots merited the attention of a cobbler. But the trousers were pressed, the battered cap sat straight on his head, his hair was cut to businesslike brevity, his moustache was a miracle of hirsute symmetry, he was impeccably shaved. And as he walked through the gates of Chelsea Barracks his shoulders were squared, his head up, his arms swinging from front to rear. An officer drove out as he entered and just in time he remembered that he could not salute when wearing 'civvies'; instead, he carried out the drill movement known as 'without headdress, salute',—his right arm dropped stiffly to his side and his head turned to the right with an almost audible click. In the distance he heard the shouted words of command and the familiar Brigade of Guards endearments: 'Left T-A-A-A-RN!

As you WEAH! Wake yourself up, you 'orrible man! B-y-y-y-y the LEFT . . . ! '

Fred Dobson, Coldstream Guards reservist, had come home.

Thus did the reservists—in many units they amounted to as much as fifty per cent of the total fighting strength—go to war. It has been written, not entirely truthfully, that they went without fuss, grousing or recrimination.

Among the married men with children there was grousing and recrimination in plenty: a man who earned between fifteen and eighteen shillings a week (a pound a week represented something like opulence before the war), sole support of a wife and children, had not been able to save a penny. Prices rose sharply the day war was declared, as did rents; many families in the poorer districts of the big cities found themselves threatened with eviction, if not actual starvation. In 1914 in the East End of London the milk-starved children of reservists were mute reproaches to England's unpreparedness for war.

The Paymaster General's department at the War Office creaked into slow and unwilling motion; separation allowances would be paid at the rate of one shilling and one penny for wives and an additional two-pence a day for boys under fourteen and girls under sixteen. Any increase in family income would have to be provided out of the soldier's pay of one shilling per day. There were the inevitable mortifying delays in payment of these allowances—delays inseparable from any aspect of military finance.

It was scarcely surprising, therefore, that not every reservist recalled to the Colours was burning with patriotism. They went back because they had signed on for seven and five and had no choice in the matter. They went back and they saved England.

The rough khaki uniforms, creased after years in mobilization stores, felt like sandpaper against the skin—more than one reservist compared them unfavourably with prison garb. The new boots were putty coloured and as hard as nails; newly issued webbing equipment was a bewildering maze of straps and buckles; the short Lee-Enfield rifle was, to many of them, a mystery.

In barracks the length and breadth of Britain sergeant-majors—never men of great patience or tolerance—groaned aloud, tore their hair and called on their Maker. When they said 'thank Gawd we got a Navy', they spoke from the heart.

The first route marches soon found the reservists' weak spots: heavy packs dragged agonisingly at shoulders; boots felt as if they were filled with broken glass; feet became swollen and blistered. At rifle firing practice many reservists were found to be all fingers and thumbs as they fired their first fifteen-rounds-a-minute practice. Platoon sergeants swore horribly and prophesied early victory for the Germans.

Medical officers' needles, too, took their toll: a perfunctory dab of iodine on bared upper arms and then the gradually blunting needle pushed hard into nipped flesh; then followed the aftermath of throbbing arms, aching heads, violent shuddering and longing for speedy death. Veterans of Omdurman and Atbara swore that they would rather face a charge of dervishes than submit to this new-fangled medical treatment. But a few of them remembered the hospitals packed with men dying of enteric in South Africa and listened to the rough sympathy of the medical orderlies—'better than getting typhoid,' said the R.A.M.C. men, 'and that's what you'll get from drinking French water.'

'*Water?*' snarled an embittered old sweat of the Royal Warwicks; 'I ain't going to France to drink no water; wine at a penny a gallon'—and he smacked his lips in gleeful anticipation. . . .

3

For Britain's Regular Army the transition from peace to war was less exacting and less uprooting: soldiering was their trade—the only trade that most of them knew—and mobilisation for war had been practised over and over again.

On practice mobilisation British soldiers had been called upon, at short notice, to cast off peacetime blue and to don the field service dress of khaki and puttees. Live ammunition had been drawn, bandoliers and pouches filled; field dressings had bulged the hems of tunics; machine-guns, water-bottles, ground sheets and G.S. wagons—items scarcely mentioned in polite pre-war military society —had put in a brief appearance. Accoutred with the full panoply of war, at times when no war threatened, the soldiers stood stoically, waiting for the bugle or trumpet which would return them to peace-time again.

For the officers these practice mobilisations had interfered with polo, race meetings, shooting, fishing and similar activities loosely lumped together under the heading of 'poodle-faking'; for the rank and file they had cut brutally into valuable beer-drinking time. Comments from officers' mess and barrack room alike were derogatory in the extreme.

But this was no practice; this was the real thing. This ammunition would be fired at a real enemy and not at targets on the range, where the battalion humorists in the butts signalled a 'miss' when the sergeant-major fired a practice; their sabres, newly sharpened, would penetrate living flesh and be withdrawn, stained with warm blood; bayonets would not be used on sacking dummies, but would be thrust into stomach, throat and groin; reservists, who had made such an unholy muck-up of firing fifteen-rounds-rapid on the range, would not do so again—if they wanted to stay alive.

For the gunners, who were drawing shells, high explosive took on a new meaning—shells would blast men to pieces; remove brains, entrails, genitals and limbs with shattering impartiality; they would be no respecters of rank and the red tabs of the staff would afford the wearer no protection.

The regular soldiers—the time-serving men—had benefited little from education and were not over-blessed with imagination. They harboured no hatred for Germany and would, in fact, have been just as willing to go to war with the 'Froggies' or the 'Ruskies'. But even the stolidest private, gunner or trooper—perhaps moronic or 'dim' rather than stolid, is the contemporary adjective, although it seems hardly fair to use any of them describing men who saved Great Britain—felt the all-pervading excitement as he handed his undress and full dress uniform into store. From now on he would be wearing khaki, the drabbest colour of all. No longer would he cut a dash in the streets of Aldershot, Colchester, Plymouth and Dublin in his blues; no longer would feminine eyes light up at his approach, because in khaki (unless the young woman had made a close study of cap badges) a cook's mate in the Army Service Corps was scarcely distinguishable from a trooper of the 9th Lancers.

The professional army in England had been waiting a week for this order to mobilise, and it came as little or no surprise when it arrived. Indeed, they would have felt the keenest disappointment if it had not—it would have meant a return to forming fours, presenting arms, tedious manoeuvres and seven days C.B. for having a stud missing from a boot.

In wet canteens in Aldershot the prevailing mood was wildly celebratory and the cheers were loud and long.

In no one unit were these mobilisation orders awaited more keenly than in the 9th (Queen's Own) Lancers, stationed at Tidworth. This was understandable: in the competitive hierarchy of the cavalry of the line, the 9th stood very high; they were a 'crack' regiment in the fullest sense of the word. Obviously, if Britain went to war, they must be in the forefront of battle.

53

Of the 9th Lancers, Field Marshal Lord Methuen, when he was Commander-in-Chief in South Africa, said: 'I cannot speak too highly of this regiment and do not suppose there is a finer regiment in the service.'

It was an assessment with which few soldiers would quarrel, and one with which the officers and men of the 9th agreed wholeheartedly: their bearing on ceremonial parade had invariably been superb; their conduct in South Africa may have been equalled by other cavalry regiments, but can hardly have been surpassed; they had been magnificent at Balaclava, invincible in Afghanistan. Of course, the 9th Lancers had competition—socially, on the polo field and at Sandown Park—but they acknowledged no superiors.

When the Adjutant, Captain Gerald Reynolds, received the heavily-sealed envelope marked *Most Secret, for Commanding Officers of Cavalry units* he knew exactly what it contained and rode in search of the C.O. of the regiment, Lieutenant-Colonel David Campbell.

Reynolds rode casually, because excessive enthusiasm or excitement were discouraged in officers of the 9th: indeed, only that morning, he had upbraided a subaltern with crushing rudeness because this young man had been rhapsodising on the subject of aerial reconnaissance as an alternative to the function of mounted cavalry in war. He found his colonel in civilian clothes—to be discovered in uniform at half-past four in the afternoon was a cardinal sin for the officers of the 9th Lancers, as it was in any other unit of the pre-1914 regular cavalry.

Campbell registered neither enthusiasm nor excitement. He merely swept a cursory eye over the printed sheets, just perceptibly raised his thick black eyebrows and said laconically: 'Shouldn't be much trouble, we've practised it enough times. Better see about getting the orders out.'

To all intents and purposes the 9th Lancers were, from that moment, on a war footing—although, apparently, in no great hurry to bring the enemy to battle. The Adjutant returned to the orderly-room and handed over his horse to a phlegmatic groom. He then had a word or two with the orderly-room quartermaster-sergeant, initialled two letters—one on the subject of treatment for snakebite, the other about the number of Methodists in the regiment—and strolled to his quarters. Arrived there, he took a bath, examined his face, decided that the occasion merited a second shave and changed into mess kit. Seven-fifteen p.m. found him sipping dry sherry in the officers' mess ante-room.

The 9th Lancers were officially at war, but in the ante-room this was not at once apparent. Dominating the scene in more ways than one was Lieutenant-Colonel David Campbell, a trim and athletic figure in his 'bum-freezing' jacket, skin-tight overalls and spurred Wellingtons. He stood directly underneath the huge oil painting of himself mounted on his own horse, 'The Soarer', which he had ridden to victory in the Grand National sixteen years earlier. Subalterns came into the ante-room and clicked their heels to a murmured chorus of 'Good evening, sir'; mess waiters scurried back and forth with sherry and cocktails; the band discreetly played selections from Gilbert and Sullivan.

Then, to the strains of '*The Roast Beef of Old England*', the officers of the 9th Lancers filed in to the dining-room. They settled themselves up and down the long table, banked with flowers and candles. The mess silver stood bravely on the table. The scene was hardly warlike.

The port circulated and the King had his due. As the officers of the 9th Lancers lit their cigars, German guns were shelling Liége. . . .

At the Headquarters of the 2nd Cavalry Brigade, whither the officers of the 9th Lancers, the 4th Dragoons and the 18th Hussars were summoned the next morning, the atmosphere was not, initially, appreciably more warlike. Standing about in chattering groups, waiting for the arrival of the brigade commander, they might have been discussing a 'needle' polo match: the war would be over by Christmas; it seemed unlikely that it would interfere with the Grand Military meeting at Sandown Park in 1915. Their tunics were rather long in the skirt; their breeches miracles of tailoring; their field boots shone like chestnuts.

Their optimistic theories were supported by Major Tom Bridges of the 4th Dragoons. Bridges had been military attaché at Brussels and stated with confidence that the war would last a bare six months, if as long. There was scarcely an officer present who visualised the long, weary bloody struggle ahead.

General de Lisle, the brigade commander, however, took a gloomier view and slapped Bridges and all the other optimists down with relish. 'Make no mistake, gentlemen,' he said gravely; 'we are in for a long and bitter war.' His words came as a cold douche; suddenly Sandown Park seemed very far away. . . .

Brigadier-General Henry de Beauvoir de Lisle, C.B., D.S.O., was no stranger to war. He had won his D.S.O. as a young subaltern in Egypt; he had fought throughout the South African war, been severely wounded and mentioned in despatches four times. He had also achieved a rare distinction: in India Henry de Lisle had captained the Durham Light Infantry polo team and staggered the cavalry and gunners by carrying off the polo cup. Such was the strange military reasoning of the period that this was regarded as a more illustrious military achievement than any of his others. If anyone had suggested in those days that the Durham Light Infantry could play polo at all, let alone lift the cup, he would have been laughed to scorn. But the Durham Light Infantry had done it at the expense of many a red-faced cavalryman and gunner.

That morning, as a result of their brigade commander's words, the officers of the 2nd Cavalry Brigade returned to their squadrons in a very much more sober and thoughtful frame of mind.

There were some disgruntled young gentlemen at the Royal Military College at Sandhurst during that first week in August; they were worried that the fighting would finish before they could take an active part in it.

There were also apprehensive young gentlemen: these were the cadets who had completed their last term and were awaiting the results of the passing-out exam. The R.M.C. was then, as now, a place of constant trial and few errors. As anxious as any of them was Gentleman Cadet Brian Horrocks, who had committed more than the average of errors. So far, his military career had been remarkably undistinguished—he had passed into Sandhurst bottom but one; he was painfully aware that he had done the minimum of work necessary to obtain his commission—indeed, it was by no means certain that he would. Military duties had come a bad second to sport in the Horrocks' scheme of things: he had, on his own admission been idle both on and off parade. He had spent a large part of his time at the Royal Military College on 'restrictions'—the gentleman cadet's equivalent of C.B. He was, in the parlance of the Sandhurst sergeant-majors, 'an 'orrible gentleman, SIR!'

To make matters worse, he had pawned his father's revolver and lost the ticket. All in all, August 4th, 1914, looked like being a black day for Gentleman Cadet Brian Horrocks. But he need not have worried. His company commander informed him that presumably the examiners had been blind or drunk or both, because by some unexplained miracle he was now Second-Lieutenant Horrocks of the Middlesex Regiment. The officer frowned. He hoped that Horrocks would speedily mend his ways and be a credit to his regiment—he had certainly *not* been a conspicuous success at the R.M.C. However, said the officer with a weighty sigh of resignation, a war must inevitably bring a sharp decline of standards. If it went on long enough, the civilians would start joining up, and if that happened then *anything* could happen . . . Horrocks[1] hardly heard him—his commission was safe. Now only two things worried him: would he get to the war in time and what had he done with that damned pawn ticket?

Aged eighteen years and six months, Second-Lieutenant Brian Horrocks acquired his first independent command—ninety-eight reservists who, he recalls, took charge of him totally and completely. He marched through the streets of Chatham at their head, ready to die the sorest of deaths. He was in France before the war was one month old.

For a fortnight or more rumours had been seething throughout the two divisions stationed in Ireland: Major-General Sir Charles Ferguson's 5th, and Major-General Sir William Pultney's 6th. By August 1st, 1914, the mounting tension could be felt in every unit in Dublin, Cork, Belfast, Newbridge and Mallow. It affected gunners at Kilkenny, Fethard, Waterford and Ballincollig; sappers at Limerick, Moore Park and Carlow; A.S.C. and medical personnel at Fermoy, Kildare and Lusk. The rumours swept the Curragh, Ireland's equivalent of Aldershot and Salisbury Plain, like a prairie fire.

In the 1st Battalion the Duke of Cornwall's Light Infantry the focal point for dissemination of rumour was, as in every unit, the other ranks' canteen. But the rumours in wet canteens were inevitably wildly inaccurate and unreliable; not for nothing were they known as latrine rumours. The 'latrine rumours' in the D.C.L.I. were neither more nor less fantastic than those circulating in the Manchesters, the 4th Hussars or the Suffolks.

Rumours of this description were usually set in motion by a private soldier who had a friend who was a despatch rider at Brigade Headquarters who knew a sergeant clerk at Division who had heard the Staff Captain telling a major at Army Headquarters that there had been an uprising of Zulus, who threatened the slaughter of the entire white population of South Africa. And who was going to quell the revolt? Why, the 1st D.C.L.I. of course—unless, by some mischance trouble was threatened in China, in which case the problem would be solved by the 2nd D.C.L.I., who were stationed in Hong Kong. The D.C.L.I. had quelled the Indian Mutiny, hadn't they? Well, then . . .

[1] Now Lieutenant-General Sir Brian Horrocks, K.C.B., K.B.E., D.S.O., M.C.

It was no part of the duties of warrant officers and sergeants of the 1st D.C.L.I. to listen to rumours: their business was to preserve the smartness and discipline for which the regiment was justly famous. But by the evening of August 4th the deadly virus had even spread to the sergeants' mess.

Late that night Regimental Sergeant-Major John Hart, that iron man of discipline, was summoned to the presence of the Adjutant. There was now no doubt, Captain Acland said, that a state of war existed between Great Britain and Germany. R.S.M. Hart accepted the news with grim satisfaction. He had fought in one war with the 32nd of Foot and was quite ready to fight in another. He was small in stature, as were many light infantrymen, but in nothing else: his moustache was fiercely waxed; from the top of his 'cheesecutter' cap to his glittering boots he was the epitome of military perfection; his normal speaking voice, clearly audible at one hundred paces, resembled a truck in low gear. If anyone had told John Hart that he was a caricature of a music-hall sergeant-major, he would not have felt unduly insulted. It was nearing midnight as the R.S.M. walked past the sergeants' mess on the way to his quarters. His lips tightened and his pace quickened as he saw a light still burning and heard the sounds of revelry within. Someone, it was clear, had seen fit to disobey his most explicit order that the mess should close at eleven p.m. To R.S.M. Hart such a gross breach of discipline only just fell short of mutiny.

The sergeants' mess of the 1st D.C.L.I. was, in truth, *en fête*. The Band Sergeant and the C.S.M. of 'A' Company had conspired against Sergeant George White, the mess caterer, and routed him: war was not declared every day, they explained forcibly, and such an occasion demanded a generous extension of drinking hours. Without a great deal of conviction Sergeant White protested that war had *not* yet been declared and that the R.S.M. would have his guts for braces if he kept the bar open after eleven p.m.—he wanted to keep his stripes, even if no one else did.

Reinforcements in the shape of three more company sergeant-majors and every quartermaster-sergeant and platoon sergeant of the battalion were on the way, and they tipped the scale against George White. At eleven forty-five p.m. every glass was primed and full-throated singing was in progress. By this time Sergeant White had entered into the spirit of the thing and was already granting generous credit facilities.

''Allo, 'allo, who's your lady friend!' bawled the sergeants' mess, blissfully unaware of the waxed moustaches and prominent nose which had just appeared through the door. The second verse was drowned by a fearful roar from R.S.M. Hart: 'AND WHAT'S GOING ON HERE, THEN?'

There was a pregnant silence, broken only by a resounding hiccough from the sergeant of Number Ten Platoon. Then—

'Don't stand there like a bloody dummy,' grated the R.S.M. at Sergeant White, who was frozen by apprehension into quivering immobility. 'Pass over a pint glass and one of them bottles of stout an' look sharp about it. . . .'

Truly, this was a night to remember; war was not declared every day.

Second-Lieutenant Robert Churchill-Longman, a bewildered officer of the Special Reserve, departed hot-foot to the 2nd Battalion the Royal Sussex Regiment located at Inkerman Barracks, Woking. The Adjutant, a stern disciplinarian, eyed him with cold dislike and asked if he had a sword. Churchill-Longman had no sword, but was informed in uncompromising terms that he would have one at their next meeting, which was likely to be of disciplinary nature in the orderly room next morning.

Churchill-Longman raced to Woking Station, caught the next train to London and went to that celebrated emporium in Covent Garden, where all sartorial problems are instantly solved. For thirty shillings he purchased an officers' sword, infantry pattern.

No, sir, said the suave assistant regretfully, it would *not* be possible to *hire* a sword: morning suits, yes; evening suits, naturally; but *not* swords . . . now, what about a valise, a sleeping bag, a fitted mess tin, a binocular case, a map-case, shirts, ties, warm underclothing, a hip flask, puttees. . . .

By no means all of Britain's small professional army lay under the hands of those who could put it to immediate active use: much of it was far away across the seas, guarding the outposts of the Empire.

There were regiments in India, China, Egypt, the Sudan, South Africa, Malta, Gibraltar, Malaya, Burma and the West Indies.

Like all British soldiers down the centuries they were dissatisfied with their lot; the soldier abroad longed for grey rainy days in Aldershot and dark luke-warm beer; the soldier in Aldershot pined for hot sun and a temperature of one hundred and five in the shade, a fly-blown native bazaar and a sight of the pyramids. The British soldier was in perpetual mourning for the day before yesterday.

The 2nd Battalion the Queen's Royal West Surrey Regiment, for instance, were on manoeuvres in the middle of the sweltering South African veldt, a full six days' march from their station at Roberts' Heights. The manoeuvres were so pedestrian, tedious and lacking in realism that Lieutenant Arthur Roberts, a subaltern of eleven years' service, found himself cursing with renewed vehemence the partial colour-blindness which had prevented him from joining the service of his choice, the Royal Navy. The directing brains of this particular exercise had all fought in the South African war and apparently had learned nothing new about military tactics; indeed, it seemed to Roberts that they had advanced little since the Crimean War. The current chestnut about the soldier who was put on a charge for having a dirty powder horn at Agincourt was still considered to be funny.

Some of the other ranks had also been in the South African war and during lulls in the battle—some of them of up to four hours duration—bored their younger comrades with interminable and largely untrue stories of frightful combat against the 'Bojers'.

Companies advanced across the veldt in line, their formation so impeccable and their dressing so perfect that cunningly sited machine-guns could scarcely have failed to annihilate them; they formed square and prepared to repel cavalry; they performed almost identical evolutions to those carried out by the Grand Old Duke of York's ten thousand men. For the purpose of this particular 'sham fight' Lieutenant Roberts' platoon were mounted infantry—they had no horses, but were expected to march as fast on foot as would the cavalry on horses. Roberts, having unsuccessfully attempted to convince his colonel that this was not possible, came to the conclusion that he was thoroughly fed up. He was also halfway to being convinced that Great Britain would lose any future war in which she found herself.

Private George Criddle was in the same angry little boat; he, too, was fed up, but he was not thinking about atrophied senior officers and tactics, save in a very limited sense. Seven years a soldier, Criddle was still a private[1]—further promotion to non-commissioned rank was effectively barred by the number of red ink entries on his conduct sheet. He spent most of his waking hours thinking of beer and there was none of this precious commodity nearer than Potchefsroom, 110 miles away.

---

[1] Private George Criddle survived the 1st Battle of Ypres and several sharp engagements on the North-West Frontier of India. To-day, still a private, he is a pensioner at the Royal Hospital, Chelsea.

To at least two soldiers of the 2nd Queen's, therefore, the declaration of war and the immediate cancellation of manoeuvres came as a distinct relief.

On receipt of the news that Britain was at war, work at that august and sybaritic seat of military learning, the Staff College at Quetta, came to an abrupt standstill, despite peremptorily worded orders from G.H.Q. at Simla that work should continue as usual.

The students at the Staff College were senior captains, all officers with illustrious military futures. The nominal roll of students in August, 1914, was an exceptionally distinguished one, for it contained no fewer than three recipients of the Victoria Cross: Captain Arthur Hore-Ruthven, 1st Dragoon Guards; Major Edward Costello of the 22nd Punjabis; and Captain George Wylly, Corps of Guides. They had been told on arrival by the General Staff Officer, 1st Grade, Lieutenant-Colonel Henry Austin, D.S.O., an uncompromising sapper, that whereas it was a splendid thing to have the letters V.C. after one's name, in order to prosper in a military career the small letters *p.s.c.* (passed staff college, but sometimes irreverently referred to as 'practically senior to Christ') were every bit as essential (this is equally true of the Regular Army to-day).

But to a professional fighting man it was not easy to knuckle down to the complexities of administration, supply and transport when his country was at war. The instructors, dedicated soldiers themselves, only half-heartedly attempted to combat the mood of elation which swept through the Staff College and indeed the whole of Quetta. The Quetta Club, scene of a million wild parties, saw the wildest one of all the night war was declared: there was riotous singing and champagne was consumed by the magnum; the band played '*Rule Britannia*' to the accompaniment of tumultuous cheering; a German waiter was debagged by some young cavalry officers and threatened with immersion in a water trough.

Some of the officers, however, heard the news in a more sober frame of mind. One of them, Captain Richard Meinertzhagen of the Royal Fusiliers, considered it:

> No occasion to be gay and hilarious . . . there is a feeling of elation at the Staff College, a state of mind I do not share . . . the prospect of this war depresses me . . .[1]

Meinertzhagen also forecast that many of the students would be dead within the year and he was proved an able prophet.

[1] Colonel Meinertzhagen in Army Diary (Oliver & Boyd).

Captain Kenneth Bruce of the Gordon Highlanders was anxiously awaiting the birth of his second child in Edinburgh. He just had time to see a tiny red-faced bundle before embarking on a ship to Egypt. On arrival in Cairo, he was just in time to join the battalion before it left for England.

There were majors on shooting leave in Kashmir and captains of Indian cavalry on the river at Henley; there were sergeants on the rough-riding course at Netheravon and corporals on musketry courses at Hythe. There were privates newly released from detention barracks in Aldershot.

The 1st Royal Sussex and the 2nd King's Liverpool heard the news with bitter amusement and envy—they had a small war on their hands as it was, on the North West Frontier of India, where soldiers slept with their rifles chained to their wrists. The 1st Lancashire Fusiliers were sweltering in Karachi, the 1st Suffolks in Khartoum and the 2nd Buffs in Madras.

The 2nd Black Watch uttered dreadful oaths in Bareilly, the 1st Highland Light Infantry got drunk in Ambala and military crime in the 1st Irish Rifles at Aden assumed hitherto unprecedented proportions.

So Great Britain went to war.

PART TWO

MONS

For it's Tommy this, an' Tommy that, an' 'Tommy, wait outside';
But it's 'Special train for Atkins' when the trooper's on the tide . . .'
Rudyard Kipling in Tommy

CHAPTER V

I

FRANCE could only hope that the tiny and vastly outnumbered Belgian Army would stand fast until joined by the French 5th Army and the British Expeditionary Force.

The Belgian General de Witte had scored a brilliant victory against the Uhlans penetrating towards Louvain—his steady volleys of rifle fire mowed down the Uhlans and seemed to point to an immediate Belgian victory. But on August 12th the great siege guns were trained on Liège and one by one the forts of Liège fell to the Germans; on August 13th two more forts fell; by the 14th all the forts east and north of the city had fallen.

The B.E.F. began to cross the English Channel on August 12th. For the next five days an average of thirteen ships—about 50,000 tons of shipping—left Southampton every day. Without any sort of hitch and without interference from the German Navy, 100,000 men went to war. The smoothness and expedition of the crossings silenced, no less than it amazed, the most rabid critics of Britain's military administration.

The B.E.F. was made up of two Army Corps. The First commanded by General Sir Douglas Haig and the Second commanded by General Sir Horace Smith-Dorrien; supporting them was General Allenby's Cavalry Division. In overall command was Sir John French. The soldiers travelled in the appalling discomfort which inevitably characterised the seaborne travel of the British Army: they were packed on the transports like sardines and there were not even the most basic amenities on board. In conditions which would bring soldiers of today to a state of near mutiny, the B.E.F. cheered, sang and roared full-throated 'NOs!' to the rhetorical question 'Are we downhearted?'

They sang the inevitable *Tipperary* and other songs of both the printable and unprintable variety. They had heard that the German Army had a General von Kluck which prompted them to sing to the tune of *The Girl I Left Behind Me*:

> Oh, we don't give a ——
> For old von *Kluck*
> An' all 'is bloody Army. . . .

The B.E.F., in fact, resembled a stag outing on a day trip to France, rather than the best trained and disciplined army that Great Britain had ever sent to war.

The loneliest member of the B.E.F. on the crossing to France was the Commander-in-Chief, General Sir John French. Once his forces are committed, a commanding general is, of necessity, a lonely man with nothing to do. He carries a fearful burden and carries it alone. On board the cruiser *Sentinel* the famed hospitality of the Royal Navy was very much in evidence and the senior staff officers passed the one and a half hours between Dover and Boulogne in extreme luxury. But French's feeling of confidence and pride was heavily overshadowed by sadness:

> I could not but think [he wrote] of the many fine fellows who had said good-bye to Old England for ever.[1]

A sombre thought, which did not occur to many other soldiers of the B.E.F.

To the British, from Sir John French down to the youngest private, the civilian population of France accorded a reception which was fantastic even by French standards of demonstrative behaviour. The first troops to disembark at Boulogne were the 2nd Battalion the Argyll and Sutherland Highlanders, wearing their kilts and marching to the music of the pipes. Amid rapturous cheering, the pipe band played '*Hielan' Laddie*', '*Cock o' the North*' and '*The Road to the Isles*'. Old men, some of them veterans of Sedan, cheered wildly, children marched and pirouetted in front of the band and women of all ages speculated ribaldly as to what, if anything, the Highlanders wore under their kilts.

The pipers marched and counter-marched and then, at a signal from the pipe-major, halted in the square. The drones began as the bladders of the bagpipes filled with air. The pipe band had practised '*La Marseillaise*' hurriedly before leaving England and the opening bars died horribly in their infancy under the baleful stare of the pipe-major. The second attempt was more successful, and the cheers redoubled as the French national anthem was heard. When the pipers paused for breath, a French brass band, not to be outdone, played '*God Save the King*' and a semi-ragtime version of '*Auld Lang Syne*'.

The mayor kissed the colonel on both cheeks; the mayoress kissed the pipe-major; the ladies of Boulogne, aged sixteen to eighty, kissed every soldier within range.

[1] Field-Marshal Lord French in *1914* (Constable, 1919).

Identical scenes were enacted at Rouen and Le Havre. Lord Kitchener, that iron man of duty and discipline, issued a stern warning to the troops and every soldier had his message pasted on page one of his paybook:

In this new experience you may find temptations, both in wine and women. You must entirely resist both temptations, and while treating all women with perfect courtesy you should avoid any intimacy.

It was easier said than done. A red-faced colonel was resoundingly kissed in Rouen's square; a Grenadier Guards sergeant-major, an august disciplinarian with fiercely waxed moustaches, was observed minus his cap badge and with a rose behind each ear; a trooper of the Queen's Bays sat helplessly on his horse as three giggling young women unwound one of his puttees and bore it away in triumph. The children, too, reaped a rich harvest in cap badges, shoulder numerals and buttons; they jostled round the grinning soldiers demanding souvenirs with piping insistence.

Sir John French went to the British Embassy in Paris, where the hospitality was on a suitably lavish scale. But General Sir William Robertson, the B.E.F.'s Quartermaster-General, probably fared better. At the Crillon Hotel the chef, a veritable priest of gluttony, produced a dinner which Robertson rated the best he had ever eaten, before or since. The next morning, knowing that Englishmen do not care to start the day on rolls and coffee, the management served a conventional English breakfast of gargantuan proportions. Nor would the *maître d'hôtel*, Monsieur Decquis, hear of presenting a bill. It would be sent to Berlin, he informed General Robertson with jocular confidence—even now he was planning a victory celebration for early December.

In the outlying villages and small towns, as the B.E.F. marched or trained to their positions on the left flank of the French Army, the treatment was the same: there were Union Jacks at every window; the soldiers were showered with fruit, flowers and chocolate. At every halt cloths were laid on tables and steaks of a wonderful succulence appeared as if by magic. So, inevitably, did wine in seemingly unlimited quantities: the young soldiers, ignorant of its potency, drank dubiously but with gathering enthusiasm; the old soldiers—'the red ink entry' men—drank with delighted appreciation.

There were shouts of *'vivent les Anglais'* and *'à bas les Allemands'* on all sides; bloodthirsty references were made to *'les sales boches'* and children, copying their elders, drew their hands significantly across their throats, yelling the while '*Coupez les gorges*'.

It certainly looked like being a lovely war.

The B.E.F. left the ports either by train or on foot and headed for the Belgian frontier. Already half Belgium was ablaze; Louvain was burning; Liège had fallen; von Gallwitz's army was within a day's march of Namur; von Kluck had almost reached Brussels. The Germans were advancing south-west on their triumphant right-hook towards Paris; they were following the main roads, with their infantry swarming along the lesser roads. In the middle of their line of advance lay Mons.

In accordance with pre-arranged plans, the British were to fill the gap on the left of the already heavily-committed French armies and take up defensive positions on the Mons-Binche-Charleroi road.

On August 22nd, the B.E.F. reached the drab, industrial town of Mons.

2

The Cavalry Division of the B.E.F. was commanded by Major-General Sir Edmund Allenby. Allenby was a big man in every way —physically, mentally and morally. He was universally known as 'The Bull', and he had many of that animal's physical characteristics. He had a jutting jaw, an imperious, even faintly cruel, expression, and a loud and booming voice. In appearance he was the almost perfect choleric general of fiction. But the nickname was appropriate to externals only. Although Allenby's manner was abrupt, if not downright rude, and his utterances were frequently explosive, he was at bottom kindly and tolerant, although neither quality was at first apparent. Troopers who stood before him in his orderly room found that his bark was frequently worse than his bite and that he had a sympathetic understanding of soldiers' problems.

His crushing rudeness to senior officers delighted all those who were fortunate enough to be listening; Allenby rarely lowered his voice and certainly not when administering rebukes. To one brigadier-general he said: 'There are fools, damned fools—and you, sir!'

His phobias about chinstraps and rifle buckets are still remembered; those who incurred his displeasure—and they were many— remembered a tongue-lashing as painful as the anger was shortlived.

He was totally without fear; he never bore a grudge; he shirked no duty, however irksome; he never sought popularity, although there was not an officer or man of his division who would not cheerfully have died for him.

The spirit of Balaklava was still abundantly present among Allenby's cavalrymen of 1914. The primary functions of cavalrymen were scouting and reconnaissance—they were the ears and eyes of the army—but at the back of every cavalryman's mind was the prospect of charging in columns of squadrons with sabre or lance.

> Theirs not to reason why,
> Theirs but to do or die. . . .

In both world wars there were a number of senior officers who have been accused of having a 'Balaklava mentality' thus implying crass stupidity, stubborn rigidity of purpose, reactionary idiocy and a host of other defects.

Rightly or wrongly, this mentality was to be found in generous measure in the 4th Dragoon Guards; if Colonel Mullen had ordered the regiment to mount and charge von Kluck's entire army, they would have sworn horribly, stood to their horses, broken from trot to headlong gallop, drawn sabres, cheered lustily and done just that. And that went for the other regiments of the Cavalry Division: the 5th and 6th Dragoons; the Queen's Bays; the 5th, 9th and 12th Lancers; the 3rd, 4th, 11th, 15th, 18th, 19th and 20th Hussars; and the Household Cavalry—the Royal Horse Guards (the Blues) and Life Guards, who had been forced by the uncouth circumstances of a World War to exchange their plumes and glittering breastplates, cuirasses, pipe-clayed breeches and jackboots for field-service khaki.

It would not be too much to say that the Cavalry Division from General Allenby down to Trooper Maguire of the 5th Inniskillings (who had just been put on a charge for filling his water bottle with red wine) were imbued with the Balaklava spirit and felt no shame thereby. . . .

The cavalry had been stripped of much of their peacetime glamour by August 1914. And there had certainly been nothing glamorous about the war to date, excepting the rapturous welcomes at Rouen, Boulogne and Le Havre.

Some regiments had been luckier than others, for there had been ramps and gangways leading to the transports at Southampton. But for the majority of the Cavalry Division the embarkation of horses had been a tedious and blasphemous business of slinging the animals, approximately 150 in each squadron, on board. Disembarkation had been equally trying. Then had followed seemingly endless marching, often in pouring rain, on the slippery pavé roads—sliding, slipping and cursing, as only cavalrymen can curse, in pitch darkness.

Interpreters, voluble and intensely warlike Frenchmen attached themselves to cavalry regiments and expressed themselves confident in early victory. Maps appeared in profusion—maps on which it would, in theory at any rate, have been possible to follow the advance of the B.E.F. across France and the Rhine to Berlin. But as it turned out, the fortunes of war were to lead the B.E.F. in the opposite direction, over country for which no maps were available.

Nor did the country just over the Belgian frontier look promising for the conventional cavalry charge; where they had hoped to find wide rolling downs over which they would gallop knee to knee in a succession of headlong charges, they encountered small smoky villages, coal mines, towering slag heaps, railway embankments and a profusion of barbed wire. All the villages and towns seemed as densely populated as Black Country towns in England: Maubeuge, in fact, bore a depressing resemblance to Stoke-on-Trent.

For the first week of the war the cavalry were, in the words of the popular song, bewitched, bothered and bewildered: there was a cascade of confused orders and they were sent here and there on abortive reconnaissance patrols.

Roads became blocked as westward-moving cavalry bumped into eastward-moving cavalry; ration limbers got lost; some of the reservists, still soft from civilian living, were beginning to feel the strain of active service and said so with dogged persistence.

But it would not be proper to say that the Cavalry Division were depressed. And at every halt the oft-repeated hopeful question was asked: 'Wonder if we'll get a ride at 'em tomorrow?'

3

The first British troops in action were the 4th (Royal Irish) Dragoon Guards; indeed, they would have felt slighted if it had not been so—although the 16th Lancers and the Royal Scots Greys have never quite forgiven them.

Known as 'The Mounted Micks', the 4th Dragoons earned their first distinction in 1736 when they drank forty bowls of punch in Dublin in a little under fifteen minutes. They quelled riots in Manchester in 1808, charged the French in the Peninsula War of 811, the Russians at Balaklava in 1854 and routed Colonel Arabi's Egyptians in 1882.

They were practically entirely Irish and a squadron nominal roll of the 4th Dragoons read like a stanza from *Phil the Fluter's Ball* or *Macnamara's Band*: Brogan, Brannigan, Connolly, Callaghan, Delaney, Finnegan, Grogan, Hogan, Hannigan, Hennessy, Logan, Maguire, Rafferty, O'Rourke, O'Toole, O'Flynn, O'Shaughnessy... They were hard riding, hard drinking and hard swearing and had a tendency to pick quarrels with horse gunners on Saturday nights. They swore terrible oaths and pilfered carrots from the cookhouse to give to their horses. Like all Irishmen, they had an amazing affinity with horses.

This was the Irish cavalryman of the period—'terrible fellers an' avid for fighting'; gentle and pugilistic by turns; hot-tempered and quick to take offence (particularly from a Scot); at one with their horses and with a fierce and touchy discipline which was all their own.

Their Commanding Officer, Lieutenant-Colonel Robert Mullen alternately railed at them, congratulated them and despaired of them; he thought continuously of them whether waking or sleeping. His feelings for his men were like those of a stern but kindly father towards wayward children who must be watched every minute of the day. His feelings for them, in fact, were something akin to love.

At first sight the scene beside the main road that leads from Mons to Brussels through Soignies seemed peaceful enough; indeed, it was strongly reminiscent of manoeuvres on Salisbury Plain: there was the same blend of picnic atmosphere, boredom and discomfort for discomfort's sake. In the thick wood beside the road, 'C' Squadron of the 4th Dragoon Guards were preparing for the rigours of another day of active service.

The squadron's horses were tethered in neat and orderly lines; sentries, with watchful eyes and rifles slung, paced up and down; there were men shaving, men feeding and watering horses; an encouraging odour of bacon indicated that breakfast was on the way. And the Squadron Sergeant-Major's injunction to 'strike a light with thim breakfasts' seemed to hold a note of belligerent urgency.

For rumours about the enemy were fast becoming translated into fact. Hitherto, reports of German movement had only come from semi-hysterical Belgian refugees—pathetic columns of men, women and children, hauling their worldly possessions in wheel-barrows and handcarts. They told of Uhlans, crack German cavalry and the equivalent of British lancers, masses of infantry, giant field guns and howitzers—a horde of field grey, pillaging and burning, as they advanced ever closer to Mons.

71

The 4th Dragoons had largely discounted these rumours, because ever since their arrival at Boulogne they had not sighted a single German.

But now more reliable and disquieting information was to hand. Breezy young men of the Royal Flying Corps in machines of Heath Robinson design—Blériots, Henri Farmans, Avros and B.E.8s—had spent busy days on reconnaissance, and had been shot at impartially by Germans, French and British: they expected to be shot at by Germans; they were not unduly surprised at being shot at by the French. But to be shot at by British troops was, as one pilot euphemistically phrased it, 'a bit over the odds'. The information given by the Royal Flying Corps was disturbing enough: something like 400,000 Germans were advancing from the north and their forward elements were less than ten miles from Mons.

And as 'C' Squadron of the 4th Dragoon Guards breakfasted on that glorious morning, they could plainly hear the distant crump of field guns and the occasional chatter of a machine-gun to the north of them. The French army on their right was obviously already heavily committed and soon it would be them. For 'C' Squadron it could not come quickly enough.

It certainly could not come soon enough for the squadron leader, Major Tom Bridges; at forty-four, Bridges already had a distinguished military career behind him, although his soldiering had not followed the conventional pattern of the cavalryman. In the South African War he had been severely wounded and twice mentioned in despatches while serving with the Imperial Light Horse and the West Australian Mounted Infantry, neither of them regular units—in fact, very irregular ones. In the Somaliland campaign of 1902 he had raised and commanded a still more unorthodox formation, the Tribal Horse; he was wounded yet again and for sustained gallantry over a long and difficult period awarded the Distinguished Service Order. Nor did his career between the wars follow the normal, uneventful pattern of the cavalry officer. He attended the staff college, a form of extended education frowned upon in many regiments and a social pitfall to be avoided. A natural flair for languages gained him the appointments of Military Attaché in the Hague, Brussels and Christiania.

But remove Tom Bridges from the somewhat rarefied surroundings of a military attaché and he was equally at home in the roughest of active service conditions: he was calm and cool in any situation, however daunting; he could go without sleep for seemingly indefinite periods—he had acquired this enviable knack in the South African veldt and the Somaliland scrub; he never required anything in the way of personal comfort; he seemed delighted to set out on any mission, however dangerous, to any place, however distant.

The presence of Tom Bridges in the comparatively humble appointment of squadron leader in the 4th Dragoon Guards appeared to need some explanation. But no explanation would have been forthcoming from Tom Bridges: his country was at war and he proposed to fight this at war the head of 'C' Squadron of the 4th Dragoon Guards.

The second-in-command of the squadron, Captain Charles Hornby, was cast in the same mould as Bridges. They had started the war together and, with God's grace, would finish it together. They were both superb horsemen—members of the regimental polo team and dashing performers in the hunting field and in steeple-chases.

The orders for 'C' Squadron, when they eventually arrived, were vague enough. The messenger of battle was the Adjutant, Captain Richard Oldrey, who came up the towpath through the woods at a casual hand canter.

Nebulous as these orders were, they represented the prospect of positive action at last:

> There are Uhlans over there—you're to send out a patrol, hit 'em hard without actually getting involved in a major scrap and then get out of it fast. Brigade want identification of the units heading this way—shoulder numerals, identification papers and so forth. Good luck.

And with a cheery wave the Adjutant cantered back to Regimental Headquarters. They were the sort of orders that Bridges understood; he had done the same sort of thing in South Africa and Somaliland—the swift disciplined rush on an enemy taken by surprise, a quick mêlée of bloody work with sabres and a fast withdrawal before the enemy knew what had hit them.

There was a note of cheerful confidence in Bridges' voice as he shouted: ' "C" Squadron, prepare to mount—MOUNT!' And every trooper as he swung himself into the saddle felt the tingling excitement of the moment.

The squadron moved off: Captain Hornby with two troops led the way, followed by Bridges and the rest of the squadron half a mile in rear.

The scene was still peaceful enough half a mile further on as

Hornby's men trotted through the woods: the sun shone brilliantly, birds sang in the trees—the thought of war seemed ludicrous.

Presently they emerged from the wood into open country and Hornby went forward with Staff Sergeant Harry Sharp. But beyond the trees there were only rolling grass fields and zigzagging through them a long expanse of unmetalled road.

Another half-mile took them to the outskirts of the village of Soignies. Then things happened very quickly.

The mouths of the three German cyclists, riding a little ahead of the party of Uhlans down the main street of Soignies, gaped open in horrified surprise when they saw the leading files of 'C' Squadron.

Hornby had no time to give any orders. Instead, he let out a hunting field yell, which was instantly taken up by every man in the troop.

Now the sabres were out and the Dragoons were galloping full tilt at the Uhlans: Staff-Sergeant Sharp's swordpoint went home once, a second and a third time . . . thirty seconds later the three cyclists lay dead as the Dragoons galloped over their bodies.

The young German lieutenant in command of the Uhlans barely had a chance to open his mouth before Charles Hornby, riding at full gallop, plunged his sabre into his ribs.

The wild but disciplined impetus of the Dragoons' charge was too much for the remaining Uhlans. With one accord they broke, wheeled, and hurtled away in ignominious flight.

It was a bad start to the war for the German cavalry. A few of the stouter hearts faced the khaki charge, but they were hampered by their long lances and in any case they were no match for the Dragoons, every one of whom was temporarily mad and obsessed with the lust to kill. Six more Germans fell to the flashing sabres before panic, total and complete, turned the charge into a rout. For Hornby, the ensuing chase over a full mile of fields combined the thrills of the polo field, the hunting field and the steeplechase. But if the Uhlans were proved to be unwilling fighters, the speed of their horses was never in question: as Hornby related afterwards, they went much too fast for 'C' Squadron.

Only when bullets from advanced elements of German infantry started to sing past their ears did Hornby remember his orders not to get involved in a major-battle: then, and only then, did he break off the pursuit, swinging the troop left in a circle to gallop back the way they had come.

Eight Uhlans had been killed without a single British casualty. Shoulder numerals and identity discs cut from the necks of the dead

74

identified the German cavalry as the 4th Cuirassiers of the 9th Cavalry Division.

Loud and envious were the cheers from the rest of the Cavalry Division as 'C' Squadron rode back to their billets, loaded down with captured lances and accompanied by half a dozen hangdog prisoners. There was plenty to cheer about: in the first action of the war, the enemy had been taught a salutary lesson. Morale, already high in every cavalry regiment, soared to even greater heights: what the 4th Dragoon Guards could do, then the 9th Lancers, the 5th Inniskillings and the Queen's Bays could do better. . . .

Before leaving England, Brigadier-General Henry de Lisle had addressed the officers of his brigade. He told them that the first officer who ran his man through with the sabre would be recommended for a high decoration. De Lisle was as good as his word: just six weeks later the *London Gazette* announced the award of the Distinguished Service Order to Captain Charles Hornby, 4th (Royal Irish) Dragoon Guards.

4

In the British cavalry the 'sabre versus lance' argument had been going on for centuries. As a result of Hornby's action against the Uhlans, many of whom had thrown their lances away, there was much fresh fuel for the inevitable good humoured, although occasionally acrimonious, exchanges.

Tight-lipped lancers, with a forest of lance tips blocking a busy road, were the targets for much chaff from Dragoons, Hussars, infantrymen and artillerymen alike. The 5th (Allenby had been their Commanding Officer before the war), 9th, 12th and 16th Lancers, proud and illustrious regiments, seemed in grave danger of becoming figures of fun:

'I should throw away the tooth-pick, mate, if I was you. . . .'
'Look out, 'ere come the Brummagem Uhlans. . . .'
There was no saying where it might all have ended.

It was argued that the lance as a killing weapon was lethal and conclusive—a man run through at stretch gallop represented a well-nigh certain kill. But the Hussar and Dragoon regiments were ready with a counter argument. How could the lancer be sure of getting his weapon back? Were not lances a ceremonial novelty, quickly separable from modern war? True, admitted the lancers, but they had sabres as well, sabres with which to thrust and slash without encumbrance. Perhaps the proof of the pudding was in the eating, and as far as the achievement of the Cavalry Divisions of the B.E.F. were concerned, both weapons seemed equally effective.

The restoration of lancer prestige fell to the 16th (Queen's) Lancers.

A patrol under Lieutenant Charles Tempest-Hicks was ambushed by a company of Jägers (German light infantry). With the first German volley, Tempest-Hicks' horse was shot from under him and two troopers were killed. But Tempest-Hicks—like Tom Bridges and Charles Hornby, he was a distinguished performer on the polo field—quickly mounted the horse of one of the dead troopers, drew the patrol into a line that would not have disgraced an Aldershot review and shouted the single order: 'CHARGE!' Half a dozen lance points went home (no one ever called the 16th Brummagem Uhlans after that) and several more Jägers were ridden down and trampled underfoot. The rest showed no more inclination for fighting than had the Uhlans routed by Hornby and fled from a stricken field and a battle which, at the beginning of hostilities, seemed to have promised a very different outcome.

Chapter VI

I

From the headquarters of the German Army at Aix-la-Chapelle, the Kaiser, in a fine frenzy of eloquence, issued the following explosive and annihilating order to General von Kluck:

It is my Royal and Imperial Command that you concentrate your energies for the immediate present upon one single purpose, and that is, that you address all your skill and all the valour of my soldiers to exterminate the treacherous English and walk over General French's contemptible little army.

It was the sort of order that von Kluck could readily understand. He was cast in the same mould as his master. Although sixty-eight years old, von Kluck had the well-preserved appearance and physical vigour of a man twenty years younger.

Forty-four years earlier, as a junior captain, von Kluck had been wounded at Sedan; even at this early age he had been favourably noticed by the higher command. And for ten years before the war he had been groomed for stardom as the man who would lead the march on Paris.

The B.E.F. were ready for von Kluck, although the long forced marches had diminished the fervour of their rendering of the songs in which he figured so derogatorily. All through the sweltering heat of the 22nd they had marched. And most of that night had been spent digging trenches; by the dawn of the 23rd General Sir Douglas Haig's First Army Corps and General Sir Horace Smith-Dorrien's Second Army Corps had sunk into the ground like moles.

The primary function of the B.E.F. was to continue the French line of resistance in a north-westerly direction towards the coast. The natural country feature which was geographically indicated for this purpose was the high road, which runs from Charleroi through Binche to Mons, and this was the defensive line which our troops were to man. But this proved impracticable: the Germans were already in possession of Charleroi and on the right the French had by now fallen back from the positions outlined in the original plan. For the British Force to have occupied the Mons–Charleroi road would have laid it open to the very great risk, if not the virtual certainty, of being cut off and completely isolated. There was no choice but to range the First Army Corps along the Mons–Beaumont road, to the rear of the position originally planned, while the Second Army Corps lined the canal between Mons and Condé. Between the canal positions and 1st Corps lay Mons itself and what became known as the Salient, partly bounded by a semi-circular sweep of the canal past Nimy and Obourg but open to the north-east. The Salient was the nearest point to the enemy, and lay directly in the German line of advance. The enemy's entry into Mons itself had to be delayed as long as possible and therefore the Salient had to be defended. This task fell to the 2nd Corps. The Cavalry Division was to throw out a screen in front of the Salient positions, to provide the usual reconnaissance patrols, and also to help fill the gap between Second and First Corps—this last involved the cavalry in a more static role than that for which they had hoped. They were later caught up in some bitter defensive fighting in the Binche area, though this did not spread to 1st Division on their right, which was hardly involved in the Battle of Mons at all.

Both tactically and geographically, the position was a bad one: the approaches to it from the north were littered with small hamlets, rows of houses, factories, and gigantic slag-heaps. The Mons–Condé Canal itself was nowhere deeper than seven feet and only in a very few places more than sixty feet wide. In the course of its sixteen miles' length there were no fewer than eighteen bridges. In fact, as an obstacle to a determined German advance the value of the canal was negligible.

The defence of the Salient was largely the responsibility of General Sir Hubert Hamilton's 3rd Division, and this division was to bear the main brunt of the Battle of Mons. It was realised that the Salient was not an ideal position and a second line of defence had been prepared behind Mons itself and roughly on the line St. Ghislain—Wasmes—Paturage—Frameries. This would straighten out the line and do away with an exposed Salient.

The popular misconception of World War One generals is of stout, choleric, port-wine complexioned incompetents who swilled quantities of claret in well-appointed chateaux many miles behind the front line. No such accusation could be levelled at General Hamilton. A man of enormous personal gallantry—he had fought in the Burmese Expedition of 1886, been present at the battles of Atbara and Khartoum and served throughout the South African War—it irked him that he should live in the comparative comfort of

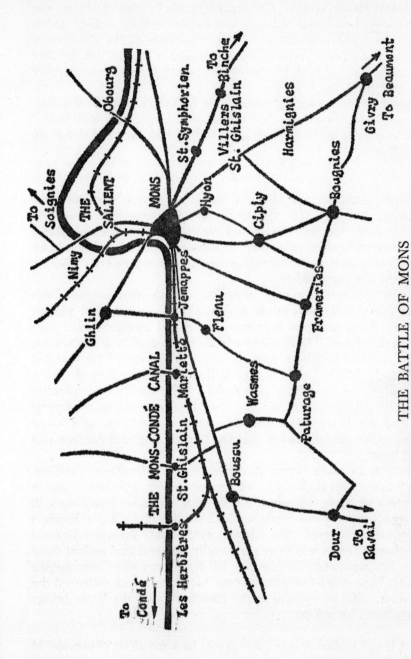

THE BATTLE OF MONS

Sketch map: Scale approximately four miles to one inch

Divisional Headquarters. Consequently, his frequent forays to the most forward and exposed positions caused endless anxiety to his staff. His A.D.C., Lieutenant Peter Wyndham of the Coldstream Guards, indignantly repudiated allegations made by his brother officers that he had a soft job: he would, in fact, have felt considerably safer in a front-line battalion.

Hamilton's long striding figure—his A.D.C., a quarter of a century his junior, frequently had difficulty in keeping up with him—acted as a tonic to the footsore men, toiling with pick and shovel on the defences.

2

When conditions are vile and the odds against survival most daunting, the Cockney—the virile and indestructible Londoner, with his ready wit, foul mouth and unquenchable humour—takes a great deal of beating. Cunning, generous, ferocious and gentle by turns; concealing a wealth of heroism under a protective irony—this is the Cockney soldier.

It was appropriate enough, therefore, that the first weight of von Kluck's thrust fell on the 4th Battalion of His Majesty's 7th Regiment of Foot—London's own regiment, the Royal Fusiliers, who were Cockneys to a man. The Fusiliers held the left flank of the Mons Salient.

No battalion had been more generous with souvenirs demanded by French children, with the result that a soldier equipped with a cap badge was something of a rarity. With totally expressionless faces, the 4th Royal Fusiliers had sung *Hold your hand out, you naughty boy*, and the French had solemnly stood to attention with bared heads, under the impression that the English National Anthem was being sung.

There were more expensive regiments than the Royal Fusiliers, better turned-out regiments and regiments with less crime. But in the years to come, wherever the fighting was most murderous, it was reassuring to know that a service battalion of the Royal Fusiliers was somewhere near. On August 23rd, 1914, Brigadier-General Beauchamp Doran was to be profoundly thankful that he had them under his command. Before they left for France the Commanding Officer, Lieutenant-Colonel Norman McMahon, had addressed the battalion. And every man in the trenches round the Nimy bridge remembered his words:

A Royal Fusilier does not fear death: he is not afraid of wounds; he only fears disgrace. . . .

Royal Scots Fusiliers in Flanders 1914, heading for Jemappes.
'And then the écossais soldiers had come . . .'

German infantry advancing over open country at Mons.
'A solid mass of grey was coming over the sky-line . . . and they came head-on.'

Colliery slag heaps at Mons.
'They encountered . . . coal mines and towering slag heaps . . .'

British Cavalry at Mons.
'They rode hither and thither as the fortunes of battle dictated . . .'

With the dawn of August 23rd came the first shell to fall on the 4th Royal Fusiliers: there came the sharp whizzing noise, then, almost before the fusiliers could hear it, a crash. From a house rose a cloud of dust and round the hole torn out of the roof a whitish-yellow cloud of smoke. Then, in quick succession, came half a dozen more, some bursting on impact with the ground and others above them in the air. Others, again, burst in trenches filled with men. In the first ten minutes the 4th Royal Fusiliers had lost six men killed and fourteen wounded; it was first blood to an enemy they had not yet even seen.

As abruptly as it started, the shelling stopped. And then, for the first time, the men of 'C' Company saw their first Germans: a cavalry patrol of seven men.

The resultant action was brief and conclusive: five of the seven saddles were emptied at the first volley; the two survivors of this fusillade galloped away into the middle distance. Stretcher bearers went out and found that four of the German cavalrymen were dead. The fifth, an officer, had been wounded in the leg and was taken to company headquarters.

On arrival, the German officer, who was clearly in considerable pain—he had received a bullet through the knee cap, just above his elegantly polished field-boot—swore most horribly in German for several minutes. As the medical officer dressed the wound, a few fusiliers, no mean performers at swearing themselves, stood looking at him curiously, until peremptorily sent about their business by the company sergeant-major:

'Wonder what 'e's saying, Bert?'

'Dunno, but I don't think he likes us much.'

'Terrible language, ain't it? 'ere, Fritz, 'ave a fag. . . .'

'Good-lookin' cove, ain't 'e?'

This was undeniably true with his arrogantly upturned moustaches and monocle hanging from a string. His identity papers told that he was Lieutenant von Arnim and the skull and cross bones on his service cap was the badge of the Death's Head Hussars.[1] In fishing parlance, he represented a tidy catch.

But that was only the beginning. The Germans attacked with four regiments of infantry and they came head-on. The weight of this frenzied assault fell on 'C' Company again. The fusiliers saw something which caused them to blink unbelievingly and push the safety catches of their rifles forward with hands that shook: a solid

---

[1] He was, in fact, the son of General von Arnim, commanding the Fourth German Army Corps.

mass of grey was coming over the skyline in column of fours: they advanced shoulder to shoulder, and as unhurriedly as if they had been on a ceremonial parade. Private Bert Denner's incredulous comment—'Lumme, there's bloody millions of 'em'—did not at the time seem to be an overstatement of the facts.

The entire skyline seemed to be full of Germans in solid square blocks. Now they were a bare seven hundred yards away. The company commander, Captain Lionel Ashburner—a sterling soldier of nineteen years' service and a holder of the Distinguished Service Order, but one of little imagination—requested Captain Henry Forster to pinch him to ensure that he was awake.

The trigger finger of every man itched almost unbearably; reservists, all thoughts of carefree civilian life forgotten, cuddled their cheeks almost lovingly into their rifle butts, while the young soldiers strove to control the trembling of their hands and the fluttering of their stomach muscles. It was a target to gladden the hearts of Lieutenant Maurice Dease's machine-gunners.

At six hundred yards Captain Ashburner blew a single blast on his whistle and platoon commanders bawled for 'rapid independent'.

The rifleman of average competence could be sure of getting fifteen rounds from his rifle in a minute; the most expert could achieve anything up to thirty. The Lee-Enfield rifle had a flat trajectory up to six hundred yards. On this day of slaughter, fusiliers who had reduced platoon sergeants to a state of near imbecility on the practice ranges found that they were killing effortlessly. It was, in truth, scarcely possible to miss. As the leading files of closely packed German infantry fell, those behind them pressed ever forward: some broke into a run, shouting wildly; others crouched behind dead comrades and returned the fire; and still they continued to fall—some dead before they hit the ground, some who would assuredly die before nightfall, some maimed for life . . . and all the time Maurice Dease's machine-guns pumped long bursts of fire into the screaming, struggling grey mass in front of them.

Realising the futility of these tactics—so deadly was the musketry of the fusiliers that many bullets were finding two billets—the Germans withdrew out of range. And this was a signal for a wild outburst of cheering from the trenches.

As they cleaned their rifles and replenished their ammunition pouches, the men of the Royal Fusiliers enjoyed a pardonable riot of jubilant exaggeration: not a single man had bagged less than twenty, which would become eighty when the opportunity came to write a letter home.

But the triumph of the Fusiliers was to be short-lived. The new attack was no suicidal advance of tightly-bunched field grey: it was preceded by a sustained and murderous artillery barrage, followed by infantry attacks into which had clearly gone careful planning— planning which had been totally absent before. It was one thing to coolly rest a rifle on a parapet, take careful and deliberate aim and fire with the reasonable certainty of killing at least one man. The slick bolt action of the trained infantrymen had already proved that beyond all possible doubt. But it was quite another to emerge from the depths of a trench, dazed and partially deafened by shellfire, to engage an enemy who was now advancing in open order in a succession of disciplined rushes: the targets were no longer simple and obvious, and it seemed that the Germans were learning sense at last. The German infantry, who had been told that the British Army was contemptible, was having second thoughts about the matter. . . .

There was a steady and mounting drain of casualties in the ranks of the Royal Fusiliers; the rain of shells was taking its toll and the Germans, having abandoned their steam-roller tactics, were bringing accurate rifle and machine-gun fire to bear on the defenders' depleted ranks. It was soon only too apparent to Captain Ashburner that unless reinforcements were immediately forthcoming, his position would become untenable. Maurice Dease's machine-gun continued to inflict astronomical casualties on the advancing Germans, as did the steady fire of the Fusiliers' rifles. But the enemy artillery fire was hotting up every minute and 'C' Company was in grave danger of being outflanked. Ashburner consequently sent a runner back to battalion headquarters with the urgent request that as many men as could be spared should be sent to his assistance.

The rapid appearance of Second-Lieutenant Jack Mead with a platoon heartened Ashburner and every fusilier of 'C' Company. For Mead, a young man of irrepressible high spirits, seemed to be a positive denial of defeat. With his fair hair and pink and white complexion—he seldom had to shave very seriously—Mead seemed more like an exuberant schoolboy cheering on his house rugger fifteen than a platoon commander engaged in the bloody business of war; in fact, just two years before, he had been doing just that. But he had barely got his men settled in their trenches before he took a jagged piece of shrapnel in his head. The force of the blow knocked him down, but seconds later he was on his feet again.

Mead continued to cheer his men with his own particular brand of public school exuberance, but he was well nigh blinded by the blood which poured down his face. His platoon sergeant, during a brief respite from the deadly work of execution, said: 'Better get back and have that fixed, sir. We'll be all right here for a bit.'

Second-Lieutenant Mead ignored him completely.

The platoon sergeant sighed and beckoned to two fusiliers. 'Get 'im out of this, you two,' he said tersely; 'and then get back 'ere at the double.'

The two fusiliers supported the volubly protesting Mead to the rear. Takes one in the napper, ran their thoughts, and he don't want to go back; just let me cop one and I'll go back quick enough. . . .

The fusiliers delivered Mead into the safe keeping of the medical orderly, Fusilier Ted Hicks. Hicks was a morose old soldier, who had scrounged his way through twenty years of undetected crime. He first of all helped himself to a cigarette from the case in Mead's tunic pocket and then bandaged the wound in the subaltern's head. He patted the bandage into place and said paternally: 'Now, just you 'ang on 'ere, sir, and you'll be all right.'

Mead's face was chalky white and the blood was seeping freely through the bandage. He stood up with difficulty and said: 'I'm going back.'

Fusilier Hicks sighed gently: if the kid wanted to be a bloody hero, then it was his own business, but he felt bound to say: 'S'posing you cop it again, sir? Then all that nice bandaging I done will be a waste of time.'

'Lightning never strikes in the same place twice,' retorted Mead and strode back to his platoon. His men, whose rifles were almost too hot to hold, accorded him a vociferous welcome.

Five minutes later Second-Lieutenant Jack Mead lay dead in the trench that he had vacated a bare twenty minutes earlier: a bullet had passed clean through his forehead.

By now the Royal Fusiliers were in evil case: Captain Ashburner was badly wounded in the head and Captain Forster, shot through right arm and stomach, died that night. Captain William Bowden-Smith and Lieutenant Eric Smith, hurriedly despatched to the Nimy Bridge with still more reinforcements, were killed within five minutes of one another. The crew of the machine-gun were wiped out and only Lieutenant Maurice Dease remained to man the gun. He had already been hit three times—in the shoulder and each leg. But he continued to pour fire into the Germans.

Colonel McMahon now realised that retreat, a hateful word to any Royal Fusilier, was imperative: only by a withdrawal could he save his battalion from almost complete annihilation.

The Royal Fusiliers had to retire across 250 yards of open ground. There was not a stick of cover and the area was swept by shrapnel and machine-gun fire. By this time Maurice Dease had been hit yet again—this time through a lung—and the machine-gun was at last silent. As long as Maurice Dease had been able to hold himself upright he had kept this gun in action. But now, riddled with bullets and with blood pouring from his mouth, he was a spent force. His great friend, Lieutenant Francis Steele—they had played the fool together at Sandhurst and joined the regiment together—picked Dease up bodily and carried him back: Dease died in Steele's arms.

I have brought the conspicuous gallantry of Lieutenant Dease to notice, Colonel McMahon reported laconically. He was awarded the Victoria Cross posthumously.

The covering fire of the machine-gun had saved many lives already, but without it there could be little hope for the 4th Royal Fusiliers. Just one man on the gun—unused belts of ammunition still lay beside it—would make an incalculable difference. . . .

Enemy shells and machine-gun fire continued to rain down on the fusiliers as they began to withdraw. Now there were some fifty men awaiting the order to quit the positions. Among them was the company sergeant-major, and he wanted to get these fifty men out alive. Above the noise of battle he shouted: 'Any of you lot know how to fire the machine-gun?'

A fusilier stepped forward. He was Frank Godley, five years a soldier, generously moustached, broad and powerful of build—a tireless cross-country runner, a tower of strength at centre-half in the battalion's football team. He had, however, never achieved any distinction as a machine-gunner; in fact, three years before the sergeant-major had endeavoured to instruct Godley in the rudiments of this complex weapon and had told him that as a machine-gunner he'd make a bloody good bus conductor. Godley had not stayed with machine-gun section very long.

But Frank Godley had volunteered, and that was good enough for the C.S.M. The sergeant-major said tersely: 'Right, Godley, get on the gun. And the rest of you, get ready to move out. . . .'

For the next hour Frank Godley stayed with the machine-gun and did tremendous execution: he was hit in the fleshy part of the leg, but continued to fire; bleeding from a wound in the shoulder, he went on pumping bullets into the advancing Germans. He was in the act of threading a fresh belt of ammunition into the gun when he was hit yet again. Only when the Germans were a hundred yards away did he smash the machine-gun to pieces and throw it into the canal.

85

It was three months later, in a German prison camp, that Frank Godley received the news that his heroic action had been rewarded with the Victoria Cross.

So ended the first, but by no means the last, battle fought by the 4th Royal Fusiliers. They had bought their initial war experience at a heavy price: they had been forced to abandon their positions and had suffered some 250 casualties in dead, wounded and missing. But on the credit side they had won two Victoria Crosses and five hundred German dead lay in swathes in front of the position which they had vacated.

The Germans may have thought that the 4th Royal Fusiliers were broken and demoralised: they were neither of these things. They asked but little: a hot meal, a few hours' sleep, a draw on a fag, perhaps a tot of rum, a wash and shave, half-an-hour in which to restore their uniforms to Royal Fusilier trimness once more; and then let them —— Allemons look out. . . .

On the right of the Royal Fusiliers the resistance offered by the 4th Battalion the Middlesex Regiment, another predominantly Cockney regiment, was no less dogged and lethal. These two battalions between them bore the brunt of the German attacks on the Salient.

The men of the Middlesex were called the 'Diehards': in 1811 they had faced a murderous fire of French shell and grapeshot at Albuhera, the bloodiest battle of the Peninsula War. They had held a hill which they had captured in a counter-attack against a French force which outnumbered them by more than four to one. Their Commanding Officer, lying mortally wounded, exhorted his troops with the words: 'Die hard, my men, die hard.' And from that moment the Middlesex had become universally known as the Diehards. The Albuhera spirit was very much in evidence in the men who took position next to the Royal Fusiliers on the right of the Nimy Bridge on the afternoon of August 22nd.

For 'D' Company the early portents had seemed good indeed. They were to take up a defensive position in the railway station at Obourg, and less than a quarter of a mile from the station was an estaminet of inviting aspect.

Almost every town in Great Britain has always had a pub near its railway station, unimaginatively called the Railway Hotel. The estaminet at Obourg bore little outward resemblance to any of these hostelries, but the stout and beaming proprietor on the front door-step told his own story. There would be beer and wine in plenty inside those hospitable doors; there might, although this theory was heavily discounted by the older soldiers, even be girls as well.

One or two men were seen to be out of step as 'D' Company passed the estaminet and it took Company Sergeant-Major Fred Trewen's roar of 'PICK IT UP, THEN—'EFF, 'EFF, 'EFF, RIGHT, 'EFF' to wrench them back to the grim realities of total war. Despite his genial exterior, the proprietor of the estaminet was a worried man: business had been practically at a standstill since the arrival of *les sales Boches* in Belgium—would *les soldats Anglais*, clearly men with formidable thirsts, be allowed to patronise his establishment? It goes without saying that the men of 'D' Company were every bit as worried on this score.

But Captain Henry Glass, the company commander, had, in the course of his lengthy service, come to know the habits of the British soldier like an open book. Thomas Atkins, despite all rumours to the contrary, is a far from helpless individual in a foreign country, and he has an infallible instinct for seeking out establishments where alcoholic stimulants can be consumed on or off the premises—preferably on. Glass also knew that if he did not grant permission to visit the estaminet during the evening, determined and thirsty forays would be made, despite any orders that he might issue to the contrary. And he had served with several of the reservists in more spacious days. . . .

On the whole, Glass concluded, it did not seem too great a chance to take. A German attack that evening seemed unlikely, and in any event the estaminet was a bare two hundred yards away. After due consultation with the C.S.M. (who was assailed by terrible thirst himself) he gave permission for thirty men at a time, fully armed and ready for action, to visit the estaminet.

The beer bore no resemblance to the dark, lukewarm frothy liquid sold in the wet canteen and the pubs in Devonport; it was amber coloured, flat and gaseous. The wine, however, came as a pleasant surprise and litres of *vin*, both *blanc* and *rouge*, disappeared down the parched throats of 'D' Company at a rate which evoked the whole-hearted admiration of the proprietor. The only thing lacking to round off the evening in requisitely mellow mood was fish and chips.

Battalion war diaries were rarely great literary achievements: adjutants in the heat of battle rarely have time to commit to paper more than is absolutely necessary. On August 23rd the war diary of the 4th Middlesex contained the single laconic entry: *Battle commenced 10.15 a.m., retirement started 3 p.m.* There was no time to write any more; indeed, there was barely time to write even that.

The attack on the 4th Middlesex was, if anything, even more violent than that on the Royal Fusiliers and the response every bit as deadly. Six battalions came head-on at the Middlesex in densely packed waves and ran into the same deadly musketry: the only complaint made by the men of the Middlesex was that they could not fire fast enough. Years later statisticians of both the Fusiliers and the Middlesex were still trying to work out which battalion had killed the most Germans, and the problem has yet to be solved to the satisfaction of either regiment.

As on the Fusiliers' front, the Germans suffered astronomical casualties and realised the suicidal futility of such tactics. Loud and vitriolic were the comments of the Commanding Officer of the Middlesex, Lieutenant-Colonel Charles Hull, about the parsimony of an Army which only provided two machine-guns per battalion— with two more the six battalions of German infantry could have been all but wiped out.

But soon the vast preponderance of German artillery began to take its toll. There was no overhead cover in the shallow and hastily dug trenches, and the 4th Middlesex soon found themselves in trouble. Having abandoned their advance in close order, the Germans were able to bring up a large number of machine-guns with which they could spray the defenders with insulting ease.

Major William Davey's 'A' Company was on the extreme left of the Middlesex line, in touch with the right flank of the Royal Fusiliers' position. Davey himself had been badly wounded early in the fighting, and the position was most perilous. In response to an urgent appeal for reinforcements, Major Walter Abell's 'B' Company was rushed up from reserve to plug the gaps in the defensive line; to the sadly depleted defenders of 'A' Company it seemed that they could not arrive in time: 'A' Company had already been reduced by one third in killed and wounded and their rifles were becoming almost too hot to hold.

They were still, however, bravely supported by the machine-gun section. The machine-gun officer, Lieutenant Lawrence Sloane-Stanley, had been severely wounded and refused to be evacuated. But the machine-guns of the 4th Middlesex, although the water was boiling in the jackets of the guns and ammunition was fast running out, remained in action until the final withdrawal.[1]

Abell's 'B' Company moved up into the front line trenches under

---

[1] This was the first occasion on which the machine guns of the Middlesex Regiment had performed in action. Appropriately enough, the Middlesex were converted into a machine gun regiment in 1935 and as such won fresh battle honours for themselves in World War Two.

a hail of artillery and machine-gun fire which tore great holes in their ranks: Abell himself and his second-in-command, Captain John Knowles, were killed on the way forward, as was Second-Lieutenant Keith Henstock. Before it reached the front line, 'B' Company had been depleted to almost half its strength. But the value of this few score rifles was incalculable and they arrived in the nick of time: the Germans were barely two hundred yards away when the survivors of 'B' Company leapt into the trenches alongside their comrades in 'A' and started to fire as fast as they could cram fresh clips of ammunition into their magazines.

It had been a near thing, a very near thing: but there was worse to come—the hour was not far off when the 4th Middlesex would almost cease to exist as a composite fighting force. Almost, but not quite.[1]

Stories of the superb discipline of the old British Expeditionary Force will circulate for as long as tales of valour can stir the hearts of men. Individual comparisons between units must be invidious, but the behaviour of 'D' Company, the 4th Battalion the Middlesex, surely merits special mention.

Captain Henry Glass, both legs broken by machine-gun bullets and bleeding profusely from a shrapnel wound in the shoulder, had led the defence of Obourg Station as long as he remained on his feet. Now he could no longer stand, but, propped up against the wall of the waiting-room, he continued to command 'D' Company as coolly as if he had been on manoeuvres on Salisbury Plain.

Glass well knew that only retirement from the railway station could save the remnants of 'D' Company from total annihilation. Glass, by pre-war standards, was a comparatively elderly officer: he had been promoted captain in 1904 and could scarcely expect to achieve a crown on his sleeve for another ten years. He knew every man, reservist, old soldier and young soldier alike, by name. More: he knew their marital status, alcoholic capacity and individual performance as soldiers. If Henry Glass had ordered 'D' Company to stay in Obourg, then they would have stayed in it dead if they could not stay in it alive.

But if they were to fight again, then the 4th Middlesex would have to give ground before this steam roller assault. Already 'A', 'B' and 'C' Companies, fighting every inch of the way as Diehards always do, were going back.

To Glass, a mass withdrawal of 'D' Company was unthinkable; nor did he propose to send his men back by platoons. Determined

---

[1] The Germans had not seen the last of the 4th Middlesex, as we shall presently discover.

to inflict the maximum damage on the advancing Germans—their leading elements were now barely four hundred yards away—he hit upon the idea of withdrawing the company a man at a time to the woods behind the railway station. Only by so doing, could he maintain the illusion that the station was strongly held and at the same time keep up an unrelenting fire.

The withdrawal started from the right of the line. As each man's turn came, he received a tap on the shoulder from the company sergeant-major—'Any bloke wot goes before I tap 'im'll be for office', was the text of the C.S.M.'s oration to the men. And not a single man moved until ordered to do so; right up to the moment of his departure, every soldier of 'D' Company continued to fire.

Captain Glass knew that he would be unable to go back. His second-in-command, Captain Keith Roy, had been killed by one of the first shells to fall into the position; command of the company therefore devolved on twenty-year-old Second-Lieutenant John Thorp, who protested vigorously against Glass's decision to remain where he was—and was consigned to hell for his pains.

As each man's turn to withdraw came, he snatched up his rifle, fired a final defiant shot at the Germans, and ran for the woods. Many did not get there; some were caught in the open by bullets and shrapnel; others, loath to break off the fight, lay out in the open and returned the German fire.

One of the last to leave was Private Victor Rogers—he was hit three times in the head before he had travelled a hundred yards, but lived to tell the tale. His last memory of Obourg Station is the spectacle of Captain Glass unconcernedly lighting a cigarette and refreshing himself, with every evidence of enjoyment, from a silver hip flask. . . .

Both the Royal Fusiliers and the Middlesex had suffered grievous losses: the Royal Fusiliers' casualties amounted to over two hundred; the Middlesex fared even worse—they had gone into battle almost a thousand strong, but on the evening of August 23rd only 275 of them answered their names at roll call. The rest were listed under the coldly impersonal headings of the casualty return: killed in action, wounded in action, died of wounds, missing believed killed, missing believed to be prisoner-of-war.

3

The 2nd Battalion the Royal Irish Regiment were not in the best of tempers; the reason was simple enough—they were in reserve.

They were sitting on the Mons–Binche road whilst ahead of them they could hear the sounds of battle, which indicated that the Royal Fusiliers and Middlesex were hotly engaged. On their right, guarding the right flank of the Salient, and prolonging the line towards Haig's First Corps, were the 1st Gordons, and beyond them the 2nd Royal Scots. For an Irish regiment, and the senior Irish regiment at that, to be left out of the first battle of the war was unthinkable.

The target for much of their choler was their brigade commander, Brigadier-General Doran, who had himself spent all his regimental service with the Royal Irish—'and phwat in the name of sweet Jasus was the man thinkin' of—his own regiment squattin' on their tails in reserve.' Before they had sailed for France, Doran had said: 'I expect great things from the Royal Irish and expect them to be always in the forefront of battle.' They were reassured to a certain extent by Major Stephen St. Leger, one of the company commanders. There was no disgrace in being in reserve, he pointed out; one of the other battalions would undoubtedly be in trouble ere long, and it would be up to the Royal Irish to get them out of it.

St. Leger was proved an able prophet: the Royal Fusiliers were withdrawing, fighting every inch of the way; both the Middlesex, and the 1st Battalion the Gordon Highlanders on their right, were desperately in need of reinforcements. For the men of the 2nd Royal Irish the call for action came at exactly the right moment, for some of the more belligerent spirits in their ranks were already hatching schemes by which they could go into action against the Germans without prior application to higher authority.

But discipline, that essential but unpopular word of the 1960s, stood them in good stead; within half-an-hour of receiving an appeal for help from the Gordons, Lieutenant-Colonel John Cox, commanding the 2nd Royal Irish, had sent two companies forward.

Gordons and Royal Irish fought shoulder to shoulder: only a short fortnight before, in a Devonport public house, they had fought one another—a gory encounter in which fists, boots and belts had been used indiscriminately, resulting in the admission to hospital of six Gordons and five Royal Irish (the score was evened later in the evening by a private of the Royal Irish who walked into a tram). But now they were together against a common foe. The fact that the advancing German infantry outnumbered them by something like five to one merely added zest to the proceedings. And so Irishmen and Scots, standing at bay, fought together and every inch of ground in front of them was littered with grey dead and grey wounded.

Today the Royal Irish Regiment no longer exists, although the sons of the men who fought alongside the Gordons enlisted in the Royal Irish Fusiliers, the Irish Guards and the Inniskillings in another World War. But as long as the older generation of Irishmen continue to carouse, brag and squabble, they will recall the deeds of the Second Battalion of the Royal Irish Regiment.

No story about the 2nd Royal Irish could be complete without reference to Company Quartermaster-Sergeant Thomas Fitzpatrick, who hailed from Dublin's fair city and was as much a part of the regiment as the Harp and Crown on the cap badge.

Life was dear and pension near when Thomas Fitzpatrick went to war for the first time in August 1914. But like many an Irishman who went into a pub for a quiet drink, met up with some friends and 'got a taste for the shtuff', so did Thomas Fitzpatrick develop a taste for war. And the story of 'Fitzpatrick's cooks' became a part of military history and by the same token Ireland's.

Fitzpatrick was like any other 'quarterbloke' of the Old Army: his horizon was bounded by rations, ammunition, indents, clothing, brushes (boot, brass, scrubbing and tooth), button sticks; badges, cap; boots, ankle, pairs, spare; and four-by-two. His knowledge of all these things was prodigious; what he knew about anything else was sometimes a matter for ribald speculation. No single man of the Royal Irish had ever visualised Fitzpatrick in battle.

But in the desperate fighting round Mons on August 23rd, 1914, Fitzpatrick knew that the regiment that he loved with singleminded devotion was in dire trouble. And 'D' Company, who relied upon him for their rations and ammunition, were in sorer straits than anyone. They had joined forces with a company of Gordon Highlanders (Fitzpatrick loathed the Gordons wholeheartedly for only last week had not two of his precious tents disappeared in circumstances which pointed directly to the acquisitive proclivities of 'thim thievin' Jocks'?).

As he went up under heavy fire with ammunition and rations for this hard-pressed force, Fitzpatrick noticed that there seemed to be no officers left. And there were men in the firing line, Royal Irish and Gordons both, who were beginning to look backwards over their shoulders—a bad sign in any fighting man.

Fitzpatrick went back to his motley command. It consisted of the more unmartial elements of the 2nd Royal Irish: cooks, orderlies, batmen, drivers and an unsavoury sextet imaginatively described on the battalion roll as the sanitary squad. They could hear the sounds of battle in front of them and were grateful for the comparative safety of their present position, And here came the fat one himself, begob, to give them a lot of blarney about his fearful experiences during a short sojourn in the front line. . . .

Fitzpatrick eyed the commissariat squad of the Royal Irish without enthusiasm for a full thirty seconds before giving judgment. 'Begod, but ye're a terrible lookin' crew, so ye are,' he announced; 'but there's fellers of ours up there alongside thim Gordons and they're in bad trouble. Now, who's amongst yez coming wid me to give 'em a hand?'

And such was the fighting spirit of this new C.Q.M.S. Fitzpatrick that there was not a cook, driver, batman, orderly or member of the sanitary squad who did not reach for his rifle and with magazine charged and bayonet fixed follow Thomas Fitzpatrick forward into the line. . . .

4

Also in action on August 22nd were the 2nd Dragoons (the Royal Scots Greys) on the right of the Salient. The Greys had not taken part in the argument about the lance; they had troubles of their own. A curt order had come from the Headquarters of the Cavalry Division, an order which seemed both cynical and insulting:

> Grey horses will make a conspicuous target in the open country, and their use cannot be countenanced. Immediate steps will be taken to darken the colour of the regiment's chargers.

The Scots Greys were probably the proudest and most exclusive of all cavalry regiments of the Line. Their motto was *Second to None*, their badge an eagle of imperious mien; their Colonel-in-Chief was His Imperial Majesty Nicholas II, Emperor of Russia. The Scots Greys had charged the French at Waterloo, with Highlanders clinging to their stirrups; they had charged the Russians at Balaklava and the Boers at Paardeberg. They had always charged with unquenchable *élan*, and now awaited, with scarcely concealed impatience, the order which would launch them at a headlong gallop against the Germans.

The Greys were justly proud of all their battle honours. They were also proud of their magnificent chargers, which had delighted the civilian populace at military tattoos. The order to darken the horses came as the ultimate insult.

Over the horse lines of the Royal Scots Greys hung a cloying, antiseptic smell as the horses were dyed with a solution of permanganate of potash; they expressed their disapproval with shrilly protesting whinnies and many a shrewdly delivered kick. Their resultant transformation into what the stud book calls 'dun' and 'liver chestnut' drew further vituperation from the Colonel.

But there was worse to come. . . .

In spite of the discoloration of their chargers, the Royal Scots Greys were ready for instant mounted action—indeed, they thought and talked of little else. But Brigadier General Sir Philip Chetwode, commanding the 5th Cavalry Brigade, had other plans for the Greys. They were sent to man a line of outposts at Péronnes, not far from Givry, whence disquieting reports had come: a large force of Uhlans and Jägers were advancing on the village and the faces of the Scots Greys grew still longer—it seemed reasonably certain that they were to be used as bait, and dismounted bait at that. . . .

Muttering darkly, the Greys handed over their chargers to horse holders—at least *they* were still mounted, although they had to ride one and lead three—and set about making Péronnes impregnable: they dug trenches, a job abhorrent to any right-thinking cavalryman, and erected barricades; they checked their arms and ammunition and waited for the Germans.

In the brewery nearby was Lieutenant George Pigot-Moodie and the machine-gun section. Pigot-Moodie had been given the section because, although an intrepid horseman and sterling soldier, his style of riding was inclined to be unorthodox—more suited to the hunting field than the barrack square.

The Royal Scots Greys' first contact with the Germans came in the early afternoon of August 22nd. Displaying either rare bravery or extraordinary stupidity, a patrol of Uhlans rode to within fifty yards of the position manned by the troop commanded by Lord St. Germans.

The troop were playing 'housey-housey' in a farmhouse. Trooper Fraser had just shouted 'hoose', thus enriching himself by twenty francs, when the sentry gave the alarm. The Uhlans were greeted by a crackle of musketry and galloped away in confusion.

Later that afternoon a patrol of four men under Lance-Corporal John Dykes went out. Every man longed to get to early grips with the enemy, but the orders issued to Dykes were explicit and categoric: they were to obtain information about enemy movement and bring it back with all possible speed.

Later in the war John Dykes was to lose an arm, be promoted to sergeant and win the Distinguished Conduct Medal. But in August, 1914, he had only one stripe and a precarious one at that. Although a first class horseman and a crack shot with a rifle, there had been little in his service so far to suggest that he was an able tactician.

The patrol trotted warily through the woods. Then, suddenly, they heard the jingling of harness and the thud of hooves. It was a patrol of Uhlans and they outnumbered Dykes's patrol by something like six to one.

'Will we ride at them, corporal?' eagerly inquired Trooper Mac-Kenzie, an excitable and belligerent Glaswegian.

'We will not,' said Dykes tersely. 'Get into those trees and look sharp about it.'

They were just in time. Seconds after they had melted into the trees the Uhlans, careless of concealment and talking loudly, trotted past them.

'What a target,' breathed MacKenzie wistfully, and indeed every man's finger itched for his rifle.

'They'll be a bluidy sight better target for young Georgie,' countered Dykes when the Uhlans were out of earshot. For by the Corporal's attentive reckoning, the Uhlans were heading directly into the line of fire of 'young Georgie's'—Lieutenant Pigot-Moodie's—machine-gunners.

He was soon proved right. At a range of five hundred yards Pigot-Moodie gave the order to fire and the seventeen Uhlans were very thoroughly annihilated.

The overshies from the Greys' machine-guns whistled in uncomfortable proximity to Dykes and his men as they headed for their outpost. 'Where's them bullets coming from?' demanded an apprehensive trooper.

'They're ours, ye stupid gowk,' said Dykes indulgently; 'but I'm thinking yon Uhlans'll no' do the goose-step again. . . .'

For the rest of the 22nd August, the outposts held by the Royal Scots Greys were targets for ceaseless shelling and suicidal attacks by Uhlans and Jägers. The Germans found the dismounted prowess of the Greys no more to their liking than had the men who had been so roughly handled by the 4th Dragoon Guards and the 16th Lancers.

The dawn of August 23rd revealed that no fewer than 250 German dead lay in front of the Greys' positions. Some score of prisoners were taken, and one of these paid a lasting tribute to the regiment's musketry. The Uhlans and Jägers, he admitted shamefacedly, were of almost divisional strength and they were convinced that they were opposed by a full brigade with a large proportion of machine-guns.

The news of the action was well received at Headquarters of the Cavalry Division; General Allenby in person congratulated the regiment. But there was sad head-shaking within the patrician portals of the Cavalry Club, sometimes irreverently known as 'The Horseman's Arms'. 'Dismounted action,' muttered the old gentlemen within the Club's patrician portals. 'That's bad, that's *very* bad.'

In the terrible days to come the pattern of cavalry action, with a few notable exceptions, was to follow that fought by the Greys on August 22nd: they rode hither and thither, as the fortunes of battle dictated; time and time again, ready for immediate mounted action, they were caught up by peremptory orders from the staff: 'Get horse holders told off and get your men into the line.'

18th Field Ambulance 6th Division at a mid-day halt on march to Hartennes,
September 1914.
'. . . *the selfless devotion to duty of the R.A.M.C.'*

German artillery passing through occupied Brussels, in August 1914.
'*The Germans had a crushing preponderance of artillery . . .*'

2nd Battalion Scots Guards leaving Lyndhurst, October 4th, 1914.
'. . . handkerchiefs were unashamedly busy as the 7th Division started on their
nine-mile march from Lyndhurst to Southampton.'

Royal Engineers' bridging train at the Aisne.
'. . . the Corps of Royal Engineers accomplished one of the finest pieces of work in its history.'

Chapter VII

I

THE battle for the Salient was now more or less over. The Royal Fusiliers and Middlesex were pulling back through Mons towards the new line Wasmes–Paturage–Frameries. On their left were two battalions of 3rd Division, the Royal Scots Fusiliers and the Northumberland Fusiliers. These two battalions between them held the vital line of the Canal from Mariette and Jemappes, past Mons itself, to the positions originally held by the Royal Fusiliers in the Salient. A German break-through in this sector would take the enemy into Mons, would cut off the battered Middlesex and Royal Fusiliers, and expose the rest of the 3rd Division to dangerous flank attacks as it made its fighting withdrawal to the new line.

In January 1915 the *Daily News*—the best informed and most widely read organ of the period—printed an epic story; 210 British soldiers, led by only one officer, held over two thousand Germans at bay in the little Belgian town of Jemappes.

The name of the regiment to which these men belonged was suppressed for security reasons, although it was known to every officer and man of the British Expeditionary Force. But, even so, each one of them was glad to read of their doings on January 10th, 1915, although they swore terrible oaths because they were referred to merely as 'a British regiment'. That could have meant just anyone! The men who held up this frenzied assault were of His Majesty's 21st Regiment of Foot—the 1st Battalion the Royal Scots Fusiliers.

There was an Englishwoman from Norwich in Jemappes some days earlier when a German advanced unit came thundering into the town with artillery, cavalry and infantry. They brought with them herds of cattle, which they had requisitioned—a euphemistic phrase when applied to the Germans in Belgium; they swaggered, bullied, drank and looted. The phrase 'hordes of fiends' has been often used in unofficial histories of the Great War. It was apt enough in Jemappes.

Nora Frankel's husband was somewhere—she knew not where—

with the Belgian Army, desperately trying to stem the grey hordes as they swept through Belgium. With her eight-year-old daughter Annette, she cowered fearfully in the cellar of their little house. The Germans were the victors, the Belgians the defeated: and the German soldiers lost little time in letting the inhabitants of Jemappes know this: their boastful shouts echoed in drunken and truculent chorus the length and breadth of the town. Many of the inhabitants of Jemappes died—men, women and children—before the Germans withdrew again.

And then on August 23rd the *écossais* soldiers had come—short, stocky, grim-faced men who wore hats with a gay red, white and black chequered pattern with two black ribbons falling down to the backs of their necks—the 'Fusil Jocks. . . .'

They were led by a soldier of singular gallantry, Captain Thomas Rose, D.S.O. He had won his decoration in the Aro expedition in Southern Nigeria and was no stranger to desperate situations: his tiny force was heavily outnumbered and the Germans were coming at them frontally and from both flanks.

Apart from Rose and a sprinkling of South African war veterans, none of the fusiliers had been in action before, but every man acquitted himself like a battle-hardened veteran.

There was not a man of this slender force, save the dead or desperately wounded, who was not fighting continuously during the afternoon of August 23rd. With no weapon larger than their single machine-gun, they stood up to artillery fire, machine-gun fire and attacks by densely packed infantry. With no reinforcements save the wounded who, if their legs would still bear them, staggered back to the firing line, they fought on. From the scant cover of slag-heaps and from ruined buildings the Royal Scots Fusiliers poured a continuous and murderous fire into the advancing Germans. Without food or water and at the end almost without ammunition, they still held their ground.

Throughout the battle Captain Rose seemed to be everywhere at once. The spirit of the leader was the spirit of the men. And the spirit of Thomas Rose was one, not so much of hope, but of certainty of ultimate victory: one of calm and confident self-reliance and firm belief in the worth of his men. Every fusilier felt that the eye of his captain was upon him; that he was at his side; that he knew not only what the soldier did, but what he thought.

With such a man to command them, lead them, discipline them, watch over them and fight for and with them, the 'Fusil Jocks' knew that they could not and would not be vanquished.

When the Scots Fusiliers finally withdrew—by now they numbered barely sixty whole men—they were very far from being defeated. By their action at Jemappes they had saved the defenders of the Salient from encirclement. In their steadfast endurance, they had performed a feat of arms which will be remembered for as long as stories of resolution and courage have the power to stir the hearts of men.

2

The 1st Battalion of the Northumberland Fusiliers was what is known as a 'tough mob'. They were recruited from the rough areas of the Border—areas where work was scarce and stomachs frequently empty: Jarrow, South Shields, Gateshead, Tynemouth; wherever there was want and depression, the 'Geordies' always seemed to come in for more than their fair share.

The men of the Northumberland Fusiliers were fierce, touchy and warmhearted; they grinned their odd, hangdog grin and spoke in a dialect barely comprehensible to men from the South. Of their efforts in war the 5th Fusiliers had a set oration: 'The owd Fusiliers is best after aal's said an' dune. We'or the laads for seein' Fritzy off the dump.'

The Northumberland Fusiliers knew nothing of the abominable atrocities committed in Belgium. The advancing Germans had left behind them a long track of foul deeds, ruin, human misery, sacrilege and desolation.

They knew nothing, for instance, of the farm near Château-Thierry: German soldiers had deliberately broken both arms of a tiny child and silenced the anguished cries of its mother by pinning her to the wall with knives in an attitude of crucifixion.

Nor had they heard of the village of Rabais, which after the passing of the Germans numbered only aged men, half-crazed women and the broken bodies of little children among its inhabitants. They would not have believed the story of the German soldier who, following an action fought at Batonville, boasted in a letter to his girl friend in Germany that he had *bayoneted several women. . . . I myself did for seven women and four young girls in five minutes. . . .*

Dear Mother,
    The wine out here does not taste too bad but I'd rather be having a pint of old and mild at the Unicorn. . . . I miss your tatie-hash and dumplings. . . .

Thus the contrast between a letter home from a 5th Fusilier and a Brandenburg Grenadier. . . .

The sack of Louvain . . . the rape of little girls in Orsmael and Neerespen . . . the machine-gunning of women and children at Aerschot . . . the bayoneting of an old woman, her sewing still in her gnarled old hands . . . the burning alive of men, women and children in Sempst. . . .

The 1st Battalion the Northumberland Fusiliers were holding the line near the bridge at Mariette. In common with every other battalion engaged in the Battle of Mons, they were mowing German infantry down by the hundred. The 5th Fusiliers were fighting as hard as anyone, but what they saw on that afternoon of August 23rd, 1914, resolved every man of the battalion to shoot faster and straighter and to thrust more savagely with the bayonet.

The German advance had checked, wavered and come to a stand-still. Then, before the blinking and unbelieving eyes of the Fusiliers, twelve little Belgian schoolgirls, all dressed in identical black dresses, emerged from a house near the Mariette bridge and ran down the bullet-swept main road.

Captain Brian St. John, commanding 'B' Company, was the first to recover the power of speech and bawled 'Cease firing!' at the top of his voice.

The Fusiliers held their fire long enough for the twelve little girls to reach the safety of a house behind them. But then the awful truth dawned upon them: the Germans had driven the children before them and advanced in serried rushes in their wake. What had started as a good 'shoot' had now become a snarling dog fight—a hacking, stabbing mêlée of bayonets, rifle butts, boots and fists. . . .

The 5th had fought the French at Mons in 1678; the Americans at Bunker Hill; the dervishes in the Sudan; the Mohmands on the North West Frontier of India. Of this fine regiment it had oft been said: 'the 5th behaved the best and suffered the worst'. But it is doubtful if they had ever been called upon to display greater qualities of discipline and steadfast resolution than on August 23rd, 1914.

In their own words, they had indeed been 'the laads for seein' Fritzy off the dump. . . .'

Sergeant Loftus of the Northumberland Fusiliers wrote home to his wife on November the 24th:

We received them in the good old way; the front rank with the bayonet and the rear ranks keeping up incessant fire on them. This sort of thing went on all day without bringing the Germans any nearer to shifting us. Nobody knew why we had to go back. . . .

But Loftus had not seen the telegram which General French had received from General Joffre at 5 p.m. on the afternoon of August 23rd. It is doubtful if it would have made any difference to his views on retirement if he had, but it gave the Commander-in-Chief plenty to worry about. The text of the telegram was disturbing enough: three German army corps—a reserve corps, the 4th and 9th Corps—and two cavalry divisions were moving on the British front and the German 2nd Corps was engaged in a turning movement on the left from the direction of Tournai.

As if this were not bad enough—it meant that the B.E.F. was outnumbered by something like six to one—the 5th French Army on the right of the B.E.F. was in precipitate retreat.

On August 24th French was to receive no messages other than gloomy ones; every report pointed to the early necessity of a general retirement. To von Kluck, the men mown down by the Middlesex, the Royal Fusiliers, the Lincolns, the Gordons and the Royal Irish in the Salient were expendable: they could be replaced. French had no reserves to draw on, he only had Haig's 1st and Smith-Dorrien's 2nd Corps.

Taking the view that sweat saves blood, Sir John French gave orders that the B.E.F. should retreat and orders were issued to Haig and Smith-Dorrien: the retreat must begin at once; there must be no stopping on this retreat; a new line was to stretch from Jerlain, south-east of Valenciennes, eastward to Maubeuge, with Bavai as the dividing point between the two corps.

3

The 1st Battalion the Lincolnshire Regiment had a jealously guarded reputation for superb musketry: their performance on the ranges in peacetime was seldom surpassed. Their steadfast discipline against overwhelming hordes of dervishes had been put to the test at Atbara in 1898. In the village of Frameries, just south of Mons, the Lincolns displayed both of these qualities to the full.

At Frameries in the early morning of August 24th the Lincolns were fresh and, by Battle of Mons standards, well fed—that is to say, they had eaten thick and nourishing stew as recently as 2 p.m. the day before.

The 4th Royal Fusiliers, pulling back through the Lincolns'

positions after their grim fight at Nimy, were neither fresh nor well fed: they were hungry, thirsty and weary. Several of them were wounded and hobbled painfully, either using their rifle as a crutch or supported by their comrades.

The Lincolns were all freshly shaved, for their commanding officer, Lieutenant-Colonel William Smith, had only recently assumed command and was firmly convinced that the clean and well-turned-out soldier fights the best; the Royal Fusiliers' water ration had been half a pint per man for the past twenty-four hours for drinking and none at all for washing and shaving. All in all, a perky young private of the Lincolns who shouted a strident: 'Are we down-'earted?' could have chosen his time and audience more carefully.

Replied a grimy fusilier, with a blood-stained bandage round his forehead: 'You may not be down-'earted now, nipper, but you —— soon will be. . . .'

In the next three hours the German 6th Division learned a healthy respect for the musketry and stubborn fighting qualities of the Lincolns, just as the Kaleifa's dervishes had sixteen years before.

Walking up and down the trenches of 'B' Company, Captain Frank Rose was quietly confident. He saw that they were good men to be in a tight corner with, and he was in little doubt that before very long the Lincolns would be in as tight a corner as the Royal Fusiliers had been.

Some were young men, hardly more than boys; some were men in their thirties—the reservists. And Rose was heartened to see that here and there were the faces of old friends—the men with whom he had fought at Atbara and in South Africa: men with ribbons up and a huge repertoire of lurid and largely untrue stories with which they regaled their younger comrades: 'Fuzzy-wuzzies—'ordes on 'em—naked as the day they was born. . . . Reckon this lot'll be a picnic after Atbara.'

But it was no picnic. In fact, in later years the handful of Sudan veterans of the battalion contended that Atbara was a picnic compared with Frameries, for in spite of their deadly two-handed swords the Kaleifa's men had no artillery or machine-guns. The Germans had plenty of both.

A continuous stream of shells was rained on the village; this was to be the softening-up process before the infantry attack. It was the considered opinion of Hauptmann von Brandis of the 24th Brandenburg Regiment that nothing could be left alive in Frameries; it looked as if it was going to be a walk-over for the German infantry. Any British soldiers who had survived this artillery bombardment must surely be too dazed and demoralized to offer any serious resistance.

But when six companies of German infantry advanced they were met by rifle fire so shatteringly accurate that von Brandis was convinced that the British had something like a dozen machine-guns. In fact, the Lincolns only had one: in the first shelling the machine-gun officer, Lieutenant Charles Holmes, and half his men had been killed or wounded.

The Lincolns fought in intense heat, with faces blackened by smoke: the German shells had set fire to a number of haystacks and the smoke hung over their positions in a choking, black pall. But their accurate fire never slackened; there were many men in the Lincolns capable of firing at the prodigious rate of thirty rounds per minute, and here was a target after their own hearts.

The Germans, meanwhile, were determined to liquidate the stubborn force which had denied Frameries to them for the whole of one long day. They had suffered fearful losses, but now the time had come to put the defenders to the bayonet.

The next artillery concentration was doubled in ferocity and lasted a full five minutes. But the Lincolns had the last laugh: before the artillery barrage started, Colonel Smith, emulating the tactics used by Captain Henry Glass at Obourg, had most skilfully extricated the battalion. The losses were not light—over one hundred men failed to answer their names at roll-call on the evening of August 24th, but the Lincolns had killed or wounded almost ten times as many Germans.

So the German infantry, now moving cautiously in short rushes, for they had a healthy respect for the Lincolns' musketry (as well they might), entered what was left of the village of Frameries and found it empty. . . .

This rueful comment from an officer of the Brandenburg Grenadiers illustrates, as no official history can, the chagrin of the Germans who finally occupied Frameries:

> Curse them, they seem to understand war, these English . . . it is marvellous how they convert every house and every wall into a fortress and slip away without waiting for our bayonets and butt ends. . . .

Of many tributes paid to the Lincolns by their enemies, this is one of the regiment's most treasured.

CHAPTER VIII

I

IN the early stages of the Battle of Mons the fighting had fallen almost entirely to the 3rd Division in the Salient: in the vernacular of the soldiers, they had 'carried the can' for the entire British Expeditionary Force.

The turn of Major-General Sir Charles Fergusson's 5th Division on the 'Canal Straight' was not long in coming. Fergusson had addressed every unit of the 5th and expressed his confidence in them.

Generals in both world wars have adopted a number of different techniques in talking to soldiers about to go into battle. The late General Orde Wingate told soldiers about to go into Burma that many of them would die of wounds, starvation and sickness; Bill Slim interlarded his address with the salty kind of talk that he had heard as a private of the Royal Warwicks. General Eric Down, a distinguished airborne leader, deflated the ego of his men by telling them that there was nothing clever or brave about parachuting; Mountbatten conquered soldiers of all races with his easy charm and raised laughs which were spontaneous rather than dutiful; Montgomery, in corduroys and richly assorted headgear, stood in front of a jeep and distributed packets of cigarettes with gay abandon.

The employment of such gimmicks in 1914—the expression 'gimmick' was not then part of the English language—would have caused soldiers to gape in open-mouthed and unbelieving astonishment: generals dishing out fags—what the 'ell next?

Charles Fergusson, commanding 5th Division, every inch a Grenadier Guardsman of the older school, employed no gimmicks: he spoke to the men in the sort of language that the soldier of the period expected from generals. Fergusson's address was inspiring, soldierlike and sobering. There would, the general told them, be no easy victories in this war. The men of the 5th Division would be called upon to stand every sort of discomfort and boredom, and there would be no picture-palace or friendly pub just round the corner. Some of us—Fergusson was careful to say *us* and not *you*, for he had been severely wounded in the Sudanese campaign—will get bloody noses.

The general permitted himself but one joke: bravery in battle would be rewarded by decorations, provided that all the D.S.O.s and D.C.M.s were not snaffled by the base-wallahs for so courage-ously dishing out plum and apple jam. He did not see fit to add, as did other generals later in the war, that cowardice would be pun-ished by the firing squad; in Ireland the 5th Division had main-tained a splendid reputation for discipline and the warning seemed to Fergusson to be neither desirable nor necessary.

It was up to every man, concluded the general, to see that the glory of his regiment remained undimmed. Stick it, he urged, even if all your officers are dead; stick it for the honour of the regiment, for it is only the regiment that counts.

2

As August 24th dawned the German attack spread the entire length of the Mons–Condé Canal and fell upon the thin line of General Fergusson's 5th Division. The first pulverising attack was launched upon Brigadier Gerald Cuthbert's 13th Brigade.

Specially chosen for the liquidation of this contemptible handful—the phrase used to describe the 13th Brigade—were the Brandenburg Grenadiers, one of Germany's proudest regiments of infantry.

But by the evening of August 24th the 12th Brandenburg Gren-adier Regiment was, in the words of one German historian:

> A mere wreck, shot-down, smashed up, a handful only left. . . . heavy defeat, why not admit it? Our first battle is a heavy, unheard-of defeat, and against the English, the English we laughed at. . . .

The Englishmen at whom the Brandenburg Grenadiers had laughed for the first and last time were of the 1st Battalion the Royal West Kent Regiment, sometimes known as 'The Dirty Half Hundred'.

Said Sir Arthur Wellesley of the West Kents in 1808:

> Not a good-looking Regiment, but devilish steady.

In 1914, also, the 50th were 'devilish steady'.

The West Kents were predominantly men of Kent with an inevitable leavening, as was usual in Home Counties regiments, of Cockneys. They came from Deptford Broadway and Tunbridge Wells; from Maidstone and the mean little streets of Gravesend, 'where the ancient shipman dwells'; from the grimy streets of Woolwich and farms in villages with names like Headcorn, Bethersden and Sissinghurst.

These were the men at whom the Brandenburg Grenadiers had seen fit to laugh. Their laughter was short-lived, for on August 24th 'A' Company, supported by two troops of 19th Hussars (Divisional Cavalry)—described by the Germans as 'enemy, strength unknown'—accounted for no fewer than 3,000 Brandenburg Grenadiers.

The slaughter at St. Ghislain on the left of the West Kents' line has been described from the German view-point by Captain Walter Bloem. Bloem, at the age of forty-six, was jolted from the cultured pursuits of novel writing and theatre management into the bloody business of soldiering with the Brandenburg Grenadiers.

> . . . a hellish inferno broke loose and in thick swathes the deadly leaden fire was pumped on our heads, breasts and knees. Wherever I looked, to the right and left, nothing but dead, and blood-streaming, sobbing, writhing wounded. . . .

The odds faced by the West Kents at St. Ghislain were ten to one—the same as those encountered at Agincourt. The men of Kent had not degenerated in the 500 years between.

August 23rd, 1914, was the longest (and very nearly the last) day in the life of Second-Lieutenant Arthur Chitty, commanding Number 3 Platoon of 'A' Company, 1st Battalion the Royal West Kent Regiment. Only one man of 'A' Company viewed Arthur Chitty with disapproval when he joined the 1st Battalion from Sandhurst early in 1914: to Private 'Onion' Hill, a morose old soldier and chronic grumbler, Chitty appeared to be little more than a child, and indeed his fair hair and pink complexion gave him an oddly cherubic and un-military appearance.

'Blimey,' said Private Hill, in tones of bitterest scorn, 'you mean to say a Gawd-forbid like that's goin' to lead us in action? Reckon 'e should of brought his bleedin' nurse along wiv 'im.'

Unfortunately Private Hill delivered himself of this scathing assessment of his new platoon officer in the hearing of the platoon sergeant, Sergeant Jim Powell. To hear a private soldier speak of an officer thus was to Powell's conventional and sternly disciplined mind a near-blasphemy.

'I 'eard that, Private 'Ill,' he said menacingly.

''Eard wot, sarge?' said Hill, wearing the expression of injured innocence which he invariably assumed when addressed by an officer or N.C.O.

''Eard wot you said about Mr. Chitty,' said Powell, as if Hill didn't know; 'Mr. Chitty's your platoon officer, follow me? And whether he wets 'is bed, picks 'is nose, plays with a duck in 'is barf or rides a muckin' fairy-cycle, you does wot 'e tells yer. Understand?'

'Yes, sarn't.'

'Less of your lip, then, AN' PUT YER 'AT ON STRAIGHT . . . !'

There is rather more to this spirited conversational exchange than may be at first apparent; it illustrated, in fact, the essence of the officer-man relationship which existed in the B.E.F.: a feeling of mutual respect and admiration.

At a time when his contemporaries at Clifton were wrestling with the intricacies of calculus and Greek irregular verbs, Arthur Chitty was in command of sixty hard-drinking and hard-swearing soldiers. On August 23rd, 1914, his age was eighteen years and three months.

His breeches were brand new and somewhat semi-circular in shape; his puttees a shade lighter than dress regulations demanded; his cap very stiff about the peak. In his kit was a recently purchased cut-throat razor which he only needed to use once a week. But his cool handling of his platoon in the holocaust of killing which followed the attack of the Brandenburg Grenadiers evoked the admiration of even Private Hill. Stealing a look over his shoulder, Hill observed Chitty nonchalantly indicating fresh targets and conceded generously to his friend and neighbour, Private George Pink: 'Our kid's doin' orlright. But 'e's so bleedin' young. . . .'

'Stop talking,' said Sergeant Powell curtly.

Now it was time for 'A' Company to retire from a position which must soon become untenable: they were under heavy shellfire from some thirty German field guns and their only artillery support, 120th Battery, Royal Field Artillery, had been put out of action.

A keen cricketer from his earliest youth, Arthur Chitty dismisses his Great War service as 'having been out first ball'. While directing the retirement of his platoon with admirable *sang-froid*—the Brandenburg Grenadiers were now less than one hundred yards away and shells were bursting on all sides—he was struck in the chest by a bullet and his left wrist was shattered by shrapnel. But as long as he could still stand and speak, he continued to encourage his men.

Two bandsmen—a trumpeter and trombonist respectively—who on the outbreak of war had surrendered their instruments for a stretcher, bravely set out towards Arthur Chitty. Chitty, his arm broken and with one lung already collapsed, ordered them back.

'Get out of this,' he told them weakly.

The stretcher bearers, with bullets crackling on all sides, exchanged a meaning glance: it certainly looked as though their journey would be wasted—copped it proper, he had; arm busted and bleeding like hell from a nasty one in the chest; couldn't last more than half an hour at this rate. But they couldn't just leave him—stretcher bearers were meant to bring in bodies, dead or alive.

'Get back,' repeated Chitty, 'and that's an order.' They left.

And then Second-Lieutenant Arthur Chitty settled himself more comfortably to die.[1]

Brigadier George Roupell is uncommunicative about the incident at Hill 60 in 1915 which won him the Victoria Cross, but on the subject of the performance of the 1st Battalion the East Surrey Regiment on the Mons–Condé Canal he has quite a lot to say, though not much about his own contribution.

The East Surreys, in common with every other battalion of the 5th Division, had a 'damn' good shoot'—the universal and euphemistic expression used to describe a writhing, struggling, squirming shambles of German dead. 'Imagine,' says Roupell, 'having as a target the side of a house. Hitting the advancing Germans was as easy as that.'

In particular, Roupell told the story of two young subalterns, Bill Morritt and Noel Ward—their combined ages barely totalled forty years—whose platoons held up overwhelming numbers of Germans for over four hours. The order to retire did not reach them and they were surrounded—cut off both from each other and from any help from the rest of the battalion. Only two courses of action were open to them—to surrender or try to fight their way out. Both subalterns chose the latter and not a man of these two platoons who died that day—approximately ninety per cent of the total strength—did so with reproach on his lips.

Both Morritt and Ward gave the order to fix bayonets and with their swords drawn charged at the head of their men into a wall of field grey. Ward died almost at once, shot clean through the heart before he had covered twenty yards; his men surged over him, with glaring eyes and bared teeth, snarling out the words of meaningless filth which sustained the private soldier in moments of extreme stress.

---

[1] Arthur Chitty did not die. He made a miraculous recovery from his wounds and was taken prisoner. Twenty-five years later he was back in France as a Lieutenant-Colonel, commanding the 4th Royal West Kents, and was awarded the Distinguished Service Order for his fine handling of the battalion before and during the evacuation from Dunkirk.

Morritt, miraculously, survived this last despairing charge; he had been wounded in the left leg and the right wrist, and his right knee was shattered by a bullet; yet another bullet, fired at a range of under twenty yards, hit his sword and broke it in half. He was taken prisoner and for the next three years was one of the most persistent would-be escapers. He was killed at his third and most spectacular attempt.

Roupell spoke also of the Commanding Officer, Lieutenant-Colonel John Longley, who was a constant inspiration to every officer and man of the battalion, although suffering from high fever throughout the action with a temperature of over 101 degrees; of Major Henry Tew, who took over command from Longley, and completely ignored a wound in his hand which severed two of his fingers.

In an order of the day General Sir Horace Smith-Dorrien said of the 1st East Surreys that they were splendid throughout. Sergeant George White of the 1st Duke of Cornwall's Light Infantry, a man sparing with his praise, said:

'I reckon them Surreys put the wind-up One O'Clock . . .'[1]

The withdrawal of the 3rd Division was rendered considerably easier by the heroism of three men: Captain Theodore Wright and Lance-Corporal Charles Jarvis of the Royal Engineers, and Private John Heron of the Royal Scots Fusiliers.

Two bridges crossed the Mons–Condé Canal: one at Jemappes, scene of the gallant action fought by Captain Thomas Rose's Scots Fusiliers; the other two miles to the west at Mariette, killing ground of the Northumberland Fusiliers.

It was obvious that a determined rush by the Germans across these two bridges might convert the orderly retirement of the 3rd Division into a rout. The situation called for urgent action by the Royal Engineers.

It was easier said than done, for there was no exploder to fire the charges under the bridges.

Theodore Wright of the 57th Field Company, Royal Engineers, swung himself hand over hand under the bridge at Mariette. For an hour and a half, twice wounded and under intense fire all the time, he struggled to set the charges.

No less gallant was the conduct of Lance-Corporal Jarvis and Private John Heron on the bridge at Jemappes.

Private Heron has never been able to explain, either to the satisfaction of historians or to his company sergeant-major, how he came under the wing of Lance-Corporal Jarvis of the Royal Engineers.

[1] Thomas Atkins's pseudonym for General von Kluck.

Heron had fought throughout the Royal Scots Fusiliers' action at Jemappes: this was war as he understood it—the enemy were coming at him, and all he had to do was to keep firing straight into the advancing German hordes as fast as he could work the bolt of his rifle. If Private Heron had been told to fix his bayonet and charge the Germans, he would have done so with equal promptitude. The war aims of the Fusil Jocks were no mystery to John Heron.

But the Royal Engineers were an unknown quantity to Heron, as indeed they were to the rest of the infantry: they were supposed to blow up bridges when they were not building them, and if someone didn't blow up the Jemappes bridge pretty soon then the Royal Scots Fusiliers were going to be caught by a horde of Germans who were getting closer every minute. John Heron looked forward to getting back home to his Ayrshire village and to killing more Germans, in that order.

But with the withdrawal of the Scots Fusiliers from Jemappes, Heron got left behind. It seemed reasonable enough to attach himself to a serious-looking sapper with the single stripe of lance-corporal on his arm. This stripe represented responsibility, if nothing else, and Heron was not anxious for responsibility at a critical time like this. Jarvis's first question unsettled Heron: 'Know anything about explosives, Jock?'

'No,' said Heron shortly; nor did he want to know anything about explosives.

'You can give me a hand,' said Jarvis decisively: 'what's your mob?'

'1st R.S.F.,' replied Heron, piously wishing that he was back with them.

'For the next hour or so,' declared Jarvis, 'you're a sapper. And don't you forget it.'

The herculean efforts of Captain Wright, Lance-Corporal Jarvis and Private Heron did not go unrewarded. The bridges were destroyed almost under the noses of the advancing Germans. Wright and Jarvis brought imperishable glory to the Corps of the Royal Engineers, and both were awarded the Victoria Cross.

Private Heron, an enthusiastic but bewildered assistant to Jarvis, was accorded a sour reception from his company sergeant-major on his return to the 1st Royal Scots Fusiliers. A month later, however, he found himself the astonished recipient of the Distinguished Conduct Medal *for gallant and distinguished services in connection with the destruction of the Jemappes bridge which materially assisted the safe withdrawal of elements of the 3rd Division. . . .*

CHAPTER IX

I

THE extrication of the much mauled but still indomitable 3rd Division went incredibly smoothly compared to the misfortunes which befell Sir Charles Fergusson's 5th Division as they in turn withdrew. On the 23rd August this division—particularly the 1st East Surreys and 1st Royal West Kents—had inflicted tremendous slaughter on the advancing Germans with comparatively small loss to themselves; the total casualties of the division had amounted to 400.

The text of the order issued to Sir Charles Fergusson from 2nd Corps Headquarters was that the 5th Division should retire to prepared positions in the line Bois de Boussu–Wasmes. The withdrawal of the division was to be characterised by a series of desperate rearguard actions which proved beyond all doubt that the men of the B.E.F., even when outnumbered by anything up to ten to one and with certain defeat seemingly inevitable, simply did not know when they were beaten.

One such action was fought in and around the small town of Wasmes.

After a preliminary artillery bombardment, dense masses of German infantry approached the village with a confidence that suggested that they thought the place had been evacuated. The 1st Royal West Kents, who had effected fearful slaughter on the Brandenburg Grenadiers at St. Ghislain, performed further deadly execution, as did the 2nd King's Own Yorkshire Light Infantry and the 1st Bedfords.

The German columns were met by concentrated rifle and machinegun fire and were flattened like grass in the path of a motor mower.

> We shot them down in heaps at St. Ghislain [recorded Major Paul Hastings of the West Kents], but that was not in the same country as the doing we gave them in Wasmes.

The courage of those advancing Germans evoked the admiration of every officer and man of the force in Wasmes, but it was the courage born of desperation and futility: time after time they advanced, but after two hours of furious fighting had made no headway; as Sergeant Jack Hunt of the Bedfords succinctly phrased it: 'It was like farting against thunder.'

The men of the West Kents, the Bedfords and the K.O.Y.L.I. fulfilled their duty as rearguard most admirably. There were dead and wounded men of all of these three battalions in Wasmes, but there were many more who laughed and cheered as they charged their magazines in preparation for yet another German assault.

Their own casualties, however, had not been light: 'B' Company of the Royal West Kents, in particular, had lost heavily, the most grievous loss being the death of Major Charles Pack-Beresford, one of the regiment's finest officers. In the Wasmes battle he proved this over and over again; he was a tower of calm strength throughout and was a magnificent example to every officer and man who saw him. With Pack-Beresford died thirty-five men and three out of the four other officers of 'B' Company who, following the example of their commander, displayed total disregard for their own safety. Command of the company devolved on the battalion's senior subaltern, Lieutenant Frank Fisher,[1] until he too was killed.

But this was no beaten force which retired in conformity with the general withdrawal of the 5th Division. The oft-repeated question, 'Why are we retreating?' was heard in every platoon. No satisfactory answer was forthcoming, but Sergeant Hunt, a sardonic and indomitable soldier of the Bedfords—he was later awarded the D.C.M. for conspicuous gallantry in the Wasmes battle—produced a theory: 'We're not retreating,' declared Hunt; 'we're just advancing in circles.'

Among the men of Wasmes who did not retire was a young private of the Royal West Kents who today lies in a French cemetery. He died a few days before his 18th birthday, having enlisted at the age of sixteen in 1913.

The manner of this boy's death differed little from that of thousands of others. He had been hit by several jagged pieces of shrapnel and Corporal Sam Haslett, as he bent over him just before the retirement from Wasmes, knew that the end was very near: the limp sagging of his back indicated, without even the most rudimentary medical knowledge, that it was broken; the trickle of blood from the corners of his mouth told of extensive internal injuries.

---

[1] The fate of 'B' Company of the 1st Royal West Kents became the pattern of many other infantry companies in the ensuing weeks. Fisher himself was killed in September; thus 'B' Company lost all its officers within one month of landing in France.

'I could see he hadn't long to live,' said Haslett, 'and he knew it too. I asked him if there was any message I could take to someone at home. His eyes filled with tears, but he was just a nipper—didn't need to shave, choked if he lit a fag and hadn't never been out with a girl. Then he said: "I ran away from home an' enlisted a year ago. Mother and dad don't know I'm here; but you tell 'em from me *I'm not sorry I done it*".'

'When I told the boys about it,' recalled Haslett, 'they cried like babies; but mind you, that's the spirit that pulled England through the war, and there wasn't a man of us who didn't think of that kiddie and his example every time we went in to fight.'

This is as good an epitaph as any soldier can hope for.

2

While the West Kents, Bedfords and K.O.Y.L.I. retired from Wasmes, eight hundred dour and determined Yorkshiremen of the 2nd Battalion the Duke of Wellington's Regiment were busily and bloodily engaged on the outskirts of the town. They presented an extraordinary appearance. A battalion which had always prided itself on its impeccable turn-out, the 'Dukes' were blackened and filthy from the coal dust which littered the positions that they had hastily taken up outside Wasmes.

But this was to be the least of their troubles.

The order to retire from the Wasmes area did not reach the 'Dukes'.

For Lieutenant Charles Ince of 'A' Company the battle was to begin auspiciously enough; he was privileged to gaze upon the finest spectacle that could have gladdened the heart of any infantry soldier: a company of Germans, marching in fours and making not the smallest effort to take cover—for all the world as if they were making a triumphal march through the streets of Paris—was advancing directly across his front. 'For me it was the finest possible introduction to war,' said Ince. 'I never saw a better target, and I spent practically the whole war in the front line.'

There was no time for fire orders. Ince was on the point of shouting: 'Number Two Platoon, five hundred enemy in front, ten rounds, rapid fire,' but soon realised the superfluity of such a procedure; it was the duty of every man to fire his rifle as fast as he could work the bolt and ram a fresh clip of cartridges into his magazine.

Ince experienced a curious lack of emotion as he watched the grey lines break and fall—so painstakingly accurate and efficient was the killing of this German company that he felt that death could not really hurt.

The grey hordes kept coming on as fast as the 'Dukes' could shoot them down and Colonel Gibbs was labouring under an anxiety which was fully understandable: his orders had been categoric—in the absence of orders to retire he was to hold his position to the last man, and the last round.

Reports from companies were depressing enough: 'A' were holding their own, but could hardly do so until nightfall; 'B' and 'C' had been penetrated at several points and only desperate work with the bayonet had saved them from being overrun; 'D' was reduced to a bare forty effective men.

True, the Germans presented a magnificent target for the artillery, but there were no supporting guns.

Now the firing from the town of Wasmes itself seemed to be dying away, an indication to Colonel Gibbs that either the West Kents, Bedfords and K.O.Y.L.I. had retired or been overwhelmed. Soon the fire from Wasmes died away altogether. Clearly, the 2nd Battalion the Duke of Wellington's Regiment had been left out on a limb.

Throughout the tumult of battle, Colonel Gibbs had been unshakeably calm. And this calmness did not desert him as he remarked to his Adjutant, Captain Denman-Jubb: 'Looks like a general retirement of the whole division. So orders or no orders we'll have to get out of it.'

This was easier said than done. Although the Germans had pulled back, it was plain to Gibbs that they were preparing for the final coup-de-grace. They came forward in dense masses, but were stopped in their tracks by a blistering volley from the rifles of the Dukes. Then, in parties of ten or a dozen men, the battalion began to pull out. Some—a few—managed to get away comparatively easily. Others—not a few—found themselves in desperate straits: isolated parties, some commanded by officers or N.C.O.s and others composed of privates only, found themselves surrounded.

One such party, the remnants of Number 12 Platoon of 'C' Company, were in a special category of heroic misfortune. When the Germans closed in for the kill, the platoon consisted of Lieutenant 'Boy' Russell and nine privates.

'Boy' Russell—although nearly twenty-five years old, he still had the appearance and manner of an ebullient schoolboy—stood in front of his nine men with his sword drawn. He could very easily have surrendered to the Germans pressing in on all sides, but the thought of a sojourn in a prison camp never entered the heads of Russell nor any of the men under his command: they would die like 'Dukes'. These ten men received the German advance shoulder to shoulder. Later, when their bodies were recovered, it was noticed that German dead lay in heaps all around them.

In another small party of 'Dukes' cut off and surrounded, there may have been men with thoughts of surrender but any such thoughts were speedily dispelled by Sergeant Fred Spence.

Spence was the type of old-style N.C.O. who caused some recruits to wonder if they had been wise to enlist. A fierce disciplinarian, he had the type of parade ground voice which was clearly audible at five hundred paces and an eye which could detect a sloppy slope from a distance of fifty yards; it is said that his shout of 'CHARGE!' that day carried a good half-mile.

So twelve brave men, hacking, stabbing and cursing, cut their way out of an encircling ring of Germans. In front of them throughout was Sergeant Spence: roaring like a bull and twisting his rifle round his head like a cane, he ran amok among the bewildered Germans who, baulked of an easy prey, scattered before the violence of the charge. Twelve men ran amok with him, and seven of them lived to fight again. Among those missing at the roll call that night was Corporal Jack Williams: he had thrust his bayonet into a German, pulling the trigger simultaneously as he kicked the man in the stomach. But he was unable to free his bayonet at once and, possibly fearing the consequences of being charged with 'losing by neglect his rifle and bayonet', he struggled to wrench it out while his comrades ran on. During this half minute a German soldier clubbed him from behind with a rifle butt and Williams ceased to take any further interest in the proceedings. When he came to, he was a bitterly swearing and fractious prisoner-of-war. . . .

It was the first major engagement for the 'Dukes' and they had bought their battle knowledge at a heavy price: 400 officers, N.C.O.s and men killed, wounded and missing, but they had held at bay six German battalions. And as they marched into Le Cateau that night they sang lustily—they had 'given the Jerries socks' and were ready to do so again at the earliest possible opportunity.

CHAPTER X

I

THE Cavalry Division at Audregnies were fed up to a man. Only the Greys, the 4th Dragoon Guards and the 16th Lancers had seen serious action in the fighting so far, and had been insufferably patronising about it to the other regiments.

To these other regiments—the Household Cavalry, the Queen's Bays, the 5th and 6th Dragoon Guards, the 3rd, 4th, 11th and 18th Hussars, the 5th and 9th Lancers—the war to date had been a bewildering and frustrating affair: it had resembled, in fact, a tedious and inconclusive exercise on Salisbury Plain carried out in extreme discomfort (cavalry manoeuvres at home had always resembled health-giving picnics, according to the dictates of the weather).

They rode hither and thither, not knowing where or why; they heard the *rafale* of French seventy-fives and the distant stutter of British machine-guns. And ever and anon they demanded: 'What the hell's it all about?'

In the 9th Lancers the mood of ennui which pervaded the 2nd Cavalry Brigade was as prevalent as anywhere, and it came from the top; Lieutenant-Colonel David Campbell was the cavalry commanding officer *par excellence*—his own horsemanship was sufficient proof of this. He had a fierce pride in his regiment and had always ridden it on a tight rein; he was also acutely conscious of the fact that the 16th had charged with lances before the 9th. For any right-thinking 9th Lancer that was insult enough.

It was just as well that the galloping Staff officer from General Fergusson's headquarters arrived at the H.Q. of the 2nd Cavalry Brigade when he did. The German advance was outstripping the exhausted 5th Division and Fergusson's men would be overrun unless the cavalry could help.

Colonel Campbell read his orders with satisfaction; this was what he had been waiting for. He read them twice and then summoned the Adjutant.

Captain Reynolds, the Adjutant, had never been a soft-spoken officer: his shout of 'TRUMPETER', said the wags of the regiment, must have been heard by von Kluck himself.

116

Preparations for action proceeded with the smooth efficiency for which the 9th Lancers were justly famous: '"A" Squadron—prepare to mount. . . . "B" Squadron—prepare to mount. . . .'

Left feet to stirrups, right legs swinging over saddles in perfect unison, reins gathered in left hands, a quick reassuring pat on the necks of horses with the right . . .

'MOUNT! Half-sections right, walk march . . ."

Right hands fingered chinstraps, for only that morning a fiery directive on the subject had come from Allenby; rifles were pressed deep into their buckets; lances were gripped tightly and 'now we'll see whether sabres are more effective than lances', murmured Colonel Campbell menacingly to no one in particular. . . .

The opportunity seemed to take an unconscionable time in coming. They moved out of the village and then halted on a rise in full view of the German artillery observers.

For fully twenty minutes—'it seemed like twenty years to me,' said Trooper Jim Crow—the 9th (Queen's Own) Lancers stood in column of squadrons on the outskirts of Audregnies as steadily and motionless as if at an Aldershot review: lance points glittered in the sunshine; the lines of horsemen were dressed and re-dressed with characteristic lack of hurry or agitation: there was complete silence, for the 9th Lancers talked on parade at their peril—a silence absolute and sinister, broken only by the jingle of bits and accoutrements as here and there a horse tossed its head. In front of the regiment, some five lengths ahead of the leading files, was Colonel David Campbell, his diminutive figure motionless in the saddle.

Echeloned to the left of the 9th were the 4th Dragoon Guards, with Colonel Mullen at their head. In front of 'C' Squadron was Major Tom Bridges imbued, as was every man of the 2nd Cavalry Brigade, with the powerful and heady spirit of the *arme blanche*.

Then the advancing Germans came into view; the cavalrymen could see advanced scouts moving across the corn fields in front of a large building which was the Quiévrain sugar factory.

Suddenly, and it seemed to the retreating infantrymen of the 5th Division almost miraculously, the volume of shelling upon them lessened. For now the German artillery had an infinitely more tempting target in the lines of exposed horsemen. If there were not guns to the left and right of the Lancers and Dragoon Guards, there were guns in plenty in front of them. But it seems that the magnificence of the target caused the German gunners to become over-excited, for the shooting, although intense enough, was execrable.

'If a British battery commander had shot his guns like that,' declared Trooper Jim Crow, 'he'd have been court-martialled.'

At first there had been scarcely a sound in the perfectly dressed ranks of the cavalry apart from the jingling of bits and accoutrements. But now, with the shells falling ever faster, the horses had begun to whinny agitatedly and paw the ground; some of them kicked out behind them, while others reared up on their haunches. Some of the more excitable animals showed signs of taking flight, and were only brought under control by ruthless use of the curb.

It was time to go. Colonel Campbell turned in his stirrups and, with a single blast of his whistle and wave of his leather-covered cane, launched his regiment into a charge which for sheer suicidal heroism must rank with the charge of the Light Brigade at Balaklava. Simultaneously, Colonel Mullen dashed forward at the head of his Dragoons.

The 9th Lancers and 4th Dragoons made a brave show as they advanced at stretch gallop towards the sugar factory at Quiévrain, thundering through the fields of golden corn: the galloping men and the accompanying sweet notes of the trumpet seemed to typify every aspect of the majesty of war.

But to the officers of the other cavalry regiments, some of whom had a grandstand view of the action, it seemed that the Lancers and Dragoons must be galloping to their doom as blindly and irrevocably as had the Light Brigade at Balaklava: by now the German artillery shooting had improved considerably; they had the range and shells were bursting among the horsemen with murderous thoroughness.

There were German riflemen among the corn stooks and they opened a rapid fire on the advancing horsemen. But as the thundering hooves came nearer, their aim grew panicky. Then the men of the leading lines of Lancers were among them, crouching low and leaning forward in their saddles. Blind panic took hold among the majority of these German scouts as they fled from the thrusting lances: there were several agonised squeals, similar to those uttered by rabbits caught in a trap, as the leading scouts took lances through their throats; one German soldier, run clean through, was carried a full fifty yards before the trooper could shake the body free of his lance; two more, in headlong flight, tripped and fell and were trampled underfoot by a dozen pairs of hooves; four more, brave men all, stood their ground and were speared with their rifles still at their shoulders.

Both regiments were caught in a withering fire. They quickened their pace and the gallop of both regiments became even more furious. 'In that mad gallop,' said Trooper Crow, 'I never consciously thought of the possibility of death, and I doubt if any other man in the charge did either.'

Nevertheless, in that inferno of shot and shell death was coming fast; saddles were being emptied every few seconds; horses pecked, stumbled and crashed, hurling their riders over their heads. In life the 9th Lancers and 4th Dragoons carried out every manoeuvre in perfect order and with parade ground precision; in death the trick did not desert them. As a man or horse dropped, and they were dropping fast, the riders on each side of him opened out. Then, as soon as they had ridden clear, the ranks closed again.

It can be fairly said that the charge of the 9th Lancers and 4th Dragoon Guards was checked and broken by the nine German batteries which were firing at them over open sights from the walls of the sugar factory at Quiévrain. But this is only partly true. The charge was halted by the scourge of the hunting field and the bugbear of ranchers, barbed wire: a high double fence, towering in its invincibility, faced the cavalry as they thundered to the attack. Against this hideous barrier they were helpless. And all the time the German shells showered down on them and the machine-guns raked their wavering lines.

There were dead men and horses—shot and blown to pieces, they at least were still and silent; there were riderless horses, crazed with terror, galloping in every direction; there were men and horses, not yet dead, who could still crawl and cry out in their anguish; there were wounded troopers with just sufficient strength to cling to their mounts' necks.

'Rally, there, RALLY!' shouted Campbell and Mullen to their regiments, and obedient to these two voices the men who were still mounted wheeled away from the wire barricade and away from the stricken field of Elouges.

As Lancers and Dragoons rallied and endeavoured to re-form, the guns of 119th Battery, Royal Field Artillery strove to support the last two battalions of the 5th Division still in contact with the enemy—the 1st Norfolks and the 1st Cheshires, the climax of whose desperate rearguard action was still to follow.

The battery commander, Major Edward Alexander—it was said of him that he ate, drank and slept gunnery—was at the top of his specialised world and here were good targets in plenty: hordes of German infantry were pouring forward from Quiévrain and debouching from Deduit Woods. As imperturbably as if he were on the artillery ranges of Okehampton, Alexander gave his orders: 'All guns, one degree right . . . one and two, add a hundred . . . three and four, add fifty . . . angle of sight—zero . . . one round battery fire . . . gun-fire . . . at gun-fire, sweep two degrees. . . .' But it could not go on for ever. Soon the position had become a shambles of dead and dying men, dead and dying horses. Although Major Alexander was fiercely determined to keep the battery in action as long as there was one gun and two men to fire it—if necessary, indeed, he would have fired it single-handed—such an unequal contest could only have one end: for every shell the battery fired, the German artillery replied with twenty; although they had silenced one enemy battery, two more, firing over open sights, had caught them in enfilade; hordes of German infantry were getting ever closer.

Over on his left he could see a party of dismounted lancers installed in some ruined buildings and slag heaps—they were some of the survivors of the charge who had been gathered up under the command of Captain Francis Grenfell, of the 9th Lancers.

In response to a message from Alexander, Grenfell rode over to the gunners' position. He came at a casual hand canter: there were bullet holes through his uniform and he was bleeding profusely from a shrapnel wound in his hand. Shells and bullets were falling about him unheeded. Alexander told Grenfell that half of his men and horses were casualties, but somehow the guns must be got away. Could the lancers help? Grenfell rode back to his party of cavalrymen without haste. He marked out a possible line of withdrawal for the guns as he went.

'The Germans,' declared Grenfell, 'will not have those guns while there are any of us left alive. Now, then, who's for the guns?'

Every officer and man able to stand—some forty in all—unhesitatingly stepped forward.

Hauling artillery pieces out of action by hand was a manoeuvre which had been infrequently practised by the Royal Regiment of Artillery in peacetime; the artillery motto *Ubique* was supposed to cover every conceivable type of emergency, but the horses took care of most of it.

But conditions on August 24th in 119th Battery were different: everyone present on the scene, from Major Alexander to a sixteen-year-old trumpeter of the 9th Lancers, was straining on the drag-ropes. . . .

There was no time to limber up, even if there had been enough horses; there was not even time to swear. The guns must be run back by hand, and it was every officer and man, cavalryman and artilleryman alike, on the drag ropes.

Major Alexander heaved on a rope, together with the boy-trumpeter and a gunner to whom he had awarded seven days C.B. only a month before; the Battery Sergeant-Major, a comfortably built warrant-officer to whom life was dear and pension near, laboured with a corporal of the 9th Lancers with the worsted spur of a rough-rider on his arm; Second-Lieutenant Charles Norman rashly put his hand on the barrel of a gun and sustained a severe burn—a practical tribute to the gunnery of the 119th Battery.

Working as hard as anyone, in spite of the wound which rendered one hand virtually useless, was Captain Francis Grenfell. Heaving and straining at the same drag rope—the gun which they were trying to extricate was bogged down in soft mud—was Sergeant Ted Pont of 119th Battery. Noticing the 9th Lancers badge on Grenfell's cap, Pont asked his companion in the work of rescue if he knew his brother—Squadron Quartermaster-Sergeant Pont.

'He's back at base, the lucky blighter,' said Grenfell.

'He was always a jammy bastard, if you'll pardon the expression, sir,' said Pont grimly. He looked at Grenfell's hand, crudely bandaged with a bandana handkerchief, through which the blood was seeping freely. 'Hadn't you better get that hand seen to, sir?'

'When we've got this gun back,' replied Grenfell; 'now then, altogether, lads—HEAVE. . . .!'

Somehow with superhuman effort the gunners and lancers got six guns back to the waggon lines. Here was Captain George Walford, wounded in both arms above the elbow, but indefatigable in his labours to get the guns limbered up.

'On the instructions of the battery commander,' recalls Sergeant Pont, 'we got going independently; I galloped my gun team up an embankment and we crashed through the crossing gates across the railway line—God only knows how. We were followed by a German ranging gun, but we were going too fast for them and somehow escaped damage. The German infantry was only two hundred yards away. . . .'

There are divided opinions on the necessity and achievement of the charge.

It is difficult . . . to see what necessity there was for the impulsive action of the 2nd Cavalry Brigade. . . . Apart from giving the Infantry a few minutes' grace before the German assault fell on them, the charge had effected nothing. The cost was high—the bulk of the cavalry division's 250 casualties of the day are accounted for by the losses of the 9th Lancers and 4th Dragoon Guards—but might have been higher.[1]

Sir Charles Fergusson had nothing but praise for the 9th Lancers and 4th Dragoon Guards when he addressed them after the action. A man ever sparing with his praise and not given to registering emotion, Fergusson's voice broke as he thanked them for saving his division; even if the charge itself had failed, he assured them, the drawing of the enemy fire from his infantry on to the cavalry had saved countless casualties.

As a subaltern of the Queen's Bays, Major-General Kingstone, C.B.E., D.S.O. and Bar, M.C., had a grandstand view of the charge; like many another subaltern of the Cavalry Division, he had watched it with the keenest envy. Says Kingstone emphatically: 'They couldn't have done anything else'; and knowing his men he adds, 'they wouldn't have done anything else anyway.'

For the exploit of the 9th Lancers in saving the guns of 119th Battery there was nothing but praise. It was fitting enough that Captain Grenfell and Major Alexander were both awarded the Victoria Cross for that day's work.

2

The charge of the 9th Lancers and the 4th Dragoons could only temporarily relieve the pressure on 5th Division, and a rearguard had to be found to protect the division's uncovered left flank. The task, a herculean one in all conscience, was entrusted to the 1st Battalion the Norfolk Regiment and the 1st Battalion the Cheshire Regiment. In overall command was Lieutenant-Colonel Charles Ballard, Commanding Officer of the Norfolks.

Only two battalions could be spared for the job—barely 2,000 men in all. As events turned out, it would have been a tough job for an entire division. Not that the men of the Norfolks and Cheshires, redoubtable battalions both, knew anything of this as they set off on the long march from the Bois du Boussu to their position on the ridge running north and south between Elouges and Audregnies. Nor would they have been unduly perturbed if they had known that they were opposed by the entire 4th German Army Corps, which

[1] John Terraine in *Mons—The Retreat to Victory* (Batsford 1960).

consisted of twenty-five battalions of infantry, six squadrons of cavalry, twenty-four batteries of artillery and fifty-six machine-guns. The prevailing sentiment among the Norfolks and Cheshires was 'let 'em all come and the more the merrier'.

On arrival at the Elouges–Audregnies road, Colonel Ballard distributed his companies along it. Lieutenant-Colonel Dudley Boger, commanding the Cheshires, was ordered to prolong the line to the left of the Norfolks.

The last company of the Cheshires to arrive—Captain Arthur Dyer's 'A' Company—had barely halted when the German attack engulfed the Norfolks and Cheshires.

There was no time to entrench and no question of readjustment of the line—when the Germans launched their attack there was only a pretence of touch between the two battalions; there was no time to site the machine-guns with a good field of fire; there was no time for orders or scientific fire control. It was every man's business to seize his rifle and begin firing as fast as he could at the advancing hordes of German infantry.

The action started auspiciously enough: although there was no time to dig trenches, both battalions had good fields of fire and the advancing Germans received a liberal dose of rapid fire.

On the subject of machine-guns Lieutenant Henry Randall, the Cheshires' machine-gun officer, was a near fanatic and his burning enthusiasm was abundantly present in the men under his command. The cynics of the battalion contended that Randall's generosity with gifts of bottles of beer as rewards for efficient gun drill was a contributory factor to the high standard of efficiency in the section. Be that as it may, the Cheshires' machine-guns came into action with a despatch which would have put their best peacetime efforts to shame: Randall's two guns added their lethal chatter to the crash of rifle fire; the attacking Germans wavered and hesitated, came on again and finally shredded away.

It was first blood to the Cheshires.

'Reckon that's worth a pint all round, sir?' inquired a jubilant private of the machine-gun section.

'A gallon per man at least,' promised Randall. 'But watch your front—they'll be back.'

The machine-guns and rifles of the 1st Norfolks were also taking a heavy toll. To the attacking Germans it may have seemed that this last rearguard was but a tiresome little obstacle to be contemptuously brushed aside; the Norfolks and Cheshires were disproving this theory in the most conclusive manner possible.

During a brief lull in the fighting—such lulls were few and far between in this desperate battle—Colonel Ballard took stock of the situation. General Fergusson had given him discretion to break off the action if and when the remainder of the 5th Division had been extricated. The bulk of the division, so it seemed to Ballard, had got clear: from his battalion headquarters in a ruined cottage, he could see what must be the last battalion to retire—the 1st D.C.L.I. or the 2nd Manchesters, but he could not tell which; he could only see ragged bunches of men with shells bursting over them as they struggled on to Elouges. The 2nd Calvary Brigade had retired and so had the supporting artillery.

Ballard knew that every minute he stayed in his present position would cost his battalion more lives and would see the expenditure of more irreplaceable ammunition. In their exposed positions the Norfolks were sitting targets for the German machine-guns; they had already suffered something like 200 casualties; the gaps between companies were so large that effective control of the battalion was fast becoming impossible.

Ballard, torn between his desire to carry out the orders which said that he must hold his position until ordered to retire and to fight his battalion again in an action which promised something better than total extinction, reached a decision.

'It's time to go,' said Ballard to his Adjutant, Captain Frank Cresswell. 'Get a message to the Cheshires telling them to retire after us.'

Ballard scribbled hastily on a message pad:

> From O.C. Norfolks to O.C. Cheshires. Enough is as good as a feast. Retire by companies after us.

He folded the slip of paper and called 'Runner!'

At a steady loping trot the runner set off for the Cheshires' position, running straight into a barrage of shrapnel and machine-gun bullets. He had covered barely fifty yards before he stopped dead in his tracks, spun round drunkenly and fell slowly forward on to his face.

'Runner!' said Cresswell again. Another man stepped forward and ran towards his predecessor. Ballard and Cresswell saw him bend down, pick up the message from the recumbent body and run on. And this runner, too, could barely have covered another fifty yards before he fell.

Finally, Captain Cresswell himself set off for the Cheshires but was never seen again. Two cycle orderlies, who were despatched later, were either killed by shellfire or captured by the Germans. Whatever their fate, the order to retire never reached the Cheshires.

The Cheshires, still fighting grimly and continuing to inflict astronomical casualties on the advancing German infantry, were in a desperate plight. Their Commanding Officer, Lieutenant-Colonel Dudley Boger, had no discretionary powers: until he got the order from Colonel Ballard to retire, he was to hold his position to the last man and the last round.

The Cheshires were in a deadly three-sided trap from which they might conceivably have escaped, had the message to retire reached them. It did not, and soon the only escape route was blocked by yet another wall of grey. They were surrounded.

Boger received reports from his company commanders—from Captain Rae Jones's 'D' on the right, Captain Dugmore's 'C' in the centre, and Captain Dyer's 'A' on the left—and they all told stories of almost identical gloom: 'can hold for another hour at the outside'; 'they're all round us and have penetrated at several points'; 'ammunition almost finished'; 'am going in with the bayonet'.

Clearly, the end of the 1st Cheshires was very near: no trenches, no dugouts, no reserves; ceaseless German infantry attacks; unremitting and accurate machine-gun fire from all sides.

As he grew weaker from loss of blood—he had been seriously wounded in the side—Colonel Boger wondered why there was no supporting artillery fire coming from 119th Battery; he wondered what had happened to the 2nd Cavalry Brigade; he wondered how the Norfolks were faring and if they had retired, and if so, why no order had reached him to follow suit.

The doom of the 1st Cheshires was finally sealed by a single German aeroplane, which hovered over the beleaguered battalion like a vulture waiting to swoop on the dead and the dying—and there were many of both.

The aeroplane circled leisurely, dipped its wings insultingly and flew away. The weary and battle-stained soldiers on the ground could only follow its progress with fearful oaths and morose speculation; it was well out of rifle range, although several men fired defiant shots in its direction, until ordered to desist by wrathful officers and N.C.O.s:

'The next man who fires a shot and doesn't have a corpse or an aeroplane to show for it goes on a charge. . . .'

The German aircraft was a spotter plane for the artillery and soon a barrage of shells was falling on the Cheshires' position. Then, as suddenly as it had started, the barrage lifted; every man who could still hold his rifle fixed his bayonet and waited for the infantry attack which must finally swamp them. . . .

Although grievously wounded—in addition to his side, he had been hit yet again in the left foot—Dudley Boger remained a tower of quiet strength and was a constant inspiration to every officer and man of the battalion. He knew, as did every other officer, N.C.O. and private, that the sands were fast running out for the 1st Cheshires. But his presence, whether at his command post or hobbling laboriously and painfully among his men, was a positive denial of defeat.

The fortunes of war decreed that Private Alf Jordan, fourteen years a soldier and the possessor of a conduct sheet just about to enter its fifth page, should command Number 12 Platoon of 'C' Company. If anyone had told Jordan before the war that he would ever command anything, he would have spat (literally or metaphorically) and uttered a rude word. But with every officer and N.C.O. of the platoon dead or wounded, the men who were left thankfully turned to Jordan for help. To his own amazement he found that he had qualities of leadership; his voice, although calm, brooked no disobedience; here was a good man to die with, as most of 12 Platoon did.

There was Lieutenant William Elliott, shot through both feet and unable to walk or stand, who refused to surrender his sword when finally taken prisoner; and just before the end came, the air was filled with the shouts springing from the throats of thirty desperate but indomitable men of 'A' Company, as they were led into a final hopeless bayonet charge by Captains Dyer, Jollife and Massy and Lieutenant Matterson. And this heroic little band, too, died to a man.

It goes without saying that the 1st Cheshires had an 'Immortal Sergeant'—indeed, they had several—but pride of place must go to Sergeant Sam Raynor. Throughout the action Raynor was a one-man wave of destruction; he assumed command of a force comprising the remnants of 'A' and 'C' Companies and held at bay a force of Germans which outnumbered them by ten to one. And by his side throughout was his staunch friend and admirer, Corporal Bill Crookes; they had started the war together and intended to finish it together.

Raynor encouraged the faint-hearted and comforted the wounded; he heaped fearful derision on any recalcitrant soldiers, but there were few of these because they feared Raynor's wrath more than German shells, bullets or bayonets. He ignored shells and bullets completely, and seemed to have as many lives as a cat.

Corporal Crookes was put out of the fight by a bullet through the hand. Weak and faint from loss of blood, he crawled to a ditch. It seemed to his wandering and bemused mind that the firing was gradually slackening. This, he thought, must be the end of the 1st Cheshires' stand. In this he was correct, but it was very far from being the end of Sergeant Raynor. When a group of German soldiers seized him, he went berserk; the Germans were not to know that he had been middleweight champion of the Army. Raynor felled one German with a straight left to the midriff; a vicious right cross to the jaw accounted for another. He was seized by two more, but kicked out savagely behind him and a scream of pain announced that his iron-clad heel had connected with a shin bone. It took the combined efforts of six men to subdue him, and at least two of these carried the unmistakable marks from Sam Raynor's flailing fists.

A German N.C.O. regarded Raynor with bitter hatred; he had felt the weight of Raynor's fist and there was murder in his heart—an Englishman, and a prisoner at that, had seen fit to strike him. The N.C.O. advanced on Raynor with his bayonet fixed. . . .

A German officer called out: 'Stop!'

The German N.C.O., wearing a sheepish and bewildered expression, halted. The officer screwed a monocle into his eye and regarded Sergeant Raynor with interest. The German officer noticed the two fraying and stained medal ribbons on Raynor's tunic, one orange and black, the other red, white and green. 'Those medals,' he asked, 'what are they?'

'South Africa,' replied Raynor; the bloke had asked him a civil question and was entitled to a civil answer.

'You fought bravely,' said the German officer. 'I am sure you will get more medals.'

He was proved an able prophet. Sergeant Raynor was awarded the Distinguished Conduct Medal.

When Sergeant Raynor found Corporal Crookes, his greeting was characteristic. He said: 'Blimey, so they got you too, did they? If I'd known you were still alive, I wouldn't have bloody well surrendered.'

There is little more to tell. The survivors of the Cheshires—a bare forty unwounded men finally laid down their arms—were rounded up and marched away to begin four years of misery in German prison camps. They marched in meticulous step; they seemed to be more like the victors than the vanquished. And the German soldiers who watched them saw for the first time the spirit of these despised English—a spirit which no amount of misery and starvation could subdue.

The 1st Battalion the Cheshire Regiment had been wiped out, but no fighting unit of any army in any war met so glorious an end. For more than thrice the length of time laid down in its orders it had held on against odds which were overwhelming.

The effort of the 1st Cheshires is perhaps best summed up by their brigade commander, Brigadier-General Count Gleichen. A man not given to extravagant utterances by word of mouth or on paper, he produced his own characteristic superlative in an Order of the Day to the 15th Brigade:

The Cheshires did thundering well as I fully expected they would.

The Battle of Mons was over and now the battered remnants of the 3rd and 5th Divisions straggled wearily back to the line Le Cateau–Cambrai, the next line of defence selected by Sir John French.

Units had become intermingled: there were Royal West Kents, Duke of Wellingtons and Bedfords mixed up together; East Surreys had linked up with Norfolks; the K.O.Y.L.I. saw strange faces in their depleted ranks—men of the Suffolks, K.O.S.B. and Manchesters.

South Lancashires were mixed up with Wiltshires, and Gordon Highlanders with Middlesex. The indefatigable C.Q.M.S. Fitzpatrick staggered in with the remnants of his bewildered but still indomitable party of cooks, drivers, batmen and orderlies.

On all sides could be heard the comfortable words of the men of this 'Contemptible Little Army', and the word 'chum', the highest rank to which an Old Contemptible can attain to-day whether he be Major-General or private, was the most comfortable of all:

'Lean on me, chum. . . .'

'Have a swig from my bottle, chum. . . .'

'Want a draw off of my fag, chum?'

'Won't be long now, chum. . . .'

These men knew that the word retirement had now fallen into military disuse; they could no longer blind themselves to the fact that this was no retirement, but a general retreat—and this was only the beginning of that retreat.

And throughout August 25th the British cavalry covered that retreat: every horse's head was down, for the nosebags were long since empty and every horseman's throat was parched because the water bottles too were empty. They rode, dismounted, marched with reins over; halted again and watered their horses at some fortuitous pump; ate their iron rations (if they had any) and cursed the staff. . . .

Thus did Smith-Dorrien's 2nd Corps and Allenby's Cavalry Division come to Le Cateau. It was August 25th now; the Battle of Mons had only started two days before.

PART III

THE RETREAT

CHAPTER XI

1

Deep in the narrow valley of the Selle, surrounded on all sides by open cultivated country with never a fence and scarcely a tree in sight, stood the town of Le Cateau.

It was a pleasant little town in August, 1914; set in countryside not unlike the Sussex uplands between Tonbridge and Hastings, it possessed much of the rural charm of this tranquil neighbourhood. In the single broad street, it seemed that every other house was a café or *estaminet*. There was to be little opportunity for the troops to patronise them on August 26th, 1914.

For General Sir John French, at least, Le Cateau presented a heartening spectacle on August 25th, for desperately needed reinforcements in the shape of Major-General Thomas Snow's 4th Division, fresh out from England, were detraining. The men were a sight to gladden any hard-pressed commander: their buttons and boots shone, their puttees were miracles of spiral perfection; their cap badges had not, as yet, fallen prey to souvenir hunters. Inevitably, their impeccable appearance drew derisive comments from the weary, grimy, battered men of the 3rd and 5th Divisions. To those who had fought in the Battle of Mons, the men of the 4th Division presented a strangely incongruous appearance, and their more seasoned comrades lost little time in letting them know it.

Among the new men there were Royal Irish Fusiliers, Royal Dublin Fusiliers, Royal Inniskilling Fusiliers and Lancashire Fusiliers; there were the kilted 2nd Seaforths; there were Royal Warwicks, King's Own, East Lancashires, Essex and Somersets. And there were those superior beings with black buttons, the 1st Battalion the Rifle Brigade.

2

The Battle of Le Cateau, so far the bloodiest and most decisive battle of the war, has been called a defeat.

The issue decided at Le Cateau was simple enough: during the retreat from Mons, Smith-Dorrien's 2nd Corps had got separated from Haig's 1st Corps. As the 2nd Corps approached Le Cateau, the Forest of Mormal and the River Sambre lay between them, effectively preventing co-operation between the two Corps.

To Sir John French Le Cateau represented nothing more than yet another milestone on the retreat. His original plan to hold a line at Le Cateau with both 1st and 2nd Corps was, he decided, impracticable. Firstly, his two Corps were separated, and secondly, he could not be sure that the French Army could hold their line on the right of the B.E.F. Indeed, a stream of reports to G.H.Q. from the French 5th Army sombrely confirmed that they could do no such thing and were already in retreat. General French could only depend on the help of two French reserve divisions on his left, hastily and indifferently entrenched to hold an enormous front towards Dunkirk. It was unlikely—indeed, it was barely possible—that they would be able to provide any effective opposition to the Germans' outflanking movement. If a German flank attack round the B.E.F.'s left were successful—and the odds on its success were considerable—then French's communications with Le Havre would be practically gone.

If Le Cateau seemed to be nothing more than a retreat milestone to the Commander-in-Chief, it represented a dilemma of the most daunting description to Sir Horace Smith-Dorrien. The orders which Sir Horace had received from French seemed clear-cut enough:

The 2nd Corps will NOT make a stand at Le Cateau, but will continue the retirement.

At the time Smith-Dorrien received these orders, the word 'retreat' had not yet come into general use, and the more dignified expression 'retirement' was used; but it made no difference to Smith-Dorrien how the future movement of his Corps was phrased.

These instructions to continue the retreat [he told the *Weekly Dispatch* in February, 1917] were orders that I could not see my way to obey; I feared that, with the men as tired as they were, further retirement might end in a rout. I considered that to show our teeth was the only way of stopping the enemy.

The 'teeth' of the newly arrived 4th Division were sharp enough: they were fresh, well fed and spoiling for a fight. The 3rd and 5th, who continued to straggle into the Le Cateau area during the night 25–26th August, were none of these things. They were, in fact, scarcely capable of putting one foot in front of the other; when ordered to halt, they collapsed where they stood and slept, heedless of the rain which poured down on them. A staff officer at 2nd Corps Headquarters reported: 'They're too damned tired to march another step, but provided they can lie down they'll fight all night.'

With men of the 3rd and 5th Divisions still reaching Le Cateau in a state of utter exhaustion, it was obviously impossible for Smith-Dorrien to move the 2nd Army Corps until the following morning, and it would not be easy even then: every road further rearwards was clogged with transport and refugees; many of them, indeed, had ceased to be roads at all—the heavy rainstorms had reduced them to impassable quagmires.

Smith-Dorrien's dilemma was this: to move at once was impossible; for the 2nd Corps to stay where they were and fight was a reversal of orders. None of his field commanders was in telephonic communication with G.H.Q., and none of them would have requested orders direct from Sir John French even if they had been: Snow, Hamilton and Fergusson were, rightly enough as it happened, imbued with the necessity for acting through the 'proper channels'. The proper channels, in this case, were Smith-Dorrien's Headquarters at 2nd Army Corps.

The decision to stand at Le Cateau was Smith-Dorrien's and his alone; there was not a soldier or student soldier in after years who did not give him honour for it.[1] The decision was unanimously supported by Generals Snow, Fergusson and Hamilton. Allenby, too, assured Sir Horace that he could count on all possible help from the Cavalry Division. At the conference at 2nd Army Corps Headquarters at Bertry, just five miles from Le Cateau, Smith-Dorrien abruptly closed the meeting and altered the course of history:

'Very well, gentlemen, we will fight.'

But if Fergusson, Hamilton, Snow and Allenby fell in readily with Smith-Dorrien's plan, G.H.Q. most emphatically did not. The Chief of Staff, Major-General Sir Henry Wilson, seemed to have become infected with some of his Chief's mercurial temperament:

> In one stride, Wilson . . . had gone from verve and fervour to defeatism . . . he was now convinced of coming calamity.[2]

'If you stand at Le Cateau and fight,' declared Wilson to Smith-

[1] General Snow went further: at the first post-war reunion dinner of the 4th Division, at which Smith-Dorrien was the guest of honour, he thanked Sir Horace for saving his division from annihilation.
[2] Barbara Tuchman in *August 1914* (Constable: 1962).

Dorrien, '*there will be another Sedan.*' He went on to tell Sir Horace that the weight of von Kluck's offensive would fall on Haig's 1st Corps and not on him and 'troops fighting Haig cannot fight you.'

With as much patience as he could muster, Smith-Dorrien explained that the 1st Corps were under no threat whatsoever; the nearest units were some eight miles off, and the rest were away beyond the Forest of Mormal and the Sambre, and, for the same reason, could give no assistance to 2nd Corps at Le Cateau.

With a baffling reversal of mood, Wilson backed down. 'Good luck to you,' he said to Smith-Dorrien before he rang off. 'Yours is the first cheerful voice I have heard in three days.'

3

At first sight the Le Cateau position, both tactically and geographically, seemed sound enough, and to hold it with the 1st and 2nd Army Corps a practicable proposition. Such had been Sir John French's reasoning when he first made a reconnaissance of the area, but it depended on the assumption that Haig's 1st Corps would be able to prolong the line eastwards. As things turned out, however, Smith-Dorrien's 2nd Corps had to withstand the shock alone.

On paper the dispositions of the 3rd, 4th and 5th Divisions, selected by Smith-Dorrien, looked reassuring enough as August 26th dawned. The 5th Division on the extreme right reached from a point halfway between Le Cateau town and Reumont to Troisvilles. Then came the three brigades of the 3rd Division: the 9th was north of Troisvilles; the 8th on the left of the 9th, to the north of Audencourt; the 7th curled round the northern side of Caudry. The 4th Division continued the line on to Esnes. But Smith-Dorrien's three divisions, two badly mauled and one woefully incomplete, were opposed by ten German divisions of fresh and fanatical troops. Against 600 guns extending along his entire front Smith-Dorrien could muster only 225; his infantry forces were outnumbered, at a conservative estimate, by five to one. He could expect no aid from Haig's 1st Corps, nor from the French. The prospect of another Sedan seemed real enough. . . .

To the layman, three divisions—something like 100,000 men—may seem to be a sizable enough force to hold a front of eight miles. But the 3rd and 5th, both sadly depleted in men, horses and guns by the earlier fighting, were almost out on their feet by the time they reached the Le Cateau positions on the night of the 25th. That left

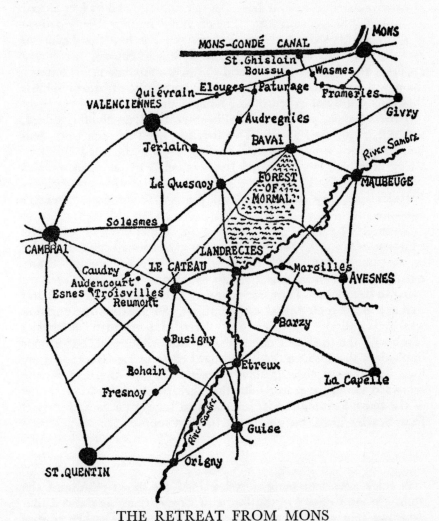

THE RETREAT FROM MONS

Sketch map: scale approximately ten miles to one inch

General Snow's twelve infantry battalions—fresh, comparatively well-nourished and bursting to give of their best. But the 4th Division, too, was very far from being complete, and in fact lacked all the essential sinews of war. The divisional cavalry, 'B' Squadron of the 19th Hussars, had not yet arrived; nor had the divisional cyclists, the field companies of the Royal Engineers, the heavy artillery, the signal company and the field ambulances. Whatever the infantry said about these men, they knew in their heart of hearts that they could not exist for long without them.

The Le Cateau position was badly entrenched; much of it, indeed, was not entrenched at all. The trenches, such as they were, had been dug by French labour, including women and even children. Every man, woman and child had worked hard and uncomplainingly, but they had not had access to the Military Manual of Field Fortifications, nor had they been present at Sir John French's councils.

Through the night of August 25th, battalion and company commanders of these dead-weary infantrymen issued the same order on the same note of frantic urgency: 'Get your men digging.' Many a platoon commander gave the answer: 'Yes, sir. But what are they going to dig with?' They were consigned to hell for their pains and told not to ask such damn' fool questions. For all that, the question was not entirely unreasonable. Every infantryman carried a 'grubber', the universal name for an entrenching tool, but a poor implement to sink into the baked hard earth at Le Cateau. Many men had thrown their grubbers away to lighten the load on the rearward march, together with their greatcoats and packs. A few of the more fortunate units managed to borrow picks and shovels from nearby farms, but they were in short supply.

4

A thick and depressing mist heralded the dawn of August the 26th, the anniversary of the Battle of Crecy: there was also a thin drizzling rain and the atmosphere was what the weather experts describe as 'muggy'.

The defenders of Le Cateau were in various stages of preparedness: some units, like the 2nd Suffolks and 2nd K.O.Y.L.I., had completed their digging and had sunk into the ground like moles; others, like the 2nd King's Own Scottish Borderers and 2nd Manchesters, had appeared on the scene in the small hours of the morning and were still feverishly digging; others again, like the 1st Wiltshires,

2nd South Lancashires and 3rd Worcesters, had been the rearguard of the retiring 3rd Division and were still coming in—at first sight these three battalions inspired little confidence, for they were in the uttermost extremes of exhaustion and resembled robots or sleep-walkers more than soldiers. But like every other battalion at Le Cateau that day, they did not know when they were beaten.

This was the state of the line at Le Cateau at 6.30 a.m. when von Kluck's guns opened up one of the most terrifying and murderous barrages in the history of war.

From dawn until the early afternoon of August 26th the battle of Le Cateau was an artillery duel, and a hideously unequal one at that. But there was never a second when our artillery was silent, as long as there was a man left able to serve the guns.

It seemed that nothing could possibly live amid the deluge of shells which fell on the positions of the infantry huddled in their inadequate trenches; to this hellish rain of death the infantry could make no reply. But the field batteries could and did, although the cost in officers, men, horses and guns was appalling.

All along the line at Le Cateau, amid the scream of shells and exploding shrapnel, unemotional voices could be heard calling out ranges, fuses, angles of sight, angles of elevation; phrases incomprehensible to the infantrymen burrowing ever deeper into the earth—they didn't know a clinometer from a dragrope—but everyday language to the men who devotedly served the guns:

'Shrapnel . . . four six hundred . . . at gunfire sweep five minutes from zero lines. . . .'

'Five rounds battery fire . . . one-oh seconds . . . stop . . . add fifty. . . .'

'Drop one hundred—five minutes more right. . . .'

'At battery fire, sweep one-five minutes. . . .'

So it went on for six mortal hours—six hours of interminable noise which deafened men, stunned men, wounded men, killed men and buried men alive.

An artillery duel so one-sided could only have one end: for every shell the British guns sent over, the Germans were replying with two dozen. Casualties, too, were mounting in the field batteries at an alarming rate: forward observation officers, spotting suicidally from crests, were being blown to pieces as they indicated new targets; signallers were killed and gun position officers had to do their own telephoning.

Many of the guns were fought by an incongruous assortment of personnel, many of them august technicians who had done no gun drill for many a long month and had confidently expected that they never would again: armament artificers were pressed into service as loaders; more than one saddler bombardier (known as a 'waxy' in the Royal Regiment) became a range setter; more than one bewildered battery clerk or officer's groom found himself pressed into service as a gunlayer; the spectacle of a senior major in command of a battery acting as 'Number One' on a gun was to become almost commonplace.

There was no shortage of good targets.

'Got in some topping bursts; must have knocked out hundreds of 'em'; this was the laconic report on the day's fighting from Captain Ernest Tandy of the 108th Heavy Battery. Artillerymen were always prone to understatement, and Tandy's assessment of the slaughter scarcely did the battery justice.

The columns of German infantry continued to move forward like an army of grey ants and the 60-pounder shells of the 108th Battery dropped among them with lethal precision, tearing great gaps in the ranks. But still the distant grey masses marched inexorably forward.

The 122nd Battery, too, were hard at it: with fuses at zero and over open sights: the casual order 'one round gunfire' was enough to obliterate an entire platoon.

Then, barely perceptibly at first, the German artillery barrage slackened. To Generals Fergusson, Hamilton and Snow this had only one meaning: the gradual cessation of shelling pointed to an all-out infantry assault at any moment. Clearly, von Kluck considered that after such a pulverising bombardment the British infantry would be too stunned, shattered and demoralised to offer any effective resistance.

Stunned and shattered the infantrymen of the 3rd, 4th and 5th Divisions undoubtedly were. But demoralised they most decidedly were not. . . .

5

At Le Cateau the 1st Battalion the King's Own Regiment bought their first battle experience at a fearful price. They were forming up to march to their appointed positions when they were caught by the fire of a German battery at 1,500 yards range. The British gunners did not hold a monopoly of splendid targets, and the King's Own in their fours were a spectacle to set any gunner dreaming.

A veritable deluge of shells fell on the King's Own and in the space of less than half an hour 12 officers and 431 rank and file were killed and wounded.

It was a scene of indescribable carnage and confusion: the mess wagon and limber carrying the machine-gun ammunition received direct hits and all the horses bolted into the middle distance; the Commanding Officer, Lieutenant-Colonel Arthur Dykes, was killed in the first minute.

It would have been a shattering experience even for a battle-hardened battalion. The King's Own, although their morale and fighting spirit were as good as any other unit of the 4th Division, were certainly not yet that: in common with every other regiment of the B.E.F., there were a large percentage of reservists in the ranks—men who had been away from the Army for anything up to five years; there were, admittedly, a sprinkling of South African War veterans who had been present at the action of Spion Kop, but this violent bombardment had caused more casualties in half an hour than the King's Own had suffered in nearly half a century.

It is to the everlasting credit of the King's Own that under the command of Major Richard Parker they re-formed and fought valiantly throughout the rest of the day.

6

The 2nd Battalion the Suffolk Regiment were holding a sector of the line just outside Le Cateau itself. As the murky dawn of August 26th faintly streaked the sky, the men of the Suffolks crouched, cramped and sodden, in their miserable apologies for trenches, gripped their rifles more tightly and prepared to give a good account of themselves when the inevitable attack came. The orders given to Lieutenant-Colonel Charles Brett by General Fergusson laid down that there would under no circumstances whatsoever be any retirement. But the dawn brought no infantry attack; instead a ceaseless deluge of shrapnel and high explosive fell on the 2nd Suffolks. In the first half hour Colonel Brett was killed by a shrapnel bullet. Later, a few men, their reason almost gone, climbed blindly out of their trenches; but if death or mutilation was likely inside the trenches, it was certain outside. It is doubtful if any unit in the early days of the Great War found itself in such evil case as the Suffolks that day. In addition to the shelling, which was killing and wounding men every minute, they were enfiladed by scything machine-gun fire.

No officer of the Suffolks was more anxious to strike a blow at the Germans than Second-Lieutenant Edward Backhouse, and a nasty wound in his right leg had done nothing to quench his determination:

> But we were so tied to our trenches by machine-gun and artillery fire that any movement on our part was out of the question; our only chance lay in waiting for the enemy to show himself when he attempted to press the attack home.

Obviously, however, the Germans had no intention of getting to close quarters with the Suffolks until they had first systematically pounded them to pieces with artillery and machine-gun fire. This moment could not be far away, for already about half the Suffolks were dead or wounded, but still the German infantry tarried.

A company of the 2nd Manchesters and another of the 2nd Argyll and Sutherland Highlanders were going to the assistance of the Suffolks but two-thirds of this brave handful died in the attempt. The advance of the Argylls and Manchesters was, in the words of Edward Backhouse, 'a most gallant affair'; they advanced at the steady, loping trot of the well-trained soldier over open ground where there is not a stick of cover; they knew with awful certainty that they were going to their deaths; they knew that any man who reached the trenches of the beleaguered Suffolks unscathed would have to be under Divine providence. The well-sited German machine-guns ripped into the Manchesters and Argylls like a knife going into butter. Less than a hundred men flung themselves panting into the trenches occupied by the Suffolks—many of them occupied only by dead and dying men, and these were unceremoniously bundled out of the trenches.

Then suddenly the artillery barrage slackened, gradually died away and was silent. To the survivors of the Manchesters and Argylls the earlier sacrifice seemed worthwhile, for the Germans would now put their infantry in to overwhelm them. Just let them try. . . .

'Watch your front,' shouted the officers of the Argylls and Manchesters who still lived—a bare half dozen.

'This is a bit more like it,' muttered Jocks and Mancunians, as they brought their rifles to the aim, for this was the 'Thin Red Line' of the Crimea all over again. The men of the Suffolks, numbed, bewildered and scarcely in their right minds after such a fearsome bombardment, were a little slower to realise that their long awaited chance had at last come. But soon they too were ready: whatever the German infantry did, it could not be worse than the ordeal which they had already suffered.

A vast press of grey clad bodies bore down upon the Suffolks, Argylls and Manchesters from front, both flanks and rear. They were met by the rifle fire and the bayonets of desperate men who were still marvelling at their survival and determined to go down fighting: thus had the 12th fought at Minden, the 91st Highlanders at Lucknow and the 63rd at Inkerman.

Above the roar of musketry a strange sound was heard—a noise which caused men to wonder if the preceding shattering events had unhinged their minds. For the noise of bugles sounding the British 'Cease Fire' could be heard from their front. Momentarily fingers slackened on triggers; such was the instinctive discipline of the old Regular Army. But not for long: the Germans, disliking this rapid fire from men who should by rights be either dead or too dazed to resist, had resorted to trickery.

Shouted officers and sergeants: 'As you were . . . carry on firing . . . take no notice of them ——— bugles. . . . watch your front . . . let 'em have it, you bloody cripples . . . RAPID INDEPEN-DENT. . . .'

But, tragically and inevitably, it was soon over. Many hundreds of motionless grey figures lay in front of these indomitable men. A round score of them had succumbed to the deadly shooting of two captains of the Argylls, 'who shot on and on, bringing down man after man and counting their scores aloud as if at a competition.'

The two officers of the Argylls were both scions of noble and ancient Scottish families: Captains the Honourable Robert Bruce, Master of Burleigh, and Angus MacLean. They were both dead shots at game and stag, but they had never encountered sport like this on the Scottish moors which they both knew so well.

Now there were still more dead and wounded among the Suffolks, Argylls and Manchesters: men shot at close range, men clubbed to death with rifle butts, men bayoneted; among them was Captain MacLean, his revolver still in his hand and his face to the enemy.

For Second-Lieutenant Edward Backhouse this was a humiliating end to dreams of glory:

So there we were—prisoners. Neither I nor any of my friends had ever given a moment's thought to such a possibility. We had fully discussed our chances of a cushy wound which would take us home after a month or so, and had, of course, realised that we might be killed. But a prisoner—I hardly knew what to think about it; my first impression was that it was rather disgraceful. . . .[1]

But Backhouse need not have worried, for the Suffolks had been very far from being disgraced. Of the battalion, General Sir Charles Fergusson had this to say:

> The blow to the Germans on the field of Le Cateau upset their plans and prevented their descent on Paris. The Suffolks were one of the units which made that blow possible. *The whole nation should be grateful to them.*

Today the Suffolks are amalgamated with the Royal Norfolks, and are known as The East Anglian Regiment. The battle honour *Le Cateau*, which is emblazoned on their colours, is one of which they may be justly proud.

7

Another fine infantry battalion was to find its Thermopylae at Le Cateau. The 2nd King's Own Yorkshire Light Infantry, like the Suffolks, were in indifferent and hastily dug trenches when the dawn bombardment started; like the Suffolks, they were ceaselessly shelled and raked with machine-gun fire. The K.O.Y.L.I. virtually ceased to exist on August 26th—they lost 20 officers and more than 600 men killed, wounded and missing—but on the credit side they had two Victoria Crosses.

Corporal Fred Holmes, that eligible young man with prospects, whom we last met in Harrogate during his two weeks' liberty from the Army, won the supreme award for valour in carrying a wounded comrade on his back over a mile of bullet and shrapnel swept ground.

In command of 'B' Company of the 2nd K.O.Y.L.I. was an outstanding soldier. Major Charles Yate (universally known as 'Cal' because of his initials C. A. L.) was no stranger to war: he had fought on the North-West Frontier of India in 1897 and been seriously wounded in the South African War. In 1904, as military attaché to the Japanese Army, he was present during the Russo-Japanese war; as a result of this unconventional service he acquired a medal of startling design to add to his Indian Frontier and South African ribbons; it was a decoration which made Yate the target for considerable chaff in the officers' mess; to the delight of his

[1] Edward Backhouse was to endure four years of captivity in Germany. In the Second World War, as a brigadier, he was captured at Singapore, and endured a further three and a half years of miserable servitude. To-day, without bitterness or rancour, he describes himself as a 'professional P.O.W.'

friends, it was revealed as the Order of the Sacred Treasure, 4th Class.

Corporal Holmes, a man of extraordinary bravery himself, admired bravery in others above all other qualities. Of 'Cal' Yate Holmes said: 'He was always in front and his constant cry was "Follow me!"'

When Colonel Cecil Romer from Headquarters of the 2nd Army Corps rode over to Battalion Headquarters of the 2nd K.O.Y.L.I., he brought with him orders which were simple enough:

There will be NO retirement for the fighting troops; fill up your trenches with water, food and ammunition.

And to these orders Yate added his own forceful rider: 'If anyone retires, it is not going to be "B" Company.'

By mid-day on August 26th Yate's command had shrunk to himself, Sergeant Jim Clarke, one corporal, three lance-corporals (two of them acting and unpaid) and twelve privates. Lieutenant Brian Denison should also be included; he had taken a bullet through the temple which had blinded him, but he had not, however, relinquished his grip on his sword and continued to encourage the men until he died.

The 2nd K.O.Y.L.I. had been subjected to almost exactly the same treatment as that meted out to the ill-fated Suffolks: the air was torn and ripped by shells; telephone wires were rent and scattered; a tornado of shrapnel descended on them for three mortal hours. And the brunt of this fearful holocaust was borne by Yate's 'B' Company. The battalion was soon surrounded. Many fought to the last and only succumbed in the final rush with bayonets; others, too weary and dazed to press a trigger, were made prisoners. Not so the remnants of 'B' Company. Yate first settled the dying Denison more comfortably. He then issued crisp last orders to the men under his command: '"B" Company will charge with the bayonet!' At the same time he promised to confirm the two unpaid lance-corporals in their rank if they came out of the charge alive. He then shook hands with every man who was still standing. With bayonets fixed 'B' Company of the 2nd Battalion the King's Own Yorkshire Light Infantry charged against the advancing Germans.[1]

[1] Some doubt surrounds the circumstances of the capture of Major Charles Yate, V.C. The most reliable account comes from an eye-witness who saw him struggling furiously in the grip of three German soldiers. He was killed in 1915 on his last and most spectacular attempt at escape from a German prison camp.

By 3 p.m. it was clear to Smith-Dorrien that it was time to break off the engagement: his artillery could make little reply to the continuing German bombardment; his infantry were being either knocked to pieces by high explosive, swamped by mass infantry attacks or both.

Fergusson's 5th Division had taken the brunt of the heaviest fighting at Le Cateau: by the afternoon of the 26th some forty of the Division's seventy guns had been knocked out and the remaining batteries were woefully short of men and ammunition. Of the infantry, the Cheshires, K.O.Y.L.I. and Suffolks had virtually ceased to exist; the K.O.S.B. and Manchesters had each lost an entire company; the Dorsets, East Surreys, D.C.L.I., Bedfords, Norfolks, Duke of Wellington's and Royal West Kents had all suffered severely.

Fergusson had seen most of this near annihilation for himself. He had not fought his division from a telephone—this would not have been possible in any case, for almost all the telephone wires had been destroyed by shellfire—but from a prancing seventeen-hand charger: eye-witnesses said that Fergusson's survival among the bursting shells, as he galloped among his scattered units exhorting them to stand fast, was little short of a miracle. In the absence of any other means of communication, the order to the 3rd, 4th and 5th Divisions was given verbally by furiously galloping Staff officers from 2nd Corps Headquarters (no one, not even the 9th Lancers, criticised the horsemanship of 'staff wallas' after Le Cateau). The orders were both curt and simple; to the artillery—'Cease firing, limber up and get out of it!'; to the infantry—'The action is broken off. Retire immediately.'

It was easier said than done. Some of the staff officers, all of them men of enormous personal bravery whatever may be said to the contrary, succumbed to shrapnel or bullet on their desperate journeys; others in the prevailing confusion, galloped headlong into German units and were made prisoners.

The order to retire never reached the 2nd K.O.Y.L.I. and 2nd Suffolks who were wiped out where they stood. It never reached the 1st Gordon Highlanders and a company of the 2nd Royal Scots in their positions at Caudry; this gallant detachment clung to their positions until 3 a.m. on the 27th and inflicted fearful slaughter on the Germans before they were overwhelmed.

The retirement of the rest of the 3rd Division was comparatively simple, however much they disliked the idea—they had given as good as they got and were firmly convinced of their superiority over the enemy. It came as a particularly bitter pill to the newly arrived 4th, who had been less severely engaged; the 1st Hampshires, in particular, had scored a notable triumph in wiping out an entire German battery of artillery before they could bring their guns into action.

The 4th Division had their share of trouble later on. Long after sunset, by which time the bulk of the 2nd Corps were clear of the Le Cateau position, isolated parties of the 1st King's Own, 2nd Dublin Fusiliers and 1st Royal Warwicks still fought on, having had no orders to disengage from battle. Many died fighting with rifle butts, bayonets, entrenching tools and bare fists in the darkness; many more, too weary even to press a trigger, were captured as August 27th dawned.

> And even of them [wrote Gilbert Frankau] a handful shot their way a hundred miles through the advancing enemy, and so came safe after many wanderings and more than one sharp engagement to Boulogne....

8

During the Battle of Le Cateau the Royal Regiment of Artillery had distinguished itself time and time again. In the retirement it continued to do so.

Some guns could not be saved: these belonged to the batteries who lacked ammunition or horses or both. But the officers and men who had served them were giving no satisfaction to the Germans; amid hails of rifle bullets and with the enemy only a few hundred yards away, they calmly reduced the guns to so much useless rubble.

Two howitzers of the 37th Battery had to be abandoned, for the crew had been killed to a man and every shell expended. Any attempt to rescue them would be suicidal, for they were in an exposed position and a grey mass of infantry was only four hundred yards away. That the howitzers should fall into the hands of the enemy was to the battery commander, Captain Douglas Reynolds, unthinkable.

'We're not going to leave them there,' declared Reynolds to the Number Ones of the howitzers, Sergeants Charles Butterworth and William Bowers.

'We are not, sir,' replied both sergeants in unison.

Reynolds nodded approvingly. Then his eye fell on the two inseparables, with their oddly Biblical combination of names: Driver Job Drain and Driver John Luke.

Drain and Luke had been staunch friends since their enlistment in the Royal Regiment seven years before; it was a friendship cemented by an incalculable quantity of beer consumed in wet canteens and characterised by their inability to ever agree on any subject. They were, however, agreed on this particular solemn occasion; they both wished to repair to the nearest estaminet at the earliest possible moment. But the eyes of their battery commander and two sergeants were upon them. 'Two volunteers,' said Sergeant Bowers briefly. 'You and you.' Drivers Drain and Luke exchanged a sheepish glance and stepped forward.

Every gunner knows the story of Reynolds, Luke and Drain—of how they each won the Victoria Cross for galloping 'split-arse', as the Royal Regiment phrased it, through a hail of bullets and shrapnel to the two howitzers; how they limbered up, with the leading files of Germans a bare hundred yards away; how, flogging desperately at their drooping horses, they galloped the guns to safety. The Royal Regiment is proud of these three men, and a painting of the incident hangs in many an artillery mess today.

Both Drain and Luke had incurred the displeasure of Sergeant Butterworth before, but on that day he felt disposed to be generous. 'Those two,' said Butterworth—both he and Bowers were awarded the Distinguished Conduct Medal and later commissioned in the field—'certainly earned their beer *that* day—even if they didn't get any. . . .'

9

So the 2nd Corps came away from Le Cateau, trudging wearily from battle to the west on the road to Busigny.

The words 'rabble' and 'mob' have been used to describe them, and at first sight this seemed to be a fair description: regiments had become intermingled, there were riderless horses and gun limbers packed with unattended wounded.

Yet this was no panic-stricken flight, although there was confusion and disorder on every side.

Men who had tobacco puffed stoically at pipes, and cigarettes were passed from hand to hand, for to the fighting British soldier a 'spit an' a draw' after battle has always been priced far above rubies. 'They resembled,' said Sir Horace Smith-Dorrien afterwards, 'a crowd coming away from the Derby at Epsom.'

It is hard enough accurately to sum up the Battle of Le Cateau. By no stretch of the imagination can it be called a victory, but neither can it be labelled a defeat. Smith-Dorrien knew that the men of the 2nd Corps were exhausted to a degree which made a further rearward move impossible. Clearly, they could not turn and counter-attack. The order 'the position will be held to the last man and the last round' was, in the circumstances in which Smith-Dorrien found himself, the only feasible order to give. Smith-Dorrien gave that order and the German advance was temporarily halted. There the matter must rest.

The inability or reluctance (or both) of the Germans to pursue the retreating army has always remained an unfathomable mystery. It happened at Mons and again, twenty-six years later, at Dunkirk. And it happened at Le Cateau. Lieutenant Francis Longman of the 4th Royal Fusiliers—they had been reserve battalion of the 3rd Division and had not been committed to battle at Le Cateau—confessed later to a sick feeling of fear at the sight of this seemingly disorganised rabble: a single squadron of cavalry or battery of artillery could have cut up the exhausted and sadly depleted 2nd Corps piecemeal.

Why the German Army did not follow up after the battle of Le Cateau has never been satisfactorily explained. There was no risk of interference from the 1st Corps, who were still some eight miles away, with the River Sambre between them. The most popular hypothesis and the most flattering to the fighting qualities of Smith-Dorrien's men is that they had been too roughly handled by the British at Le Cateau to allow of pursuit. The fact remains that the Germans did not pursue and the 2nd Corps trudged painfully on to the crossroads.

Here harassed staff officers endeavoured to restore order out of chaos and their shouted commands gradually penetrated the numbed mental faculties of the men: 'Transport and mounted troops straight on, 3rd Division to the right, 5th Division to the left. . . .'

The town of St. Quentin lay directly in the path of the retreating 2nd Corps. And into St. Quentin trudged the bone-weary men of the 1st Royal Warwicks and the 2nd Royal Dublin Fusiliers. They were part of the newly arrived 4th Division and had come to Le Cateau with high resolve to give of their best. But now, having fought and marched for nearly forty-eight hours without respite or sleep, they were in the uttermost extremes of exhaustion—more dead than alive; a spent force; drained of everything save the desire for oblivion in sleep.

They should have been preparing to repulse the attack from the advancing Germans who were hard on their heels; they should have been cleaning their rifles; they should have been taking steps to prepare a meal. But even hunger—and none of them had eaten for twenty-four hours or more—went by the board. When the order to halt was given, they collapsed in inert heaps in St. Quentin's main square, and no amount of cursing, kicking and cajoling by the few officers could move them.

As exhausted as anyone were the Commanding Officers of the two battalions: Lieutenant-Colonels John Elkington, in command of the Warwicks, and Arthur Mainwaring of the Dublin Fusiliers. But for them there was to be no sleep. The two colonels were approached by the *Maire* of the town; they explained that their men were too exhausted to move on and they would therefore have to fight a rearguard action against the advancing Germans.

The *Maire* was horrified; there would be a fearful artillery bombardment of the town; women and children would be killed and vilely mutilated, and their deaths would be on the colonels' consciences. The British, he suggested, should stay in the town until the Germans arrived and then surrender.

To Elkington, the senior of the two commanding officers (he fervently wished that he were not) it seemed that the *Maire's* argument was cogent enough. He could organise no effective resistance with men who were already half dead with fatigue. He had only two choices: to save life or to expend it wantonly. Eventually it was decided that the men should pile their arms at the railway station and surrender when the Germans arrived in St. Quentin. The two commanding officers gave the *Maire* a written assurance that they would surrender in order to save the town from bombardment. The matter might have ended there, had it not been for the arrival in St. Quentin of two squadrons of the 4th Dragoon Guards under the command of Major Tom Bridges.

Bridges regarded the scene in St. Quentin's main square with horror: some three hundred British soldiers lay sprawled on the ground like so much unswept rubbish. There were no rifles to be seen and the few officers, who had by now despaired of ever galvanising the men into movement, sat around in disconsolate groups. It was a scene of indescribable inertia and despair. Four Dublin Fusiliers, clearly determined to make the best of the situation, had, by unspecified means, procured some bottles of wine. Locked in an unprofitable embrace, they staggered about among their sleeping comrades giving a spirited but off-key rendering of *Molly Malone* and other Irish ditties.

Bridges sought out the two commanding officers and listened to their story. He then spoke to some of the men, who informed him that they had already surrendered and would only leave the town if a train was sent to fetch them.

Undeterred by the presence of two officers considerably senior to himself, Bridges relieved the *Maire* of the document of surrender and then informed the recumbent soldiers that they had exactly half-an-hour in which to get ready to march. He further informed them that he would not leave a British soldier alive in St. Quentin.

The Warwicks and Dublin Fusiliers exchanged sheepish glances: this tall and confident major of cavalry was a very different proposition to the two colonels whose fighting spirit seemed to have been broken. For a brief moment it occurred to Bridges that he might have gone too far: he was not in command of the troops in St. Quentin and if two commanding officers had decided to surrender then strictly speaking he had no right to interfere with their decision. His other thought was that he wished he had a military band: a stirring march or two would work wonders with such men—such is the compulsive power of military music. There was no band, but Bridges found the next best thing. There was a toyshop nearby and from the pop-eyed proprietor he purchased a tin whistle and a drum. The whistle Bridges gave to his trumpeter and instructed him to play every tune he knew; the drum he took himself.

Bridges let out the strings to their fullest extent and put them over his head. Then he squared his shoulders, threw out his chest and, bringing up his elbows in a line with his chin, he beat two taps loudly with each stick; slowly at first, and then gradually faster and faster until the taps blended together in a long, loud roll. The trumpeter, catching the crazy infection of the moment, played *The British Grenadiers, Tipperary* and, for the benefit of the Irish, *Lillibulero*. The soldiers sat up, rubbed their eyes and stared incredulously: the spectacle of a cavalry major playing a toy drum was clearly the manifestation of some obscure war neurosis. But gradually the men started to laugh and then to cheer. Mouth organs were produced and joined the tin whistle in strident harmony. Within half-an-hour, Bridges's shock treatment had worked: the square was a mass of cheering men, all thoughts of surrender forgotten.

Thus did the Royal Warwicks and Dublin Fusiliers return to the war. And later they were to acquit themselves splendidly in the bloody fighting which followed.

For Colonels Elkington and Mainwaring the 'St. Quentin Incident' brought a grim aftermath: they were both court martialled for, in the grey words of the Army Act, 'shamefully abandoning their posts, which it was their duty to defend'.

Both were found guilty and sentenced to be cashiered. For Mainwaring it was the end of thirty years of honourable, if unspectacular, service. It was very far from being the end of John Elkington; he like many another broken and disgraced ex-officer before him, joined the French Foreign Legion and fought with it throughout the rest of the war. He was awarded the *Croix de Guerre* and *Medaille Militaire* and lost a leg. For John Elkington, at least, the 'St. Quentin Incident' had a happy ending: after the war the King invested him with the Distinguished Service Order and reinstated him in the British Army.

Chapter XII

I

It is now time to follow the fortunes of General Douglas Haig's 1st Corps. Mons and, later, Le Cateau were almost entirely 2nd Corps battles. On August 23rd, the day on which General Hamilton's 3rd Division was continuously and bloodily engaged in the Mons Salient, the 1st Corps on the Mons-Beaumont road sustained less than fifty casualties, from stray shells. Indeed, a young officer of the Scots Guards wrote in his diary that August 23rd had been a *day of rest*.

When French decided that the B.E.F. must retreat, the as-yet-uncommitted 1st Corps could only comply with the general order. The Corps went back through Bavai and Barzy, well to the right of 2nd Corps; Haig's line of retreat took 1st Corps over to the farther side of the River Sambre and this, combined with the dense Forest of Mormal, further widened the gap between the two corps.

On August 25th, the day before General Smith-Dorrien's delaying fight at Le Cateau, the 4th (Guards) Brigade fought a splendid rear-guard action at Landrecies and thus gave Haig's 1st Corps what was really its initial blooding.

But if the men of 1st Corps had done little fighting, they had done a great deal of marching: they had taken up a succession of defensive positions, but German attacks against them never materialised; they received orders to advance, which were promptly countermanded. They did not know whether they were coming or going. Possibly it was the endless digging which tried their patience most of all; digging, the dreary chore inescapable to infantry soldiers in any war. The oft repeated bleat of the infantry in the Second World War 'first we digs the ———— 'oles an' then we fills the ————s in again' might well have originated from a man of the 1st Corps in 1914.

The digging was all the more depressing because the trenches were often never occupied. And as they toiled through the heat of the day, stripped to the waist, their backs became painfully sunburned. Then it was on with the rough, hairy flannel shirts and the thick tunics; on with the packs, with the straps biting cruelly into blistered shoulders.

'Marching, marching, marching,' they sang to the tune of the hymn *Holy, holy, holy, Lord God Almighty* and 'Gawd send the day when we'll —— well march no more. . . .'

2

The 1st and 4th (Guards) Brigades had been fretting in disciplined inactivity since arriving in France. True, they had marched an incalculable number of miles in blazing heat, keeping their meticulous dressing as guardsmen always do. But as yet they had done no fighting—the fighting so far had been done by the 'line mobs'.

The 4th Guards Brigade, comprising the 2nd and 3rd Coldstream, the 2nd Grenadiers and the 1st Irish, felt justifiably insulted. And the march on the afternoon of the 25th August to the little village of Landrecies looked like being yet another wearisome foot-slog with probably nothing to eat and no enemy to fight at the end of it.

When the Guards Brigade marched into Landrecies just before dark on the afternoon of 25th August the village presented a sufficiently depressing aspect: the broad main street was deserted except for a few very old men and women and hungry and predatory dogs sniffing hopefully in the gutters.

But a clash with the Germans was clearly imminent. The road leading out of Landrecies swarmed with hundreds of refugees, all equipped with the paraphernalia of headlong flight: children and furniture loaded on to wheelbarrows; women with babies at their breasts; pianos, sideboards and grandfather clocks—pathetic remnants of small-town respectability—loaded on to carts. The refugees were heartened by the sight of the guardsmen. The Germans were coming, but these large and cheerful men who whistled and sang as they marched would assuredly drive them back.

The guardsmen settled in their billets, eased packs from aching backs, searched morosely for cigarettes and tobacco and wondered if the officers would give orders for them to open their iron rations. No such order was forthcoming.

The four battalions were positioned at each of the three exits from the village: the 2nd Grenadiers on the western side; the 2nd Coldstream on the south and east; the 3rd Coldstream to the north and north-west; with the 1st Irish Guards responsible for the barricading of the streets with anything they could lay their hands on.

The 4th Guards Brigade, declared Brigadier-General Robert Scott-Ker, would stay in Landrecies until relieved; if they could not stay in it alive, then they would stay in it dead.

Coldstreamer Paddy Smythe's most vivid memory of Landrecies is of a smell—a delicious and mouth-watering smell of baking bread. Having been told by an unsympathetic corporal to think less about his stomach and more about cleaning his rifle, the smell of baking became well night unbearable. Finally he could stand it no longer. Keeping a wary eye open for officers and N.C.O.s, Paddy slipped into the house next door. He emerged with a large loaf of unbelievable golden-crusted succulence and still hot from the oven. He also had a pat of butter of a wonderful brilliant yellow. Six clasp knives and six sets of strong teeth made short work of that loaf of bread. Said a guardsman with his mouth comfortably full: 'Reckon old Paddy orter get the V.C. for that.'

But the feasting was of short duration. An insistently pealing bugle told the men of the 3rd Coldstream that there was fighting to be done.

Two hundred yards from the village, the main street branches out into two roads, each leading into the Forest of Mormal. At the junction of the roads was Number Two Company, commanded by Captain the Honourable Charles Monck.

Darkness had fallen early and the sky was overcast, unrelieved by any moon. Suddenly the incongruous sound of singing was heard in front of Number Two Company's position. The voices were strong, cheerful and unmistakably French. Unmistakably French, that is, to any Englishman. Fortunately for Captain Monck, however, he had with him Henri, the battalion's French interpreter. And to Henri it sounded as if the voices were too guttural and harsh for Frenchmen. But in answer to Monck's shouted challenge, the reply came back '*Amis—Français*' accompanied by shouts of '*Vive l'Angleterre*' and '*A bas les Allemands.*' As Monck said afterwards, nothing could have sounded much more French than that.

Then things happened very quickly.

The leading elements of the advancing men, dressed in French and Belgian uniforms, suddenly charged forward. In the ensuing skirmish Guardsman Arthur Robson on the machine-gun was bayoneted and the gun captured. Captain Monck was knocked down by a press of bodies.

The machine-gun was recaptured, but only with fearful effort: a corporal and six guardsmen charged into the mêlée, and after swift and deadly work with bayonet and rifle butts brought the gun back intact.

Then the German attack came down on the whole 3rd Coldstream front like a smith's hammer on the anvil. They surged down the main street of Landrecies in closely packed waves and were greeted by accurate fire. At first the Coldstreamers fired strictly according to the drill book; that is, no man fired until an officer gave the order: 'Enemy in front, five rounds—FIRE!'

But clearly this method could not work against an enemy who still came on, walking over their dead comrades, heedless of losses. Murderously accurate as the fire of the Coldstream was, they must surely be overwhelmed by sheer weight of numbers. Major Torquil Matheson, the battalion second-in-command, soon realised that it was, metaphorically speaking, time to throw away the drill book. When the advancing Germans, seemingly undeterred, were six-hundred yards away, he issued an amended order: 'Rapid independent.'

And still the Germans, urged on by their officers from behind, pressed on down the broad street. Resolutely seeking death, it was not denied to them.

Torquil Matheson seemed to be everywhere at once during the battle. His tall figure strolled unconcernedly among the men, 'for all the world,' said Paddy Smythe, 'as if he were in the Royal Enclosure at Ascot.' He put new heart into the men with his total disregard of personal danger.

Torquil Matheson led the defence for four hours. But it was the second machine-gun which tipped the scale against the Germans. It was somewhat late in coming into action because it had been covering another approach to the village. But once it arrived at the head of the street it poured a hail of fire into the closely packed Germans— a fire in which nothing could live.

The attack checked and wavered as more men fell; there were now so many corpses littering the street that an unwounded man could hardly struggle forward.

And then, suddenly, panic took hold and the Germans broke. Officers roared threats and encouragement, but were shouldered out of the way and trampled on as the terrified men surged back: they threw away rifles to facilitate flight; they fought one another to avoid that flailing fire; suddenly, they resembled stampeding animals caught in a forest fire.

As daylight broke on the morning of August 26th the weary men of the 3rd Coldstream stretched their cramped limbs and stared unbelievingly down the street. There was, in truth, little enough of the street to see, for the piles of German dead lay like so much unswept rubbish.

The casualties of the 3rd Coldstream were miraculously light, considering that they had been heavily outnumbered. The Germans had been firing from the hip and their shooting had been wild; the Coldstream's killed and wounded amounted to 120 men.

3

General Sir John French, naturally enough, came in for much sharp criticism for his insistence on the continuation of the retreat:

> He had given way to the conviction that the campaign was lost . . . he thought no further of the purpose that had brought him to France, but only of extricating his forces from the danger zone . . . such was their commander's anxiety to remove them from von Kluck's enveloping army that he gave them no rest . . . the B.E.F. had to be preserved from being involved in a French defeat.[1]

Indeed, at British G.H.Q. pessimism and near despair were the prevailing emotions. Colonel Huguet, French Liaison officer attached to G.H.Q., was doing nothing to buttress morale, and his mood of gloomy defeatism depressed everyone who came in contact with him. In a report to French headquarters, he wrote:

> The British Army is beaten and incapable of any serious effort. The 1st and 2nd Divisions still present some aspects of cohesion; the same may be said of the 4th, but the 3rd and 5th are nothing more than disorganised bands, incapable of offering the smallest resistance.[2]

Nor was a message from French's Chief of Staff, General Sir Henry Wilson, to General Snow, commanding the 4th Division, calculated to inspire confidence:

> From Henry to Snowball: throw overboard all ammunition and impedimenta not absolutely required, load up all your lame ducks on all transport, horses and mechanical, and hustle along.

To a less level-headed soldier than Snow, such an order might have suggested an ugly illusion of undignified panic. Snow's only reaction was one of furious anger: the début of his 4th division in battle had, by common consent, been a splendid one and he was ready to fight the battle of Le Cateau all over again if necessary.

---

[1] Barbara Tuchman in *August 1914* (Constable, 1960).
[2] From John Tereraines *Mons, The Retreat to Victory* (Batsford, 1960).

The order for the continuation of the retreat was inevitably unpopular with General Smith-Dorrien, whose troops were the most battle-weary and exhausted: he regarded his situation as entirely favourable; after the blow struck at Le Cateau there were only small parties of Germans pursuing him and these were keeping at a respectful distance.

But it seemed that Smith-Dorrien could do little right in Sir John French's eyes: he had been rebuked for his stand at Le Cateau, although French admitted that:

> The saving of the left wing of the army under my command on the morning of August 26th could never have been accomplished unless a commander of rare and unusual coolness, intrepidity, and determination had been present to personally conduct the operation.[1]

But Smith-Dorrien was to earn further censure from the Commander-in-Chief for taking too optimistic a view of the situation. Optimism, indeed, had become a dirty word at G.H.Q.

The disapproval expressed by Smith-Dorrien and Snow was as nothing compared to the storm of protest which emanated from the Headquarters of the 1st Corps. It was as well that Brigadier-General John Gough, V.C., Chief of Staff to the 1st Corps, had not seen Colonel Huguet's assessment of the 1st and 2nd Divisions: *they still present some aspects of cohesion.* Gough was a veritable fire-eater; he desired nothing more than that the 1st Corps, composed of the finest fighting troops in the world, should strike a shattering blow at the Germans at the earliest possible moment. So far, although they had marched incredible distances, they had hardly fired a shot.

But the discipline of the old British Army, whether at a Corps Headquarters or in a section of riflemen, permitted no divergence from orders from above.

The order was retreat, and retreat it had to be.

4

The news that the retreat was to be continued was received without enthusiasm in the B.E.F. The 2nd Corps, admittedly, had been retreating (but fighting as well) for five days and accepted the fact that a further retirement was necessary with comparative stoicism.

[1] Field-Marshal Lord French in *1914* (Constable, 1919).

For the 1st Corps, however, it came as the ultimate insult. Apart from a brief and bloody action fought by the 1st Royal Berkshires in Maroilles and the slaughter inflicted by the 3rd Coldstream at Landrecies, they had not as yet been committed to hard action.

There was clearly audible muttering among the commanding officers of the 1st Division and to the G.O.C., Major-General Samuel Lomax, a belligerent Cameronian, much of it sounded only moderately subordinate.

'The orders, gentlemen,' he said, 'call for a further *retirement*'—in common with many other senior officers of the B.E.F., Lomax did not use the word 'retreat' now or subsequently. 'For a retirement there must be a rearguard—a job for one battalion.'

A brief silence was broken by a strong and cheerful voice, strongly reminiscent of a truck travelling in low gear: 'A job for the 2nd Munsters, sir.' It was Major Paul Charrier, temporarily in command of the 2nd Battalion the Royal Munster Fusiliers, and a very exceptional man.

Charrier, it was freely acknowledged in the 1st Division, was something of a law unto himself: he had a refreshing scorn for dress regulations and was never seen, either in winter or summer, wearing any other headdress except an old-fashioned pith helmet of dramatic design with the green and white flash of Munster prominently displayed.

'Very well, Charrier,' said Lomax. 'The 2nd Munsters will furnish the rearguard.'

'Thank *you*, sir,' said Charrier, and went off to urge on his Munster Fusiliers.

The action fought by the 2nd Munsters at Etreux has become the classic example of the performance of its function by a rearguard. It was also to see the end of the 2nd Battalion the Royal Munster Fusiliers—the old 104th of Foot.

The last day of his life started well for Major Paul Charrier: the rest of the 1st (Guards) Brigade were going back, but not the 2nd Munsters: they were in happy isolation and determined not to budge; they would retire only when ordered—'and probably not even then', grimly forecast Brigadier-General Ivor Maxse, who knew his men.

The 2nd Munsters were, in fact, expendable, although they did not yet know it. It would have made no difference to their fighting spirit if they had.

The Germans, thinking that they were opposed by at least a complete brigade, attacked the village of Etreux with seven battalions of crack infantry. They came at the Munsters in dense and confident masses, roaring out their battle song *Die Wach Am Rhein*.

The 2nd Munsters' first and last battle of the war was to go on for twelve hours and, amid the roar of musketry, the voices of men who are now part of Ireland's history could be heard over and over again. There was Company Sergeant-Major Seamus McEvoy roaring, 'Come on, me boyos—the Irish never lost a Friday's battle yet!' and Captain Hector Jervis who, before he fell gravely wounded, despatched six Germans with his revolver at a range of less than ten feet.

The machine-guns, most ably handled by Lieutenant Cedric Chute, took a heavy toll; when Chute fell dead, Sergeant 'Johnno' Johnson took over. When the ammunition ran out, Johnson smashed the guns to pieces with the Germans hard on him and then, in a fine frenzy of rage, he threw the component parts of the now useless machine-guns into their faces.

Paul Charrier carried them all: his final laconic message—the last news that Brigadier-General Maxse was to hear of the Munsters—was typical of the man:

Am holding on to position north of Fresmy. Being attacked by force of all arms. Getting on well. Germans are driving cattle in front of them; we are killing plenty of both. Good chance of fresh meat for dinner tonight. Am now going in with the bayonet.

Wherever the fighting was thickest and the number of Munster Fusiliers thinnest, Charrier's huge figure, topped by his prominent helmet, could be clearly seen. He had led three bayonet charges and been wounded twice—on both occasions he had scorned any medical treatment—in the fourth charge he took a bullet through the head; he did not rise again.

By now every senior officer was either dead or wounded, and command of the battalion evolved on Lieutenant Erasmus Gower, the battalion's senior subaltern. Gower was a man cast in the same mould as Paul Charrier, and it was soon clear that the Munsters would not go under without more fighting.

Gower collected the survivors—by now a bare two hundred men—in an orchard and positioned them facing the four points of the compass.

By now the Germans were no longer singing—the German dead littered the village of Etreux and a hundred more were to fall in this final frenzied onslaught.

11th Hussars on the march northward from the Aisne to Flanders in the
Doullens District in October 1914.
'. . . wonder when we'll get a ride at 'em?'

British troops resting in a Belgian village.
'. . . it looked like being a lovely war.'

7th Division on the quay at Zeebrugge, October 7th, 1914.
'*It had taken them a long time to get within striking distance of the war . . .*'

Two infantrymen at an advanced post under cover of a hedge at Ypres.
'*No man of the B.E.F. went back until he had to . . .*'

The 2nd Royal Munster Fusiliers ceased to exist; their contribution to the retirement of the 1st Division had been a priceless one. For as the Germans rounded up those last few score of still fiercely defiant Irishmen, the remainder of General Lomax's division were some twelve miles away. . . .

5

On September 14th the 2nd Battalion of the Queen's Royal West Surrey Regiment disembarked at Southampton. They had come from the peace and sunshine of South Africa to take their place in the fighting line in France. Amid the paraphernalia of stores and baggage which littered the wharf they could see a gun—a single thirteen-pounder; but it was no ordinary gun. The barrel was pitted and scarred in a dozen places; the shield had been splintered into matchwood; of the wheels and spokes only a tangle of twisted metal remained.

'Gave that one a hell of a hammering,' remarked Private George Criddle, and added feelingly: 'Hope they've got plenty more of 'em.'

They had, by then, tragically few, but Criddle was not to know that. The presence of this gun remained a mystery until it was removed to the Royal Artillery depot at Woolwich, where it can be seen today. The story of this gun begins at Néry.

On the morning of September 1st the scene in the picturesque little village of Néry seemed peaceful enough, although the village was blanketed in thick fog. The 1st Cavalry Brigade (The Queen's Bays, 5th Inniskilling Dragoon Guards and 11th Hussars) were billeted there and as dawn broke, or tried to break through the fog, they were morosely contemplating the prospect of another day of retreat.

In the lines of the Queen's Bays men were grooming, watering and feeding horses, cleaning rifles and saddlery. Troopers, stripped to the waist, were washing and shaving in canvas buckets; tea was being brewed and the encouraging odour of frying bacon testified to the imminence of breakfast.

Although the fog and the prospect of still more retreating was sufficiently depressing, it was generally agreed in the Bays that life could be worse.

One officer of the 1st Cavalry Brigade did not share this view:

Lieutenant George Tailby of the 11th Hussars was on dawn patrol with a corporal and six troopers; the fog was so thick that the men of the patrol were constantly bumping into one another. As one trooper remarked to another, with a wealth of unprintable detail, it would be just as easy to bump into the Germans.

By the crudest of coincidences, that is exactly what did happen.

Tailby and his Hussars literally bumped into a column of German cavalry; he just managed to discern the shape of their helmets and the forest of lance tips. The patrol barely had time to gallop back to Néry before shot and shell were falling thickly on the village. It was afterwards revealed that the German force consisted of no fewer than six cavalry regiments, each with two batteries of six guns attached.

By this time the fog had lifted and the Queen's Bays and 'L' Battery were horribly exposed. The first half dozen salvos of shells fell among the Bays and the horses immediately stampeded. At first the rearward charge of the horses with the dismounted troopers in pursuit had an ugly illusion of panic, though it was in fact no more than the swift reaction of the cavalry man to go after his horse; a cavalryman without a horse was, according to the unsubtle reasoning of the cavalry, totally useless.

The main weight of this tornado of shot and shell, however, fell on the men, horses and guns of 'L' Battery; in the first twenty minutes two of the three guns were hit: they were flung crashing upwards and their crews wiped out. In the space of this twenty minutes five officers and forty-nine men of 'L' Battery had been killed or wounded.

Five were left to fight the only remaining gun: Captain Edward Bradbury, Battery Sergeant-Major George Dorrell, Sergeant David Nelson, Driver Bill Osborne and Gunner Harry Darbyshire.

The last fight of 'L' Battery has been accurately enough described as 'an absurd and preposterous duel'. The fire of artillery, rifles and machine-guns was all concentrated on this one gun.

But the men serving it were determined that this gun would not be silenced. Today, officers and men who served in the Néry Battery speak of it with near reverence and it is still a source of gratification to reflect that the last shot in this brief and bloody engagement was fired by this single battered and bloodstained thirteen-pounder at the backs of the enemy. Of the twelve German guns, eight were captured by the British.

Three Victoria Crosses were awarded to 'L' Battery for that day's

162

work: Captain Edward Bradbury, although he had a leg blown off early in the action, propped himself up against the gun and continued to direct the fire until he died from loss of blood; B.S.M. Dorrell and Sergeant Nelson continued to fire the gun, while Driver Osborne and Gunner Darbyshire—they were both awarded the Distinguished Conduct Medal—brought up shells.

6

The action fought by 'L' Battery was typical of a dozen others fought by an army determined to express its resentment of the continued retreat; the job of rearguard, normally the least envied task, was eagerly sought after.

In the retreat the B.E.F. marched 136 miles as the crow flies ('and how many as the bleeder 'ops?' Private 'Onion' Hill wanted to know), and 200 miles as the soldier marches.

Along the endless roads which converge upon Paris could be seen many old friends—some marching, some riding, some clinging to horses' tails, some painfully hobbling, but all indomitable.

Riding at the head of the 9th Lancers, his small, dapper figure erect in the saddle, was Lieutenant-Colonel David Campbell. And behind him rode Squadron Sergeant-Major Bill Gomerson, Corporal John Christie and Trooper Crow. Major Tom Bridges and Captain Charles Hornby of the 4th Dragoon Guards, anxious for 'another ride at 'em', were not far behind.

There were cavalrymen like Troopers Frank Sims of the Household Cavalry and Patrick Hefferman of the 5th Lancers, asleep with their arms round their horses' necks; A.S.C. men like Sergeant George Gilkes and Driver Walter Dobson, drooping over the reins of their G. S. waggons; gunners like Albert Deering, Peter Key and William Fry, lolling semi-conscious in their saddles.

The endless boots and remnants of boots of the infantry—'boots, boots, boots, boots; moving up and down again; there's no discharge in the war'—Sergeants George White, Ted Hunt and Fred Spence; C.Q.M.S. Fitzpatrick and his Cooks; Paddy Smythe of the 3rd Coldstream Guards; Fred Firks of the 2nd Grenadiers; and many more. . . .

'I did not know,' said a Staff officer, 'that men could be so tired and still live.'

'We were walking corpses,' said Paddy Smythe; 'we were dead men falling to bits—we looked like it and we smelt like it.'

Yet somehow, under the magic compulsion of discipline and

regimental pride, they struggled on—the 'Nobbys', the 'Smudgers', the 'Shiners', the 'Dustys', the 'Knockers', the 'Tugs', the 'Jocks', the 'Taffies', the 'Paddys'.

So the B.E.F. went back—back to the very outskirts of Paris itself.

PART FOUR

THE MARNE AND THE AISNE

They was movin' into action,
They was needed very sore . . .

Rudyard Kipling in *Snarleyow*

Chapter XIII

I

OF course, they must be dreaming; it could not be true that
they were no longer marching, forcing one blistered and
bleeding foot in front of the other. Soon they would wake
up to the officers' and sergeants' shouts of 'On your feet! Get
moving!' and they would stagger blindly on for another thirty odd
miles, but it was a lovely dream while it lasted.

But it was no dream; the retreat, which had covered almost two
hundred murderous miles, was over. They had crossed the Marne
and were spread out on a line from Villers-sur-Morin to Fontenay,
with a French army on either flank.

The B.E.F. lay about in fields and meadows and under trees in
orchards. They took off the remains of their cracked boots, cut away
their socks and observed with amazement that they had five toes on
each foot. They wriggled these toes ecstatically in the cooling
streams.

The A.S.C. achieved miracles of logistics and produced fresh meat
as a change from biscuits, bully beef and Maconochie's stew. 'What
a feed I had,' said Bombardier Mark Mills, in the manner of a
man who has just emerged from the Savoy Grill. 'A pound of beef,
apricots, a pint of milk and lots of tea. . . .'

The B.E.F. certainly presented a heartening spectacle to Generals
Haig and Smith-Dorrien when they toured their commands on the
evening of September 5th.

Of the two Generals, Smith-Dorrien was the better qualified to
pass judgment on the fighting capabilities of the British soldier.
He, an infantryman, had experienced active service in its most
dangerous and uncomfortable sense, whereas Haig had buttressed
the British Empire in more gentlemanly fashion (his severer critics
have made much of the fact that in the 1898 campaign in Egypt a
camel loaded with claret accompanied him to war) with the
cavalry.

In France, Smith-Dorrien had been in constant range of gunfire
(and frequently nearer than a Corps Commander should have been)
while Haig had prosecuted the war more comfortably—in his

Headquarters mess the food had invariably been lavish and well served.

September 5th had been a day of almost complete rest, and it had worked wonders: the men had washed and shaved; they had eaten a square meal; there had been an issue of cigarettes and tobacco—essential attributes to the well-being of the British soldier in any theatre of war.

And soon the sound of cheering could be heard in the bivouacs of the B.E.F.—a roaring crescendo of sound which could be heard, it was said, by von Kluck himself.

The British Expeditionary Force was to advance.

2

Most of the British soldiers in the retreat (although not all of them) had heard the name of Joffre. He was a French general, wasn't he? Couldn't be a German, or he'd have 'von' in front of his name.

While the British Army trudged back towards Paris, 'Papa' Joffre spent most of his waking hours sitting in the shade of a vine; much of the time, indeed, he gave the impression that he was asleep. He did no paperwork, for which, like many other great generals, he had a profound loathing; he was rarely seen to look at a map; and some of his staff officers doubted whether he knew how to read one. Subordinates disturbed his lengthy sojourns in the shade at their peril.

The afternoon of September 5th was exceptionally hot and to most of the staff of French G.H.Q. situated at Bar-sur-Aube it seemed that Joffre was asleep; he had been sitting, silent and absolutely motionless, in the shade of a weeping ash for three hours. Something of a gourmet, Joffre had lunched well—too well, in the opinion of some of the younger and more flippant staff officers.

The inaccuracy of this diagnosis was very apparent at six o'clock. Joffre rose abruptly from his comfortable anchorage and walked briskly into the Operations Bureau. Ten minutes later he had set in motion plans for the Battle of the Marne—a battle which transcended in its colossal magnitude any previous conflict recorded in history; a stupendous struggle which spread from the valley of the Moselle in Lorraine, round Verdun to the valley of the Ourcq.

3

The Battle of the Marne was predominantly a French battle and a French victory. It had all the ingredients which produced the exhilaration and near hysteria which have always accompanied French victory, whether at Calais or Twickenham: Joan of Arc and General Joffre were mentioned practically in the same breath.

History remembers the Battle of the Marne for the rolling back of the German Army when it seemed to have Paris at its mercy; for the brilliant generalship of Joffre, Foch, Franchet d'Esperey, Gallièni and Maunoury. Perhaps the popular fancy was caught most of all by the rushing up of the 'taxi-cab' army from Paris, when 600 taxis, each carrying five French soldiers, twice made the sixty-kilometre journey to the front line.

Amid the nationwide rejoicing which followed the four-day Battle of the Marne, the British contribution tended to be forgotten. The much reduced and battered B.E.F. played its part valiantly enough. but from the very nature of the contest it was bound to be a comparatively small one; the wonder is that they were able to play any part in it at all.

The Germans probably numbered more than seventy divisions, as against rather more than forty French and five British.

The five British divisions had not been allowed for in von Kluck's strategy: by all the rules of war, he calculated, the five infantry and one cavalry divisions of the B.E.F. must be considered useless: after the battles of Mons, Le Cateau and the Retreat, they need hardly be taken seriously.

At first sight it seemed that von Kluck's assessment of the fighting potentialities of the British Army was a correct one: their losses of 589 officers and 18,140 men had not been made good; no substantial reinforcements had yet appeared and there seemed to be no immediate prospect of getting any. The supply situation of the British Army was parlous in the extreme: in the retreat quantities of clothing and equipment had been lost, captured or thrown away. To complicate matters further, the sea bases, from which everything from a machine-gun to a bootlace had to be obtained, had been moved from Havre and Boulogne to St. Nazaire.

The men of the B.E.F. were scarcely recognisable as the weary scarecrows who had struggled back from Mons: every man marched meticulously in step—sergeants only shouted 'PICK IT UP, THERE!' from force of habit; they roared out *Tipperary*, although during the misery of the retreat some men had even forgotten the words.

The faces of the civilian population were no longer sullen and reproachful, for now *les Anglais* were advancing and would continue to do so; by Christmas *les sales boches* would be driven out of France, never to return.

As the advance continued, a subtle change came over the marching British soldiers. At first they had recaptured the mood of August 17th, when they had first landed at Boulogne and Havre: they were as cheerful and confident as they had been then, and their singing was, if anything, louder than ever. But along the line of the Grand Morin river, from the town of Coulommiers through Rebais and beyond La Ferté, they saw the effects of the German invasion for the first time. Having looked hard and scarcely believingly, the singing and chaff gave way to a quiet, grim determination which boded ill for the enemy.

Where there had earlier been acres of corn land there were grim stretches of ashes and dust. Houses had been wrecked and razed to the ground. Churches had been burnt and the flowers on graves trampled flat; crosses had been trodden underfoot and tombstones smashed to pieces. The British soldier was, in the main, an unimaginative man. But even the most obtuse private realised that if this could happen in France, then it could happen in England also.

4

On the afternoon of September 8th, the 9th Lancers were advance guard to the 2nd Cavalry Brigade with Lieutenant-Colonel David Campbell riding at the head of the leading troop. Directly in the path of the 9th lay the little hamlet of Moncel.

The normal population of Moncel was rather less than two hundred souls, but by the afternoon of September 7th they had nearly all fled. There remained only a few old men and women, young girls and children. Germans or no Germans, they were going to remain in their homes.

The self-appointed *Maire* of Moncel was a belligerent septuagenarian who had fought the Germans at Sedan. He set about instilling confidence into his flock by telling them that the British would soon arrive and must be given a fitting welcome; something of a tactician in his own right, he pointed out that the British had been forced back by weight of numbers, but very soon would be attacking again. In the meantime, Moncel was theirs.

But instead of British soldiers, there came to Moncel a reconnaissance squadron of German Dragoons, splendidly mounted horsemen and full of truculent arrogance. The most arrogant and truculent of them all was their commander, Hauptmann Schniff. The villagers stood about in uneasy groups as the Dragoons clattered through the small street, and their hearts were sick within them; from these men they could expect only abuse and tyranny.

The reception of the Dragoons from the inhabitants of Moncel fell far below Schniff's requirements, but there were wine and women for the taking—both commodities essential to the well being of victorious German cavalrymen. The Dragoons speedily set about the introduction of '*kultur*' in the village.

The treatment meted out to the inhabitants of Moncel was typical of countless other atrocities committed during the German advance—in Rebais, Coulommiers, Nogent, Chateau-Thierry, La Ferté.

A woman was outraged in the presence of her husband; the Sedan veteran was shot while valiantly going to the aid of another; one of the young girls, cornered by two dragoons, seized a chopper and split the skull of one of them: his comrade then raped her and ran her through with his sword.

As night fell the people of Moncel huddled fearfully together and listened to the sounds of pillage: the crash of broken glass and furniture, raucous laughter and the roaring of songs of victory.

Colonel Campbell well knew that Moncel was occupied by advanced German cavalry, but he was not concerned about their strength. He rapped out a single crisp order: 'Left wheel, into line —GALLOP!' drew his sword, set spurs to his horse and went headlong for the village. In the excitement of the moment, Campbell had forgotten that he had changed horses that morning; his previous mount had gone lame and his new horse, a raking black with a wicked eye, had been given a generous portion of oats—the Colonel's groom was subsequently put on a charge for this act of over-indulgence.

In steeplechases at Sandown Park, David Campbell had never been an exponent of the 'waiting race'. He had never, however, 'gone on' with more verve than in the action of the 9th Lancers at Moncel: the horse (appropriately enough named Crasher) had taken complete charge of the Colonel, and he was a good hundred yards ahead of the leading files of lancers: 'I rode straight on, hoping for the best—there was a disagreeable-looking wall of lances in the way.'

Hauptmann Schniff, realising that British cavalry was approaching, raced to a small outhouse at the end of the village where the telephone line ended, and informed his brigade headquarters that he had run into British advanced cavalry units and that he was expecting an attack in force at any minute. It came before he had replaced the receiver on its hook.

Half the German dragoon squadron had mounted when the 9th Lancers swept into the village; the rest were dismounted. The 9th, cheering and thrusting with sabre and lance, went through the German squadron like a knife into butter; Hauptmann Schniff took the point of Colonel Campbell's sword through his neck and at least thirty of the dragoons were speared.

The charge at Moncel was to be the first of many fantastic escapes from death for David Campbell: he was hit by a chance bullet through the leg and his right arm was pierced by a lance. He fell backwards over the hindquarters of his horse, 'and it seemed that the whole regiment galloped over me'. The Adjutant, Captain Reynolds, was also badly wounded by a lance thrust and was actually skewered to the ground. In a gallant attempt to extract the lance from Reynolds, Lieutenant Frank Allfrey was killed, though the wounded Reynolds was got back safely. The casualties in the ranks of the 9th Lancers amounted to less than a dozen.

The German dragoons retreated precipitately to the north side of Moncel and galloped straight into a cunningly-sited trap. Among the corn stooks was a dismounted squadron of the 18th Hussars, under Major Charles Leveson. The Hussars poured a hail of accurate rifle fire into the dragoons.

'Given 'em something to think about,' commented Leveson grimly as he watched bodies topple from horses. 'We'll cease firing for a minute and see what they do next.'

'Reckon they've had enough,' hazarded a trooper.

But the trooper was wrong. Although they had suffered heavy losses, both from the lances of the 9th and the rifles of the 18th, there were still brave men left in the German dragoon squadron. They were a crack cavalry regiment and they were determined to prove that when it came to a charge the British did not have the monopoly of courage. There seemed little doubt as to the intentions of the dragoons; through his glasses Major Leveson could see them wheeling into line.

'Good God!' exclaimed an excitable subaltern in a voice of extreme disbelief, 'they're going to charge us!'

'Serve 'em right,' said Major Leveson grimly. 'We'll let 'em come on a bit and then let 'em have it.'

The charge of that squadron of German dragoons can only be described as suicidal. The day was clear and they stood out in sharp relief as they set off on that last despairing gallop. Now they

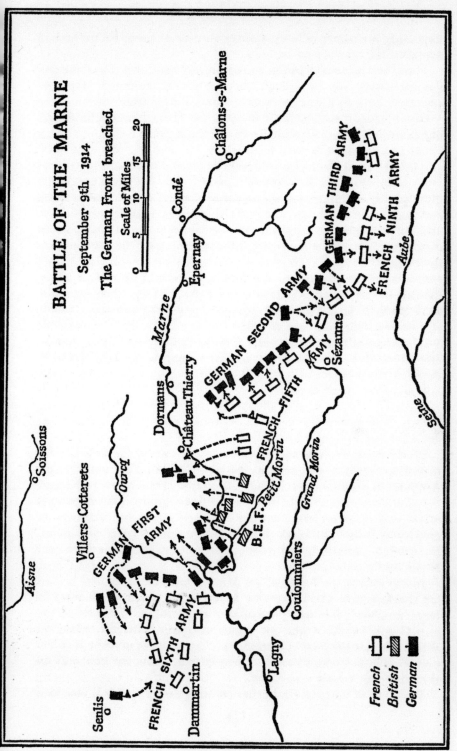

BATTLE OF THE MARNE

September 9th 1914

The German Front breached

Scale of Miles

0 5 10 15 20

French
British
German

Reproduced from The First World War by Cyril Falls by kind permission of Messrs. Longmans, Green and Co. Ltd.

were only a quarter of a mile away . . . three hundred yards . . . two hundred. . . .

There was some uneasiness in the firing line of the 18th Hussars; the charging dragoons seemed alarmingly close, and in a matter of seconds it seemed that they must ride over the Hussars.

But Charles Leveson (he had won his D.S.O. in South Africa under similar circumstances) knew his business.

'At one hundred, let 'em have it!' he shouted. 'Not a shot until you get the word, and then two good volleys. Aim low!'

Now the dragoons were only a hundred and fifty yards away and there was no slackening of the impetus of the charge. The hussars, cuddling their cheeks to their rifle stocks and with trigger fingers already taking the first pressure, picked their men. Major Leveson stood nonchalantly in the open, idly slapping his field boots with a light cane.

One hundred yards. . . . Leveson blew his whistle and all along the line of hussars rifles spat as every man fired as fast as he could work his bolt. In the space of approximately thirty seconds, practically every saddle had been emptied.

Of that squadron of dragoons, which had clattered so triumphantly into Moncel, it is recorded that only ten escaped this fusillade from the 18th Hussars.

Moncel had been avenged.

5

While the French Armies were locked in battle, the B.E.F. were marching into a wide gap between the German First and Second Armies. Expecting to be brought to major battle at any moment, they fought only a series of desultory actions against isolated pockets of resistance, stragglers cut off from their units and skirmishing cavalry patrols. Although the B.E.F. acquitted itself well in all these minor actions, it had little opportunity to play a decisive part in the battle.

It was during the Battle of the Marne that British soldiers beheld for the first time the heartening spectacle of German prisoners in large numbers; this was particularly gratifying to the men of the 2nd Corps, for there was not a unit of Smith-Dorrien's command which had not left men behind to start four years of under-nourished privation in German prisoner-of-war camps. Now the boot was on the other foot with a vengeance.

The sight of the grey-clad prisoners straggling rearwards provided a salutary tonic to the men of the B.E.F. Prisoners-of-war of any race wear a hangdog and shamefaced expression, and the Germans captured during the Marne battle were no exception: there seemed to be nothing invincible about these bedraggled men who shuffled along so listlessly and were clearly only too glad to be out of it.

Corporal Fred Firks of the 2nd Grenadiers recalls with satisfaction his first sight of German prisoners—'reckon they must have been Prussian Guards—we had nothing in our Guards to equal their size.'

September 10th saw the capture of still more prisoners: some emerged from woods and ditches with their hands up—it seemed that they could not surrender quickly enough: these were the stragglers who, in the uttermost extremes of exhaustion, had been left behind in the retreat from the Marne.

Many German soldiers were found dead drunk in haystacks, barns and ditches: these were the men who had found the strain of continuous retreat too great and had taken refuge in the oblivion of intoxication on wine found in the deserted villages.

September 10th marked the end of the Battle of the Marne.

It seemed to be success all the way for the B.E.F. on the advance to the River Ourcq. A notable little action was fought by the 1st Lincolns near Nanteuil, where they wiped out a German battery; the 2nd Royal Scots captured 200 prisoners in the village of Orly; the 9th Brigade took 600 north of Germigny and the 6th another 400 at Haute Vesnes. Between Bellot and Sabloniere, the 1st Camerons and 1st Black Watch took, in the guarded words of battalion intelligence reports, 'some prisoners': a great many more Germans had succumbed to the bayonets of the 'Jocks' (the number of prisoners taken by the Highland regiments inevitably seemed to be on the small side).

Now the B.E.F. was getting into its stride. But there was one more river to cross, and that was the Aisne.

CHAPTER XIV

I

FOLLOWING the comparative walk-over of the Marne battle, Sir John French seemed to have good cause for optimism regarding future operations: the German forces were in full retreat all along the line; the reports from Belgium were entirely favourable—the Belgian Army had made a fine sortie, which had resulted in the scattering of the German forces in the area of Antwerp and had delayed the movement of German reinforcements south.

September 13th was a day of almost uninterrupted good news; French troops crossed the Marne between Epernay and Vitry-le-Francois, and occupied an impressive array of towns and villages; the Russians had inflicted a crushing defeat on the Germans on the River Niemen. That morning Sir John French issued his historic Order of the Day:

I ordered the British Forces to advance and make good the Aisne.

But the Commander-in-Chief's optimism was to be short-lived. For the comfortable gap between the German 1st and 2nd Armies, which seemed to offer an opportunity for further rapid and triumphant advance, was closed by the Germans in the nick of time with the fortuitous appearance of the newly-formed 7th Army, a hastily scratched up but undeniably formidable adversary. The Germans were now holding the heights above the Aisne in force, and from first-class positions.

The Official History records:

The passage of the Aisne is likely to be remembered in the annals of the Army as a very remarkable feat, consisting as it did in forcing a passage frontally without any possibility of manoeuvre.

There was, of course, considerably more to it than that. A frontal assault, with inadequate artillery support, depends on one factor and one factor only: the determination of the soldiers who do the assaulting.

The Menin Gate, Ypres.
'The Prussian Guard, advanced north and south of the Menin Road . . .'

2nd Battalion Gordon Highlanders on patrol near Ypres.
'. . . and then let them—Allemons look out . . .'

1st Battalion Queen's Royal Regiment on mobilisation, August 1914.

... and the same Battalion on November 9th, 1914.

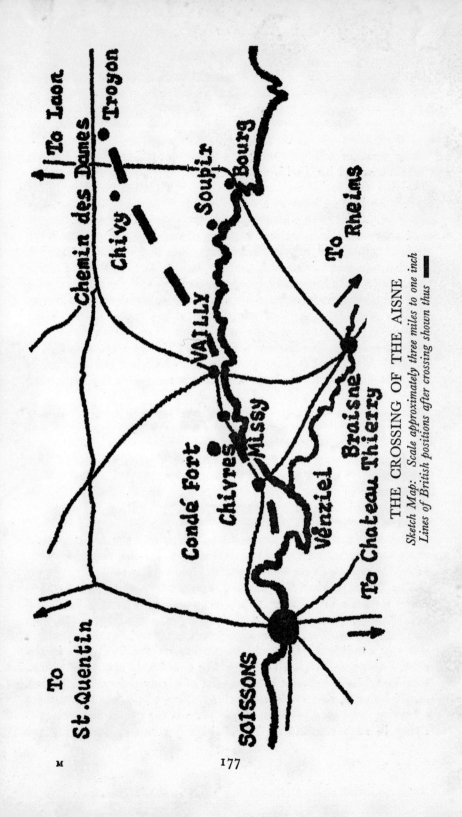

To Laon

Troyon

Chemin des Dames

To Ramel

Chivy

Soupir

Bourg

VAILLY

To Rheims

Condé Fort

Chivres

MISSY

Vénziel

Braisne

To Chateau Thierry

To St. Quentin

SOISSONS

THE CROSSING OF THE AISNE

Sketch Map: Scale approximately three miles to one inch
Lines of British positions after crossing shown thus ▬▬

At first sight the River Aisne appeared to be an almost impassable obstacle: it was a sluggish and unfordable stream of some 170 feet in breadth and nowhere shallower than 15 feet. There had been no fewer than eleven bridges across the river in the disputed area, but now there were only one or two.

The weather did not help; the perverse nature of the French climate asserted itself with cruel violence. A continuous downpour of driving rain had started on the Saturday, which never stopped for more than half an hour at a time; it seemed as though all the rain in the world had been concentrated in the valley of the Aisne. Every road became an impassable quagmire of knee-deep slime: the mud resembled liquid glue, and men, horses, guns and wheeled transport found themselves inextricably bogged down. The state of the roads prevented the delivery of rations in many units and the soldiers, who had come to regard empty stomachs as an essential connotation of modern warfare, tightened their belts a few more holes. They resigned themselves to meagre portions of Fray Bentos bully beef and sodden biscuits—if they were lucky; if they were unlucky, a helping of a new and deplorable confection which had just been introduced to field service rations: a nauseous mess with the intriguing name 'Profiteer's' on its label.

'It was ninety-nine per cent gristle,' declared Corporal Fred Firks violently, 'and if anyone made a profit selling muck like that, then I'll go to hell at the double.'

The B.E.F. was ill-equipped for a wet weather campaign; the large majority of the men had thrown away their greatcoats during the retreat. More fortunate than some were the men of the Dorsets who found some oat sacks in a granary; wrapped round the shoulders they made some sort of substitute for greatcoats.

The rain continued to descend in torrents and the Aisne became more swollen with every hour—a swirling, muddy mess of water, which at every minute threatened to burst its banks.

The Royal Flying Corps—the 'eyes and ears' of the Army— could do little or nothing to aid reconnaissance: the gallant and indefatigable young men in their atrophied machines spent an incalculable number of exhausting hours in the air, but the appalling weather conditions rendered observation on the far banks of the river impossible. Given anything like reasonable clarity of vision, they could have brought back reports of enemy defensive positions. As things were, they could see nothing, though this did not put them off trying, and continuing to try, in spite of the risk to themselves of flying in such conditions. The British generals commanding the divisions entrusted with the crossing of the Aisne could only assume (wrongly, as it happened) that the Germans were continuing their retreat; the only course of action open to them was to push on and hope for the best.

The ground to the north of the Aisne was probably as strong a defensive position for the Germans as could be found between the Urals and the Bay of Biscay: about a mile from the river the ground began to climb to a high plateau, and before the outbreak of war, while the rest of Europe basked in untroubled peace, German staff officers had systematically reconnoitred every last inch of it. They had done their work well: everywhere there was the sort of field of fire that the soldier dreams about; there were ideal places for the siting of heavy artillery; a complete system of elaborate trenches had been prepared and there was a comforting number of old stone quarries and caves which ran the length of the heights.

The German position was undoubtedly one of great strength, and it seemed that a frontal assault against it must be doomed to fail. It was against this bastion that Sir John French was to hurl his ragged, weary, hungry, depleted and rain-soaked five divisions.

That they succeeded was due, in a very large measure, to the almost incredible skill and courage of the Royal Engineers. Advance patrols arrived at the south bank of the Aisne at various points, and all sent back the same melancholy report: the river was a swirling and impassable torrent and the bridges with one exception had all been destroyed; there were no boats.

To add to the atmosphere of desolation and frustration, the weather became steadily more vile; there was a sudden sharp drop in temperature and an icy wind—presently increasing to gale force— chopped round to the north-west; it lashed and tore at the soldiers, who had by this time been reduced to a state of sodden misery. The depression of that fearful day hung over the troops all through the afternoon, evening and night of September 12th. As night fell, some units managed to secure shelter in the neighbouring villages and barns, but there was little enough available.

From every brigade came the urgent call for the Sappers, and in the next forty-eight hours the Corps of Royal Engineers accomplished one of the finest pieces of work in its history.

The Sappers worked under conditions of appalling difficulty and danger, and their task was rendered the more difficult because the German guns had the exact range and were able to shell them at will.

Within forty-eight hours the Royal Engineers, working under the direct fire of the enemy's massed artillery and machine-guns, had constructed or adequately repaired no fewer than fourteen bridges along a fifteen-mile front, each spanning about seventy-five yards of river in full flood.

At Vailly, two companies of Royal Engineers struggled to complete a pontoon bridge. The river bank on their side was adequately covered by trees, but as the bridge neared completion, the harassed engineers came under fire from a large fortified hill, the Condé Fort, which loomed up some two miles to their left and dominated the valley. In spite of the shells, the bridge was finished—now it was the turn of the cavalry.

There was to be no easy passage of the Aisne for Chetwode's 5th Cavalry Brigade. But once across, they promised themselves, they would show the true worth of the Royal Scots Greys, the 12th Lancers and the 20th Hussars. All three regiments had been in sanguinary action already and had emerged the undoubted masters of the Germans; it only remained for them to cross the Aisne and make the issue doubly certain.

The country on the other side seemed to give promise of decisive cavalry action.

The first attempt at a crossing, pursued as it was with enormous personal bravery, was doomed to failure: German artillery, sited in the Condé Fort overlooking the river, had the exact range; as soon as the cavalry appeared in the open, beyond the bridge, shells began to rain down, killing, wounding and maiming men and horses alike. In the space of five minutes fifty men and horses had been killed.

Chetwode soon realised that to press on with the crossing would bring about the near annihilation of his entire brigade and wisely ordered their recall.

The eventual crossing of the pontoon bridge at Vailly was a triumph for cavalrymen and sappers alike. This was due in a large measure to the presence of Captain Theodore Wright—he had earlier won the Victoria Cross for gallant and persistent attempts to destroy the bridge at Mariette. Wright resembled an imperturbable London policeman directing endless streams of traffic at Hyde Park Corner. The German artillery fire had slackened but little, and Chetwode and Wright both knew that it was now or never. The casualties were heavy now but the most tragic was the death of Theodore Wright, killed by shrapnel as almost the last troop of horsemen crossed.

2

Throughout September 13th and 14th the valley of the Aisne became an inferno of hellish noise. The rival artillery exchanged an unceasing flood of projectiles; the air was filled with bursting shrapnel and the unnerving chatter of machine-guns; the Germans had brought up giant 8-inch siege guns with a range of 10,000 yards and for the first time the B.E.F. was under the fire of guns far heavier than anything in the British Army; the huge high-explosive shells became familiarly known as 'Jack Johnsons' and 'Black Marias'.

As night fell, the German searchlights sought out the infantrymen and cavalrymen as they struggled across on rafts and in single file across precarious pontoon bridges; the guns and Maxims blasted them without ceasing.

It was, in fact, a triumph for the old British Regular Army discipline. 'Go on,' said Private Paddy Smythe, 'grouse about the old-fashioned discipline if you want to. But we'd never have got across that river without it!'

So, by nightfall, on September 14th, the British Army had 'made good the Aisne' according to orders.

3

The passage of the Aisne, a fearsome enough undertaking, was one thing; the holding of the positions so hardly won was quite another. The Germans counter-attacked with vicious fury from their commanding positions above the river. Now it was beginning to become an altogether different type of war. The British soldier, never a good hater, went to France in August with no loathing for the Germans in his heart. But in September, 1914, the emotion of hate gradually came to the British soldiers. The first germs were engendered during the advance from the Marne: they saw the dead bodies of men, women and children who had been wantonly butchered. Company Sergeant-Major George Hunter of the 2nd Welch Regiment carried the memory of an elderly Frenchman who had been nailed to a tree. Private Patrick McClusky of the Connaught Rangers, never forgot seeing a little girl left impaled to the floor with a bayonet.

There was hate in plenty after the fight for Troyon on September 14th. The first objective of the 2nd Battalion Royal Sussex was the sugar factory which stands near the cross roads on the Chemin des

Dames, some five miles north of the Aisne. Led by their Commanding Officer, Lieutenant-Colonel E. Montrésor, always a conspicuous figure mounted on a white horse, they seemed to be encountering remarkably little opposition—a stray rifle shot here and there and a few half-hearted bursts of machine-gun fire, but nothing worse than that. Then, to the amazement of the Royal Sussex, a party of some two hundred Germans marched towards them with several white flags prominently displayed.

Colonel Montrésor stared; it was incredible that two hundred soldiers should be surrendering without firing a shot. 'Extraordinary,' said the Colonel, 'I should have thought they'd have put up some sort of a fight. Still, I suppose we'd better go and round 'em up.'

These were the last words he ever spoke: from well-sited and concealed machine-guns in the sugar factory and from both flanks, a hail of fire tore into the exposed men of the Royal Sussex. In the space of two minutes the battalion strength was reduced by a third, the colonel, second-in-command and adjutant being killed by the first bursts of fire.

An almost exactly similar calamity befell the 1st Northamptons and the whole battalion, in the words of Second-Lieutenant Edward Needham, became 'furious and embittered'. The same thing, with few variations, happened to the 3rd Coldstream and the 1st Dorsets. The paucity of prisoners taken during the Battle of the Aisne by these four battalions was no coincidence.

It did not require an act of treachery to instil hatred and savage fighting spirit in the men of the 2nd Battalion the Highland Light Infantry, the City of Glasgow's own regiment. Recruited almost entirely in the Gorbals district, the H.L.I. have always been (and still are) something of 'problem children' in the peacetime British Army: they have always had a propensity for breaking windows, wrecking bars and waging street fights, sometimes armed with secreted bayonets and broken glass, against English, Irish, Welsh and other Scottish regiments: during any period of history the regiment has inevitably been well represented in detention barracks.

It was unfortunate for the Germans holding the ridge at Verneuil that they killed one of the battalion's senior subalterns, Lieutenant Sir Archibald Gibson-Craig.

Gibson-Craig led 'D' Company to the attack; an athlete of some renown, the men had difficulty in keeping up with him. He fell forty yards short of the German trenches. With howls of rage, the Scotsmen surged over him and then they went berserk.

The sector occupied by 'D' Company became the scene of a snarling dog fight. One hundred Germans were killed by 'D' Company alone, and of these at least fifty were bayoneted whether they put their hands up or not. Later, the Commanding Officer, Lieutenant-Colonel Arthur Wolfe-Murray, guardedly inquired if any orders had been given concerning the taking of prisoners.

'I didnae hear ony, sirr,' was the usual reply. The Colonel, who knew his men, did not pursue the matter further.

We last met Private George Wilson, Edinburgh newspaper seller and reservist, trudging in his cracked boots to Maryhill Barracks on his recall from the reserve.

As the H.L.I. were consolidating the position at Verneuil, a German machine-gun in the woods nearby began playing on the battalion with such disastrous accuracy that it soon became clear that either the machine-gun must be silenced or the position evacuated.

Without orders from anyone, Wilson set off towards the gun alone. His short stumpy figure could be seen walking unhurriedly towards the wood; his slow pace was deliberate, for he was searching for a good position from which to overlook the enemy.

Presently he found a place which afforded him good cover. Then, as calmly as if he were on the range at Aldershot, he fired three rounds. In peacetime Wilson had qualified as a marksman, and his aim was unerring—three of the machine-gun crew fell dead.

Now he was running towards the Germans and they hastily swivelled the machine-gun round to fire at him. The officer in charge of the gun fired his revolver at Wilson, but his aim was panicky and the shots missed. Pausing in his unhurried advance just long enough to come to the aim, Wilson shot the officer neatly between the eyes.

Now it was time for the bayonet, and Wilson fell upon the two surviving members of the machine-gun crew; he thrust with his bayonet, withdrew and thrust again.

There was no machine-gun fire coming at the H.L.I. now, and officers, N.C.O.s and privates alike rose from their trenches and cheered as Wilson stumped back. In addition to his rifle (on which, with characteristic self-advertisement, he had hung a German helmet), he carried the machine-gun and two boxes of ammunition.

'Damn it all,' said Colonel Wolfe-Murray when he was able to speak, 'the feller's a blasted one-man army.'

George Wilson received the Victoria Cross for, in the words of the official citation, 'matchless heroism'.

Any account of the Aisne fighting should include the name of Bombardier Ernest Harlock, of the 113th Battery, Royal Field Artillery—Ernie Harlock, the man the Jerries couldn't kill.[1] He stood six feet and three inches tall and he could handle heavy artillery pieces as if they were children's toys. Before joining the Royal Artillery, Ernest Harlock had worked ten hours a day, seven days a week, on a Hampshire farm near Alton for a weekly wage of seven shillings and his keep. Like all West Country farm-workers he was slow of speech and deliberate of movement.

Bombardier Harlock was the layer of a gun of 113th Battery, Royal Field Artillery. During the advance towards the German positions on the north bank of the Aisne his gun was in action in an open field. A 'Jack Johnson' exploded near the gun and killed the Number One; three jagged splinters from the same shell hit Harlock in the fleshy part of his right thigh, and a gunner bringing up ammunition looked at him in bitter envy—an easy two or three weeks in hospital, hazarded the gunner, and it might even be a 'Blighty' one. A subaltern with the guns said to Harlock: 'Back to the dressing-station.'

'It's nothing, sir,' said Harlock. 'I can carry on.'

'Dressing-station,' repeated the subaltern, 'and that's an order.'

A painful half-hour hobble brought Harlock to the dressing-station, and one quick look inside convinced him that this was no place for him. It was exactly like a hundred other makeshift dressing-stations on the Aisne front; it looked like, smelt like and in fact was a charnel house—there was blood everywhere; bloody forms lying on bloody sacks; bloody bandages in bloody buckets; men with bloody hands stooping over bloody flesh. Three doctors and a dozen R.A.M.C. men were handling something like three hundred wounded, and they were still coming in every minute.

It would be idle to pretend that there were not many soldiers who were only too glad to be there, but Bombardier Harlock was not one of them. Ten minutes later he was back on his gun.

Almost immediately he was hit again—in the back. And this time the subaltern sent him back with an escort, another bombardier who had been lightly wounded. 'This time,' said the subaltern grimly to Harlock, 'you stay there. Understand?'

On arrival at the dressing-station once more, a harassed R.A.M.C.

---

[1] Eventually they did, but it took a torpedo to do it. The then Sergeant Ernest Harlock, V.C., was on a troopship which fell victim to a U-boat in 1917.

sergeant took one look at Harlock and said: 'Hospital for you.' He indicated an ambulance on to which prone forms on stretchers were being loaded. Ernest Harlock thought briefly of all the things that wounded front-line soldiers dream about: white sheets, cups of tea in bed, a packet of fags, perhaps even a pretty nurse to hold his hand. Then he thought of his gun, which he suspected was being grossly mishandled by the flannel-footed gunners who were left to serve it. Harlock then said to the R.A.M.C. sergeant: 'Never mind about me. I'm going back to my gun.'

113th Battery was in action all that night and Number Two gun, both laid and fired by Bombardier Harlock, continued to pump shells into the German positions. The subaltern, who had twice ordered Harlock to the rear, had been killed and the remaining three men, inspired by Harlock's example, proved that they were something like real gunners after all.

It was not until he had fainted from loss of blood—he was hit again during the night—that Ernest Harlock made his third and last journey to the dressing-station, this time on a stretcher. And in hospital in England he learned that he had become the sixth gunner to win the Victoria Cross.

There were four other Victoria Crosses awarded in the Battle of the Aisne, but each of these was for the saving rather than the taking of life. Wilson and Harlock would have been the first to concede that they were no less gloriously won.

The peacetime civilian years had not been over kind to Fred Dobson, Coldstream Guards reservist, as we discovered when, clad in somewhat seedy mufti, he marched into Wellington Barracks on his recall to the colours. If his seven years in the Coldstream had not been lucrative, they had provided three meals per day—the dubious affluence of pre-1914 industry had not always been so munificent.

Dobson early discovered that very little had changed in the 2nd Coldstream Guards since he had finished his time; the old Brigade of Guards' discipline and comradeship were the same, and Dobson gratefully absorbed them after the hard-won privileges of being a civilian.

In the Aisne battle he soon showed his worth. A corporal and four guardsmen had been sent out on a risky job of reconnaissance in thick mist; the mist afforded them some sort of protection, but when it lifted they were sitting targets for German snipers.

Two out of the five were instantly shot, and only one of them managed to reach our lines. The other two, both gravely wounded, lay out in the open. To leave them where they were meant twelve hours or more of exposure before they could be got in under cover of darkness. Guardsman Dobson volunteered to try to get them in at once. On the face of it, the undertaking appeared to be an impossibility, for to reach the wounded men Dobson had to cross two hundred yards of bullet-swept open ground in full view of the enemy.

When Dobson reached the two men—it took him an hour of crawling—he found that one of them was dead; the other, with skilled medical attention, seemed to have a good chance of living. Dobson dressed his wounds and crawled back to the 2nd Coldstream lines.

On the return journey he brought with him Corporal 'Topper Brown and a stretcher. They lifted the wounded man on to the stretcher, and amid a flurry of bullets—two men carrying a stretcher was a target which the German riflemen found irresistible—they reached their own lines; by some unexplained miracle, neither Dobson nor Brown were hit. Dobson was awarded the Victoria Cross and Brown the Distinguished Conduct Medal.

No less gallant was the conduct of Private Ross Tollerton of the 1st Cameronians. Like George Wilson, he was a Scot but of a very different type: Wilson was the prototype H.L.I. soldier; hard-swearing and belligerent—the conventional genus of tough Glaswegian. Tollerton was a quiet, soft-voiced man with the instinctive good manners of the Western Highlands.

During an attack by the Cameronians on a strongly held position Tollerton saw Captain John Matheson fall badly wounded. Although he himself had been hit in the head and the hand, he carried Matheson on his back to the shelter of a cornstack. 'Bide here a wee while,' Tollerton bade him, 'and I'll be back for you.'

He then took his place in the firing line once more and with his own wounds untended remained there all day. That night, in the face of heavy shelling and even more intensified infantry assaults, the Cameronians received the order to retire. They went back without Private Tollerton, for he had returned to the wounded officer.

Matheson had lost a great deal of blood and was suffering agonies from thirst. Tollerton propped up his head on his knee and gave him water from his bottle, with frequent injunctions 'to take it slow, sirr, or ye'll choke'.

The officer, both legs broken by machine-gun fire, was totally unable to move. For three days and nights Tollerton tended him. There was little he could do for his charge except bind his wounds with his puttees and give him water to drink; for his own wounds Tollerton did nothing whatsoever. Tollerton's courage and perseverance were rewarded, for both Matheson and he survived the ordeal. Tollerton was awarded the Victoria Cross.

The third of these V.C.s went to the Welch Regiment; the 2nd battalion of the Welch Regiment was attacking the village of Chivy against an enemy immensely superior in numbers and cunningly positioned. In the van of the assault was 'B' Company, led by Captain Mark Haggard, nephew of Rider Haggard, the author.

Haggard fell, hit by a burst of machine-gun fire; he was a long way ahead of the rest of the company and when he fell some of the impetus died out of the attack; they were pinned to the ground by machine-gun fire and it seemed that nothing could possibly live in the patch of open ground between the company of Welch and the German position.

Pinned down with the rest of the company, Lance-Corporal William Fuller looked round; a hasty reconnaissance told him that no officers of the company remained on their feet; with Captain Haggard either dead or wounded, it seemed as though the attack must fail.

Without orders from anyone, Fuller dashed out into the open. Bullets were kicking up the dust at his feet as he ran, but he did not stop until he reached Haggard's body. Hoisting Haggard over his shoulder in a fireman's lift, he staggered back to 'B' Company.

A few men gathered round Haggard and Fuller, who was dressing his wounds. The end was clearly very near, but Haggard somehow found the strength to urge his company forward again. He could do little to help them, but it was enough. He said weakly: 'Stick it, the Welch.' As one man the Welshmen charged forward again and the objective was taken. Lance-Corporal Fuller received the Victoria Cross.

In the first five days of the Battle of the Aisne the casualty lists of the British Army made melancholy reading; on average 2,000 men per day were killed, died of wounds or were wounded. The figure would have been even higher were it not for the selfless devotion to duty of the regimental medical officers of the R.A.M.C.

Without sleep and with a miserable dole of drugs and medical comforts, they saved life in appalling conditions—by day in makeshift dressing-stations with shells bursting all round them, and by night with only a dying battery of an electric torch to guide them.

Ten years' service as a peacetime regimental medical officer had convinced Captain Harry Ranken, R.A.M.C., that things were often not what they seemed to be; in these years he had encountered malingerers of both the professional and amateur variety in all their variegated forms. Indeed, Ranken reckoned that he could smell a malingerer as soon as the morning sick parade was fallen in.

There were no malingerers in the Regimental Aid Post of the 1st Battalion the King's Royal Rifle Corps (the 60th) at Hautvesnes on September 19th and 20th: there were only men with lower jaws shot away, fearful cavernous wounds in stomach and chest, fingers, arms and legs missing, and faces a soggy red mess.

There was nothing particularly exceptional about this scene of carnage on the Aisne front; there were a score or more of almost exactly similar regimental aid posts over the entire length of the front. It was exceptional only for the gallant conduct of Captain Harry Ranken, R.A.M.C., who in this grim place of healing was to win a posthumous Victoria Cross.

The 60th, in common with every other infantry battalion engaged on the Aisne, had 'caught a packet': by the late afternoon of September 20th, Ranken had already handled something like one hundred cases—for many of them there was little he could do—and they were still coming in in a seemingly endless procession.

All the time, near the regimental aid post of the 60th, could be heard the shrill whine of the 'Jack Johnsons'. One of these shells scored a direct hit and a piece of shrapnel removed Harry Ranken's left leg at mid-thigh. He paused just long enough in his work of mercy to amputate what was left of the leg and to apply a tourniquet which temporarily arrested the bleeding. He was actually attending to yet another casualty when he died from shock and loss of blood.

4

For four days and nights the Germans used the familiar steamroller tactics to break our line: they pounded our trenches ceaselessly, and such was the preponderance of their artillery that for every twenty-five shells that came over the British gunners could only answer with one.

The infantry attacks followed the same tactics as the Germans had used at Mons and Le Cateau: densely packed masses of men, heedless of casualties, hurled themselves against the thin British line and were mown down in their thousands.

The surroundings in which our men fought, slept and ate were unbelievably foul; a reversion to conditions at which any self-respecting caveman might have jibbed. The men of the B.E.F. were acclimatised to mud, for they had lived in the foul, glutinous slime since arriving in France and were resigned to being mud-caked for as long as the war lasted. Mud was one thing; the chalk in the heights above the Aisne was quite another and infinitely more unpleasant.

The rain never ceased; the water mingled with the chalk and produced a revolting milk-coloured slush in which British soldiers stood to fire, sat down to eat and lay down to sleep—or die. The men of the B.E.F. were perpetually soaked to the skin, their faces were caked with greyish clay which gave them a ghost-like appearance and they were chilled to the marrow. Considering their ghastly privations and exposure to the very worst which the French climate could do for them, the rate of sickness was amazingly low and a glowing tribute to the good health of the British soldier.

After two days and nights of shelling, the battalion on the right of the 3rd Rifle Brigade pulled back and the riflemen had to go too. The next morning they were ordered to counter-attack and get back the ground which had been lost.

The subsequent action was a routine little skirmish, which merited a bare two lines in the intelligence summary: a brief and bloody affair of hacking, stabbing and clubbing with bayonet and rifle butt. Corporal Fred Rozee of the Rifle Brigade took a good three inches of German bayonet just below his left kneecap, which left a gaping hole from which blood poured out continuously.

Corporal Rozee, something of a 'do-it-yourself' expert even fifty years ago, acquired a piece of gauze and round the gauze he wrapped part of his first field dressing. With this he plugged the wound and spent the next six days and nights in a trench up to his knees in water. The cold water, he explains to-day, did a lot to numb the pain in his knee.

There was, too, the story of a private in the 1st Royal West Kents, told by Captain Henry Buchanan-Dunlop while on sick leave from France. During a brief lull in the fighting on the Aisne, the private turned to Buchanan-Dunlop and asked: 'May I retire, please, sir?'

'Why?' demanded Buchanan-Dunlop.

'I've been hit three times, sir,' said the soldier with quiet satisfaction. That night he died in the Regimental Aid Post.

At this stage of the fighting on the Aisne there came a most welcome addition in the form of Major-General William Pulteney's 6th Division. Like the 5th, they had been in Ireland before the war; like the 4th when they first arrived at Le Cateau, they were the target for much good-natured derision from the veterans who had been out from the beginning.

In the 6th Division were the 1st Battalion the East Kent Regiment (the Buffs), the 1st Leicesters, 1st King's Own Shropshire Light Infantry, the 1st Royal Fusiliers (fiercely determined to match the performance of the 4th Battalion, who had already won two V.C.s), the 1st North Staffords, the 2nd Leinster Regiment, the 3rd Battalion the Rifle Brigade, 1st West Yorkshires, 1st East Yorkshires, 2nd Sherwood Foresters and 2nd Durham Light Infantry.

They all looked well-turned-out, clean and, most noticeable of all, young: the men of the first five divisions seemed to have aged ten years in the month they had spent in France and Belgium; by contrast the men of the 6th looked almost laughably youthful and inexperienced.

The veterans, it goes without saying, ragged the men of the 6th unmercifully and told them stories of the horrors of warfare which were at most one-tenth true; they offered them souvenirs—spiked helmets and lances were the most popular currency—in exchange for new boots and greatcoats.

For the men of the 6th Division there was no preliminary training in trench warfare, no probationary 'shake-down' period in a quiet sector of the line, for in the Battle of the Aisne there was no such thing. They went straight into the front line and stayed there.

As was inevitable with 'green' troops, the early hours of the new-comers in the front line were not distinguished. They were used to replace units which had suffered most severely, and the Germans had an uncanny knack of smelling out sectors of the line containing untried troops—sometimes with disastrous results.

They found themselves shivering in a wet misty dawn, peering anxiously along their rifles at the enemy lines only about a hundred and fifty yards away. They were nervous, and the enemy knew it. When the Germans attacked in the usual dense masses, the front ranks were swept away by rifle fire, but it did not have the same sustained and lethal accuracy as that of the old hands. In their early initiation period the 6th Division were to lose quite a number of trenches.

The B.E.F. was now organized into three Army Corps: Haig s 1st Corps was still made up of 1st and 2nd Divisions; Smith-Dorrien retained 3rd and 5th Divisions in his 2nd Corps, but 4th Division, which had come under his command at Le Cateau, now joined the 6th Division to become 3rd Corps, under General Pulteney.

5

Nowhere, at any time, did the Germans penetrate the British line on the Aisne. Between September 14th and 18th there was scarcely any let-up in the frenzied German assaults which came in by day and night, but they never got further than the forward trenches.

One of these attacks—it was typical of a hundred others—was launched against the 2nd Battalion Grenadier Guards; an attack in six closely packed ranks with reserves following. The first two ranks appeared at four hundred yards from the Grenadiers in their trenches: one moment the faint rim of ground in front of them was bare and empty, the next it was alive with bobbing spiked helmets. Nonchalantly the officers gave the order: 'At two hundred, let 'em have it. Aim low.'

Now nothing can be seen in front save a solid jam of advancing men, firing from the hip as they come nearer. When they are two hundred yards away every machine-gun and rifle opens fire at top speed and with perfect accuracy; before twenty yards has been covered more than half of the men in the first two ranks are down. Now they are beginning to step over the bodies of their fallen comrades, and with every ten yards covered the slaughter becomes more deadly; now, just fifty yards from the Grenadiers' trenches, those behind are literally clambering over the dead and those who climb are shot down and fall upon the writhing parapet of bodies.

The attack is beaten off, but only with fearful effort; the German dead lie where they are, probably for the next three or four days. And after the battle follows the inevitable disgusting aftermath: the rain-sodden bodies become swollen and bloated, and with their gradual decay comes the smell—the vile, foetid odour of death; the sweet, sickly stench which is like no other smell on earth.

A brief notice appears in the Intelligence Summary at the Headquarters of the 4th (Guards) Brigade:

On the afternoon of September 17th we gained a small local success. Enemy casualties are estimated at approximately 500; own casualties one officer killed, two officers wounded; 25 other ranks killed, 70 wounded. . . .

It was not much to read about in the newspaper in England, if indeed it ever appeared. Similar actions had been fought on the Aisne front the day before; almost identical ones would be fought on the morrow. In England morose breakfasters remarked that there was 'nothing in the papers as usual'.

But one ensign and twenty-five guardsmen would never mount another guard at Buckingham Palace. It was not much, but it was certainly not nothing. . . .

There were four days of fighting like this—four days in which the Germans beat their heads against a brick wall. Then the attacks became half-hearted and gradually they faded away altogether. The Battle of the Aisne degenerated into desultory shelling, desultory night raids, desultory patrols; it was, in fact, the beginning of the soul-destroying static trench warfare which was to go on for four fearful years.

But there was worse, much worse, to come. . . .

'It was bad in the Retreat,' said the men of the B.E.F. 'It was bad on the Aisne. But neither of them were in the same county as the doing we got in the north.'

They were referring to the First Battle of Ypres.

PART FIVE

THE FIRST BATTLE OF YPRES

Chapter XV

I

YPRES, late October 1914: clearly, they had all been there far too long. This was at once apparent from the staring, red-rimmed eyes which told of an incredible number of days and nights on end without sleep; from the gaunt and wasted faces covered in thick and filthy stubble—there was little enough water for drinking, let alone for washing and shaving; from the begrimed and trembling hands which now had but one function—to ram a fresh clip of ammunition into a rifle's magazine, to work the bolt and to press the trigger.

Loading, aiming and firing—actions as automatic to the British regular soldier as cleaning teeth, lighting a fag or going to the latrine—had now become a fearful effort. Rifles were choked with mud, and rifle oil was in short supply.

Machine-guns? The mere mention of these instruments of destruction raised a laugh from the men in the trenches, if a stinking, unrevetted hole, three feet deep, full of water and more than likely tenanted by at least two corpses, could be called a trench. No battalion leaving for France in August had started with more than two; the present allocation was more like one per brigade and there was probably no ammunition for that one.

Artillery support? Another hollow laugh from the men in the stinking holes. A field battery, firing 700 shells per day, would have been sadly inadequate; the present ration was *ten shells per gun per day*, always assuming that there were enough artillerymen to serve the guns and usually there were not. The gunners were patching up the line in a hundred different places armed with rifles and bayonets if they were lucky, entrenching tools and bare fists if they were not. And this was true of many other unlikely personnel in this fearful battle: cooks, drivers, officers' servants, sappers, grooms, signallers, bandsmen, stretcher-bearers, drummers, trumpeters, orderly-room clerks—they were all front-line soldiers, and a break anywhere in this thin and sagging line could have meant irreparable disaster for Great Britain.

They were so weary that a man could sleep through a four-hour-

195

long bombardment; they were so thirsty that they drank the stagnant water in their trenches; their stomachs were shrunk and straining for food; they would have bartered their souls for a draw at a fag; they were begrimed with assorted vermin which thrive on filth. They were, in the words of John Coleman, an American War correspondent, 'a terrible crew; they were like fierce, wild beasts'.

These were the men of Ypres at the end of October, 1914.

The 'Contemptibles' had been slowly overwhelmed by superior numbers at Mons; they had fought the Germans to a standstill at Le Cateau; they had endured the humiliating misery of the Retreat; they had crossed the Marne and battered their way across the Aisne, holding firm against everything in the way of artillery fire and infantry attacks that the Germans could throw at them. But never in the Great War so far, or in any other war before or since, had the British Army found itself in such dire straits as during the First Battle of Ypres.

In places the line was so thin that there was a man for every seven yards of front; in others there was a line of shallow pits, each containing two men, at intervals of fifteen yards. Here and there were gaps of 30, 40 or 50 yards; into these gaps were flung infantry-men, cavalrymen, gunners, sappers, A.S.C. men; fit men, sick men and wounded men. Even dead men had their uses, and many of them had to wait a long time for burial: when there was no time and probably no tools with which to dig trenches, a corpse, whether it were that of a man or a horse, provided a useful rampart from which to fire. A closer look at these men is revealing.

The kilted Highland regiments are easily recognizable, and we find that the 1st Black Watch consists of Captain Victor Fortune and 109 men; the 1st Cameron Highlanders are comparatively strongly represented: they have their commanding officer, Lieutenant-Colonel David McEwen, one company commander, Captain Ernest Craig-Brown and 140 men still on their feet. The Commanding Officer of the 1st Royal West Kents, most bloodily engaged since the very beginning, has recently celebrated his 21st birthday: Second-Lieutenant Henry White. A hasty consultation with the West Kents' only other surviving officer, Second-Lieutenant John Russell, revealed that White was the senior by six months. But the West Kents seem comparatively affluent in manpower, for 180 N.C.O.s and other ranks have answered their names at roll call and among them are two familiar ones, Sergeant Jim Powell and Private 'Onion' Hill.

The 1st Queens can muster only Lieutenant John Boyd and 32

men; the 2nd Royal Scots Fusiliers consists of two twenty-year-old second-lieutenants, Walter Clutterbuck and Alan Thompson, and 70 men; the 2nd Queens, 2nd Warwicks, 1st South Staffords and 1st Royal Welch Fusiliers are so depleted in numbers that they have been formed into a single battalion—of approximately two companies' strength.

The 1st Scots Guards have Captain Robert Stracey and 69 men; the 1st Coldstream, 150 men—every single officer has been either killed or wounded. The Brigade of Guards at Ypres suffered astronomical casualties—proportionately, regiment by regiment, possibly the highest of the whole B.E.F.—and the reason is not hard to find: their attacking line was always that little bit straighter and more determined; in desperate last-ditch stands the position was always held that little bit longer; the order to 'hold to the last man and the last round' was always interpreted in its most literal sense.

2

How had the British Army come to this sad state, and what was it doing in Ypres?

Towards the end of September, when stalemate was gradually setting in on the Aisne front, Sir John French had approached General Joffre with the proposal that the British Army should move northwards: more troops were about to be landed in the north of France and French considered it desirable that the British Army should act in one body. In addition, the lines of communication of the B.E.F. would be shortened if it were nearer to the coast.

Most serious of all, from the British viewpoint, was the German menace to the Channel ports. If Boulogne, Calais and Ostend were seized by the Germans they would be able to threaten the transport of troops from England to France and to block the vital avenues of sea-borne traffic converging on London. They could, in fact, even launch an invasion of England.

> The stakes for which we were playing (wrote Sir John French) were nothing less than the safety, indeed the very existence, of the British Empire.

So started the 'race to the sea'. The German and Allied armies were locked together, each striving to outflank the other. A gap of twenty-five miles lay open to the Germans, and this gap was a wide-open gateway to Calais and the Channel Ports. It was for the British Army to bar that way.

The withdrawal of the Army from the positions on the Aisne, the taking over of these positions by the French and the transfer of the British Army to Flanders called for masterly staff work. To withdraw a company or a battalion from the firing line was difficult enough; the difficulties attending the switch of an entire army without the enemy knowing seemed insuperable. Said General Sir Horace Smith-Dorrien:

> I always regard the conception and execution of this great flank move as providing the largest nail in the coffin of the enemy in the whole war. But for this, I am unable to see how the Germans could have been stopped from seizing Calais and Boulogne.

Joffre agreed to French's proposal to move the B.E.F. to Ypres, and on the night October 1st–2nd, the withdrawal of the British troops from the Aisne began; it must rank as one of the most astonishing feats of the war. The British held a front of twenty-six miles in length. Along this front, or in reserve immediately behind, were some 70 battalions of infantry, 15 regiments of cavalry and 80 batteries of artillery. The German lines were, in a number of places, only two hundred yards or less from the British trenches.

To heap derision and abuse on the gilded Staff has always been a favourite pastime of the British regimental soldier, but even their most rabid critics could find no fault with the move from the Aisne. The organisation was so perfect that when the moment arrived there was scarcely a single hitch: artillery gun positions were meticulously handed over; communications were rearranged; British battalions moved out and French battalions moved in; and the Germans apparently had no inkling of what was happening or, if they had, they gave no sign of it.

All movement was by night. During the day, the British soldiers stayed out of sight so that no sign of their departure could be seen by enemy aircraft. No offensive action was taken by either side, and amazingly the Germans seemed to accept the situation at its face value. The British Army crept away from the Aisne like a thief in the night. . . .

Our soldiers left the Aisne positions in cheerful mood: any change from the miserable discomfort and tedium of static trench warfare must be for the better. All portents seemed to be good: the

French climate underwent a magical change and days of bright, warm sunshine gave way to nights of radiant moonlight.

There were, of course, the inevitable long marches, but halts were frequent and took place in such picturesque places as Mareil-sur-Ourcq, Senlis and Abbeville—all of these places represented to the battle-weary men from the Aisne front a brief glimpse of Paradise. Along the route were comfortable billets and baths; baths in which weary men could wallow in unlimited hot water and emerge, as Private 'Onion' Hill neatly phrased it, 'smelling like a whoreshop'.

No one knew their exact destination except that it was 'somewhere in Belgium'. Now the country was becoming flatter, and keen-eyed cavalrymen noted this with satisfaction—flat ground with good galloping surface meant mounted action.

But during that first week of October even the most unimaginative private was struck by ominous changes: the vineyards and beautiful uplands of the Aisne country and the peaceful forest glades of Compiègne had been left far behind and in their place was a flat manufacturing district, the Black Country of France. The fine weather went as quickly as it had come; it grew steadily colder and there were swift, lashing storms.

A new name cropped up in conversations on troop train or at roadside halt—a curious name, which the soldiers pronounced 'Eeprez' and later inevitably referred to as 'Wipers'. They were headed for the ancient Flemish town of Ypres and within less than a month those of them still left alive were to wish themselves back in the chalky and waterlogged trenches on the Aisne.

CHAPTER XVI

I

BELGIUM—'Gallant Little Belgium' as she was always known
in 1914—had captured the sympathy of the world. But mere
sympathy was not enough. Alone in August, 1914, she had
striven to hold back the armed might of Germany; Great Britain
had come to her aid, but she too had been driven back, in the
Battle of Mons.

Great Britain had done all that she immediately could for Belgium; France could do nothing, for she had more than enough
troubles of her own; the same applied to Russia. That only left
the United States, but America in the early days of the Great War
did little more than ask: 'Why doesn't somebody do something?'

The news from Belgium in the first week of October, 1914, was all
consistently bad. Most of it emanated from the beleagured city of
Antwerp. Napoleon called Antwerp 'the pistol aimed at the heart
of England.'

> Antwerp [wrote Winston Churchill] is not only the sole stronghold
> of the Belgian nation; it is also the true left flank of the Allied front in
> the West. It guards the whole line of the Channel Ports (Dunkirk,
> Calais and Boulogne); it threatens the flanks and rear of the German
> armies in France; it is the gateway from which the British Army might
> emerge at any moment upon their sensitive and vital communications.[1]

While the Battle of the Aisne degenerated into stalemate, General
Sir John French had been giving a lot of study to the position of the
Belgian Army at Antwerp: if the Germans captured Antwerp, as
appeared very likely, then the Channel Ports would be seriously
threatened and an invasion of Britain would become more than a
remote possibility. Nor was the German High Command slow to
appreciate the importance of Antwerp. As early as September 9th,
before the Allied crossing of the Aisne, orders had been issued by the
Kaiser himself that 'immediate steps should be initiated for the
reduction of the fortress'.

[1] From *The World Crisis* by Winston Churchill.

Before the war, Antwerp had been considered to be impregnable; it was admirably adapted by nature for a prolonged siege, having access to the sea on one side whilst to landwards the city was practically encircled at an advantageous distance by the rivers Scheldt, Rupel and Nethe. Antwerp's forts, too, seemed formidable enough; but the inner ring of forts, placed at regular intervals of 2,200 yards at an average distance of about 3,500 yards outside the *enceinte* of the city itself, had been planned and built mostly prior to 1869; the outer forts were designed in 1879. They were certainly impregnable to bombardment by any artillery gun of that period, but not to the 16-inch howitzers which the Germans had trained on the city.

The Belgian soldiers considered that, man for man, they were superior to the Germans in fighting qualities and they had already proved this in many bloody encounters. But they were dog-weary after two months of continuous marching and fighting; they were woefully ill-equipped and numerically hopelessly short of the German strength. General de Guise, Commander-in-Chief of the Belgian Army, decided that the surrender of the city was inevitable.

And so the ghastly pilgrimage from the doomed city started: something like 150,000 people of all ages made their escape by sea and at least a quarter of a million more poured over the Dutch frontier on foot. By midday on October 8th, Antwerp was no longer a city, but only the husk of one: the streets, usually a hive of activity and gaiety, were shuttered, silent and deserted; the population was now reduced to nurses and their wounded, a few city officials, half a dozen newspapermen and a sprinkling of dubious citizens who had good reason to know that they had nothing to fear from the Germans.

On the evening of October 9th the Burgomaster made formal surrender of the city to the Germans and Antwerp's agony was at an end.

2

In September, 1914, the 7th Division were encamped at Lyndhurst. It was a hastily scratched-up formation, but its presence at the front was desperately needed. It was, in fact, a superbly confident and disciplined force; as far as the men were concerned, they could not get to war soon enough.

The news from France had been of the sketchiest—there were no war correspondents with the B.E.F.—and it seemed that the show might be over before they got there. This was a state of affairs too terrible to contemplate.

There had been rumours of retreat and defeat; Mons and Le Cateau were just vague names on a map of France. But they would soon have the Germans on the run, and they would all be home for Christmas and then back out to the sunshine again.

The 1st Royal Welch Fusiliers, the 2nd Warwicks, the 2nd York-shires, the 2nd Royal Scots Fusiliers and the 2nd Wiltshires had come from Gibraltar and Malta. The 3rd Dragoon Guards and the 2nd Gordon Highlanders had been in Cairo. Some of the division had been in South Africa; the 2nd Queens and 2nd Bedfords at Roberts' Heights, and the 1st South Staffords in Pietermaritzburg; there had also been two cavalry regiments in South Africa, the 1st (Royal) Dragoons and the 10th Hussars at Pochestroom.

And so these regiments came home and on arrival in England they were shaken up like some military cocktail and became the 7th Division, under the command of Major-General Thompson Capper, C.B., D.S.O., who, even before going to France boasted two rows of gaily coloured ribbons which told of service at Chitral, in the Sudan and South Africa.

But the 7th Division was not yet quite complete, and the late-comers were regarded with amused tolerance by the tough veterans from overseas: these two battalions had not been abroad for many years and their foreign station was said to be Pirbright—the 1st Grenadier Guards and the 2nd Scots Guards had been on ceremonial duties in London (although the red tunics and bearskins had given way a month earlier to khaki). And last but not least came the 'donkey wallopers'—the 1st and 2nd Life Guards and the Royal Horse Guards (the Blues): only a short month before, in all their splendid regalia, they had clattered down Pall Mall on Sovereign's Escort and changed the guard at Horse Guards on the stroke of 11 a.m.

Lyndhurst, unlike Aldershot, Colchester, Dover and Shorncliffe, had never been a soldiers' town, but it rose to the occasion man-fully. After a lengthy sojourn overseas, most of the men of the 7th Division had, as the British soldier described his rare periods of financial affluence, 'a bit in their credits'. They were predominantly bachelors, and were intent on spending their money in the shortest possible time.

The long main street teemed with khaki: the soldiers thronged the public houses and threatened to drink them dry; they swarmed into the few cafés and consumed mountains of fish and chips and faggots and peas. They ogled the young women, flattered the middle-aged and called the old ones 'Mum', helping them across the street to the accompaniment of outrageous comment. They spoiled the children atrociously and showered them with sweets; they adopted stray dogs and cats, took them back to camp and illicitly fed them on army rations; they wrote their names on the wall of the town's only public convenience.

Then suddenly, on the afternoon of Sunday, October 4th, they were gone: handkerchiefs were unashamedly busy as the 7th Division started on their nine-mile march to Southampton, for in a short fortnight they had brought to the humdrum little New Forest town a brief glamour and commercial boost that it had never known before, and has not known since.

Comparisons between the first seven Divisions is not easy: the 3rd bore most of the brunt of the Battle of Mons; Le Cateau was almost entirely a 4th and 5th Division affair; on the Aisne the 1st and 2nd possibly showed to the greatest advantage; the 6th, after a shaky start on the Aisne, covered themselves with glory in the later fighting.

At first sight, however, in matters of morale, discipline, keenness and fighting efficiency, the 7th seemed to carry off every palm. To a soldier this was easily enough understood: like a top-class rugby football club, the 7th were able to take the field with all their best players. There were no reservists in their ranks.

To stifle any outcry from reservists—were not Dobson of the Coldstream, Holmes of the K.O.Y.L.I., and Wilson of the H.L.I., all recalled from the reserve?—some explanation of this statement is necessary. A reservist, with his colour service and anything up to five years' civilian life behind him and another thirty or more stretching invitingly before him, must inevitably be something of an unwilling warrior; he has, as it were, lost some of his cutting edge as a soldier (but they soon acquired it again, as the Germans found to their cost at Mons, Le Cateau and on the Aisne). The fact remains, however, that almost every unit of the original B.E.F. had a large proportion of reservists in its ranks, in some as many as sixty per cent. The infantry battalions of the 7th Division had come home from the more astringent atmosphere of overseas service (the 2nd Queens, 1st South Staffords and 2nd Bedfords thought nothing of fifty-mile route marches across the South African veldt); they were peacetime entities—a war was simply incidental; practically every man had at least five years' service; they were trained to a fine peak of professional efficiency.

They were all crack shots—their musketry was of a higher standard than that of the other six divisions. They were, on the whole, tougher and harder men—if they missed the target on the range, they did not say: "Supposing that had been an enemy?"—they said: 'F—— it, there goes my f—— proficiency pay."

CHAPTER XVII

I

O N THE evening of October 7th the 7th Division landed at Zeebrugge.

It had taken them a long time to get within striking distance of the war; the men from South Africa—the Royals, the 10th Hussars, 2nd Queens, 1st South Staffords and 2nd Bedfords—had not arrived at Southampton until September 19th: by that date Mons and Le Cateau had taken their place in history.

Their early days in Belgium were not auspicious for the 7th Division, although on disembarkation at Zeebrugge the troops were accorded the same rapturous reception as their predecessors at Havre and Boulogne. They did not go straight into a battle like Mons, Le Cateau, the Marne or the Aisne; nor did they find themselves forced into a precipitate withdrawal like the Retreat. They did not, in fact, go into battle at all, but a week later they were every bit as exhausted and footsore as the men who had taken part in the Great Retreat.

Antwerp, the city which they had primarily been sent out to defend, had fallen and the men of the 7th found themselves caught up in the flight of the remnants of the Belgian Army and the stream of refugees pouring out of the city. They marched and counter-marched all over Belgium: from Zeebrugge to Bruges; thence to Ostend and Ghent; from Ghent to Pitthem, via Roullers. They marched along roads blocked from end to end with Belgian refugees: rank upon rank of old men and women, young girls and children; perambulators filled with the pathetic remnants of household effects; carts pulled by decrepit ponies and dogs. Very early they were faced with the grim realities of total war against Belgium. The 7th Division was used to long marches, but they were soon as exhausted as their comrades of the 2nd Corps had been after Le Cateau. Expecting to go into action almost at once, they merely marched and cursed an enemy that they could not see; spoiling for a fight, they heard rumours of the presence of the Germans, only to find still more refugees and still more miles of foot-bruising pavé road to be covered. The growing impression among the men of the 7th

Division was that if all they were going to do was more route-marching, they might just as well have stayed in Lyndhurst, for there, at least, the population did not clutter up all the roads.

On October 14th the 7th Division, half-way to being convinced that the war would be finished before they had reached it, came to Ypres; they had marched a total of forty miles in a little under forty hours. For the 7th the war was just about to begin. The advancing Germans were quick to appreciate that this was an isolated British division without supports and reserves, and they accordingly formulated plans for its speedy annihilation.

To the weary men of the 7th Division who entered it on October 14th, Ypres seemed as peaceful and welcoming as Lyndhurst after a long route march through the New Forest. The quaint, old-fashioned Flemish town, lying sleepily by the side of a tree-shaded canal seemed very remote from war.

At every cottage door there were rosy-cheeked women with tempting jugs of wine—there were few teetotallers in the 7th Division—and wide-eyed children, who demanded souvenirs, but only got chocolate instead.

The 7th Infantry Division and Major-General the Honourable Julian Byng's 3rd Cavalry Division took up their positions five or six miles east of Ypres, on the line Houthem–Gheluvelt–St. Julien; they got there in the nick of time. They were the only British soldiers between the advancing Germans—a force of almost a quarter of a million men—and the Channel Ports.

For three weeks from October 16th there was not an officer or man of the 7th Infantry Division and 3rd Cavalry Division, save the dead and desperately wounded, who was not fighting continuously by day and by night. For the first few days they fought the Battle of Ypres single-handed.

Between infantry and cavalry there was no difference in role. In the 3rd Cavalry Division were the 1st and 2nd Life Guards; the Royal Horse Guards (the Blues); the 10th Hussars and the 1st Dragoons (the Royals). They were superbly mounted and had arrived on Belgian soil bristling with confidence.

By the evening of October 16th there was no sign of peacetime glitter nor even of horses. The shine on leather and brass had been replaced by stinking mud and the horses were in charge of the very minimum number of horseholders.

The experience of Captain John Dorrington of the Royals, a brilliant polo player and steeplechase rider, can be taken as typical of the transition from dashing horse soldier to the mole-like existence of a front-line infantryman in Flanders:

> I have half my troop, twelve men in all, with me in a shallow trench . . . the rest of the squadron are spread out a hundred yards on each side of us . . . in ten days I have washed twice and had my boots off once. Horses? I've almost forgotten what a horse looks like. But the men are splendid—as happy as schoolboys. . . .

There were a few strangers among the all-regular 3rd Cavalry Division: they were the Northumberland Hussars—the first of many splendid regiments of Yeomanry to go out to France. Sir John French's description of Yeomanry is as fair as can be expected from a 19th Hussar of the pre-Boer War school:

> The old type of hunting farmer is not so fully represented as formerly, yet a valuable leavening of this class still remained. They were, for the most part, commanded by country gentlemen of position and influence, accustomed to hunting, polo and field sports.[1]

Not ideal qualifications for modern war, one might be excused for thinking; but the German infantry, however, took the Northumberland Hussars very seriously indeed in Polygon Wood, if the hundreds of grey corpses in front of their position was anything to go by.

2

They were all in the front line at Zandvoorde, Kruiseik, Polygon Wood, Zonnebeke, Gheluvelt: grooms, signallers, cooks, orderlies, batmen, trumpeters and drummers—particularly drummers. Charles Downham was a drummer in the King's Company, 1st Battalion Grenadier Guards; his lack of inches (he stood only five feet three inches tall) made him a somewhat incongruous figure in the King's Company, for the minumum height requirement for this exclusive body of giants was six feet three inches. For all that, the company commander, Captain Arthur Weld-Forester, described him as being worth a battery of field artillery.

The job of a drummer in action was a hazardous one: the carrying of messages from company headquarters to battalion headquarters or one of the other companies. Many were the messages that Charles Downham carried, although he seldom knew what they were all

---

[1] Field Marshal Lord French in *1914* (Constable, 1919).

about: folded scraps of paper, torn from field message pads, the writing blurred and shaky, the signatures barely decipherable, but the meaning always clear. These scraps of paper contained news of an enemy break-through, a trench lost, an objective successfully counter-attacked . . . news that was often of vital importance.

Every journey undertaken by Charles Downham was perilous in the extreme; there were no communication trenches and he had to travel across expanses of broken ground, swept by artillery, machine-gun and rifle fire. But the messages to and from the King's Company always got through.

Another diminutive drummer was to perform prodigies of valour at Ypres on 20th October: Drummer William Kenny of the 2nd Battalion, the Gordon Highlanders. He was to gain the first Victoria Cross won by the Gordons in the Great War.

There is something irresistibly funny about a very small man beating the big drum in a military band. The big drummer, one would have thought, should be a big man with mighty arms and a chest like a barrel, for the big drum is no light weight. Drummer Kenny, like Charlie Downham, stood five feet and three inches in his ammunition boots. In the ten years before the war, the pipes and drums of the 2nd Gordons had delighted audiences from Edinburgh to Delhi, from Aldershot to Cairo. And during these ten years William Kenny had lent his very considerable presence to the proceedings, making up for his lack of inches by the demoniac vigour with which he belaboured the big drum.

During the desperate action fought by the 2nd Gordons at Zonnebeke, Kenny seemed to bear a charmed life and, in the words of the official citation:

> Throughout this gruelling battle . . . he continued to carry messages of vital importance under the heaviest fire. Thus were the small and often isolated groups holding the front enabled to co-operate in resisting every tactical device of the enemy.

To every Gordon Highlander, from the Commanding Officer downwards, the sudden and unexpected appearance of 'Wee Wullie' in a score of desperate hard-pressed sectors of the line acted as an immediate tonic.

Drummer Kenny did not only carry messages. A sergeant, a corporal and three privates, all of them wounded, owed their lives to him; showing incredible strength, he carried them to safety under heavy fire.

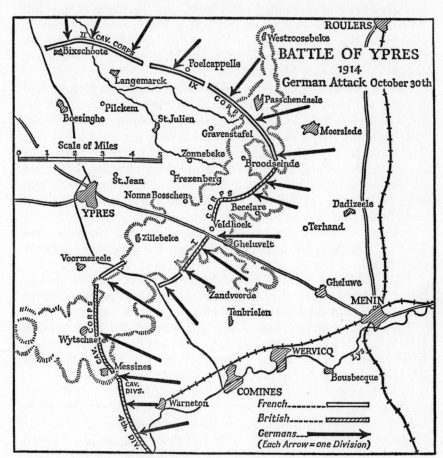

ROULERS

BATTLE OF YPRES
1914
German Attack October 30th

II CAV. CORPS
Bixschoote
Langemarck
Poelcappelle
IX CORPS
Westroosebeke
Passchendaele
Moorslede
Boesinghe
Pilckem
St.Julien
Gravenstafel
Zonnebeke
Broodseinde
Scale of Miles
0 1 2 3 4 5
St.Jean
Frezenberg
Nonne Bosschen
II CORPS
Becelare
Dadizeele
YPRES
Veldhoek
Terhand
Zillebeke
Gheluvelt
Voormezeele
Zandvoorde
Gheluwe
MENIN
Tenbrielen
CAV. CORPS
Wytschaete
Messines
CAV. DIVS.
WERVICQ
Lys
Bousbecque
Warneton
4th. DIV.
COMINES

French _____
British _____
Germans _____
(Each Arrow = one Division)

Reproduced from The First World War *by Cyril Falls,*
by kind permission of Messrs. Longmans, Green and Co. Ltd.

The ferocity of the German attacks on the 7th Infantry and 3rd Cavalry Divisions multiplied every hour, and the plight of one unit differed little from that of another. It is likely, however, that no two battalions found themselves in more trouble than the 1st Grenadier Guards and the 2nd Gordon Highlanders at Gheluvelt, astride the notorious Menin Road.

The 1st Grenadiers, the left-hand battalion of the 20th Brigade, had suffered the most severely: they were attacked frontally, from the flank and from the rear. Before the German infantry swarmed into their positions, they had been subjected to most intense artillery fire. The commanding officer, Lieutenant-Colonel Maxwell Earle, was wounded; the second-in-command, Major Hugh Stucley, was killed within five minutes of assuming command. Altogether the Grenadiers lost 19 officers killed and wounded and 470 men. The Gordons fared better, but they too had over 300 casualties.

A party of about one hundred Grenadiers and Gordons were lying in a ditch: they had no officers and few sergeants—possibly three in all.

They had been literally *blasted* from their positions, for the so-called trenches which they had been occupying afforded no cover whatsoever, and they might as well have been lying out in the open.

They were unhappy and a little shamefaced, for there was no gainsaying the fact that ground had been lost; the Germans were a hundred yards nearer to the Channel Ports. The great majority of the Grenadiers and Gordons wanted nothing more than to re-take the position from which they had been so murderously ousted. Some of them were in favour of counter-attacking immediately; there were a few, but only a very few, of the more faint-hearted who were in favour of going back even further, but they were speedily silenced with fearful oaths and dire threats by the few remaining N.C.O.s.

The artillery barrage had, for the time being, slackened—something for which the Gordons and Grenadiers in the ditch were profoundly thankful. But the irritating and shameful fact remained that the Germans were still in *their* trenches—the trenches *they* rightfully owned—and this they could not tolerate.

To this still belligerent but disorganised and leaderless force came Lieutenant Otho Brooke of the 2nd Battalion the Gordon Highlanders. His tartan breeches, although liberally bespattered with Flanders mud, bore the unmistakeable stamp of Savile Row; his Glengarry was worn at a rakish angle, his right hand resting lightly on his sword hilt.

He could not have come at a better time. He walked along the line of the ditch; here and there he cracked a joke with his High-landers; they were not particularly funny jokes, but Brooke knew that they were the sort of jokes the men must have. He had a friendly and encouraging word, too, for the Grenadiers.

Then Otho Brooke issued a single crisp order: 'Fix bayonets, and give 'em hell.'

The roar from a hundred desperate throats struck terror into the hearts of the Germans as the Gordons and Grenadiers charged across a hundred yards of open and bullet-swept ground, where there was no stick of cover of any description. Otho Brooke carried them all: waving his sword and yelling encouragement, he was shot through the heart just twenty yards from the Germans. The men surged over his body into the trenches and beyond, for many of the Germans fled panic-stricken before this onslaught: Gordons and Grenadiers stabbed and hacked and cursed; triggers were pulled at a range of a few inches; rifle butts cracked down on heads, driving spiked helmets into brains. Just ten minutes after Otho Brooke had given his last order, the Gordons and Grenadiers were back in their original positions.

'This time,' said a grim-faced Grenadier sergeant, whose bayonet dripped, 'we stay here.'

And they did.

3

Every other battalion of the 7th Division found itself in much the same case as the Gordons and Grenadiers: the Royal Welch Fusiliers, fighting with their characteristic Celtic tenacity, were reduced to 41 men; the 2nd Wiltshires, who had left England on 5th October, 1,100 strong, were cut off. Ringed round on all sides, their ammunition almost exhausted, they charged the enemy in all directions with bayonets and clubbed rifles. The commanding officer, Lieutenant-Colonel John Forbes, was taken prisoner and congratulated by a senior German officer on the resistance put up by his battalion—they had been opposed, he informed Forbes, by seven German battalions. Inevitably, there were far more grey corpses than khaki.

The 2nd Royal Scots Fusiliers, encircled by enemy and isolated from the rest of the 21st Brigade, fought to a finish and the company roll call of Captain Robert Burgoyne's 'C' Company illustrates the desperate straits in which they found themselves: only twelve men (and seven of these were more or less seriously wounded) were left.

The 2nd 'Fusil Jocks' had, however, dealt out fearful slaughter before they went under. Lieutenant Hector Stewart, ordered to stop a flank attack, took twenty men—all that was left of 'B' Company—and posted them at intervals in a wood. In the resultant battle, Stewart, a deadly marksman, personally accounted for seventy Germans with a rifle because, as he admitted afterwards, he was 'a damned poor shot with a revolver'. Another party of twenty fusiliers, under a corporal, had been detailed for the melancholy duty of burial of German dead. They dug the first grave to the regulation depth of six feet; they heaved a body in, and threw the earth atop of it. It would, calculated Private Masters, take them another six hours, assuming that they devoted twenty minutes to each corpse. 'An' don't they stink awfu' bad. . . .'

'No sae much o' yer mooth,' said the corporal unsympathetically.

But it seemed that there were still live enemy to be dealt with. A party of twenty Germans approached the fusiliers at their grim task. The Scots had piled their arms, but they had their picks and shovels. And picks and shovels in the hands of blood-mad Scots are weapons to be reckoned with. Displaying energy which had been markedly absent during the gloomy business of interment, the fusiliers fell on those Germans with slashing shovels and driving picks: the resultant bloody shambles added another hour to the burial detail. . . .

But in spite of all this gallantry, the sands for the 2nd Royal Scots Fusiliers were fast running out. Their fate was similar to that of the 1st Cheshires at Audregnies, for repeated messages to retire never reached them. Lieutenant-Colonel Alistair Baird-Smith had only the orders from Brigadier-General Henry Watts of two days previously to guide him—the uncompromising order to 'hold on like hell.'

The 2nd Royal Scots Fusiliers did just that.

Captain John Vallentin, a junior captain of the 1st South Staffords, found himself commanding not one battalion, but two—a composite force of the 1st Staffords and 2nd Royal Warwicks, totalling 350 men.

Vallentin had been slightly wounded in the early fighting and been admitted to the officers' ward of the 7th Division hospital at Ypres. When he was brought in it was comparatively sparsely populated. But not for long. As the battle gathered fury, they started to come in by the score: officers on stretchers, officers painfully hobbling, officers dying, officers already dead.

By November 6th his wound was the least of Vallentin's troubles: he had developed dysentery and a high fever; the medical orderly who had taken his temperature that morning had morosely confided that it was 102. Propped up on his pillows, his face gaunt and wasted, John Vallentin felt the proximity of death. And if death were coming to him, then he would find it with the 1st South Staffords—the old 38th.

Vallentin searched the incoming wounded officers for a sign of the Staffordshire knot on a tunic collar or cap: he soon spotted one, for the Staffords had 'caught it' at Kruiseik and had lost thirteen officers and 440 men in two days.

'Where will I find the battalion?' Vallentin asked this officer.

'Probably you won't,' returned the other pessimistically, 'and there's damned little left of it.'

John Vallentin struggled into his muddy uniform. He was weak and shaking from fever, and his wound throbbed painfully. But his sword was in its frog, and he was once more ready for battle. On arrival in the thin but unbroken line of South Staffords and Royal Warwicks, Vallentin found that he was the senior officer of the composite battalion and his deeds on that day and the next were to win him the posthumous award of the Victoria Cross.

Some of the heart had gone out of the Staffords and Warwicks—they had been told that relief was on the way, but there was no sign of it and it seemed that there never would be. John Vallentin put their heart back. Drawing on some incredible reserve of strength, he seemed to be everywhere at once: he derided the faint-hearted; he directed the wickedly accurate fire which brought half a dozen German attacks to a standstill; he led three bayonet charges. It was in the third of these charges that he stopped six machine-gun bullets and died with his sword in his hand and his face to the enemy.

4

When the 2nd Battalion the Queen's Royal Regiment left Lynd-hurst for France they went without Captain A. N. S. Roberts, and 110 other ranks: they were to be the first reinforcements. When the battalion reached Ypres, they were soon needed. The journey out took Roberts to Le Havre, where he languished in the sea of glutin-ous mud which went by the name of a rest camp; thousands of others had sat waiting in this mud before him; hundreds of thousands more were destined to do so later in the war. Roberts found himself in command of 1,500 other reinforcements for the 7th Division: Grenadiers, South Staffords, Warwicks, Royal Welch Fusiliers. On arrival at Ypres on November 5th, he presented himself to the

Divisional Commander, Major-General Thompson Capper. Capper, Roberts recalls, was sitting at his headquarters with a handkerchief held to a chronically 'weeping eye'; if the truth were known, the general was very near to weeping in earnest.

'How many men have you brought?' demanded Capper.

'Fifteen hundred, sir.'

The general produced a mirthless laugh. 'If it were fifteen thousand,' he said grimly, 'it still wouldn't be enough. . . .'

The next day Captain Roberts was snatching a brief rest prior to going into the line. A young second-lieutenant of the Royal Welch Fusiliers appeared, accompanied by two soldiers carrying what appeared to be an impossible amount of baggage for one officer: it seemed that in matters of personal comfort this young gentleman was leaving nothing to chance. He was Second-Lieutenant Francis Orme, and his age was eighteen years and nine months. Just one month earlier he had emerged, without any great distinction, from the Royal Military College, Sandhurst.

Second-Lieutenant Orme had crossed the English Channel in a state of acute alarm: not for his own safety, but because the fatuous drivel talked in England about the future of the war had influenced even the Army itself: the war, declared certain well-informed pundits, could not possibly last another month. Just let it last another fortnight, ran the uncomplicated thoughts of Francis Orme, and he would be happy enough.

Francis Orme favoured Roberts with a tremendous salute and said: 'I wonder if you could tell me where the 2nd Royal Welch Fusiliers are.'

Roberts jerked his thumb towards a group of sixty or seventy men sitting in a ditch. 'There they are.'

The subaltern stared and gulped: 'And—er—who's in command?'

'I suspect,' said Roberts carefully, 'that you are.'

And he was, though not for very long. The remnants of the 2nd Royal Welch Fusiliers went back into the line that evening, and before another day had dawned the name of yet another had been added to the long list of the regiment's fallen officers—Second-Lieutenant Francis Orme.

5

The 7th Division had bought their first battle experience at a fearful price; by November 7th, when they were relieved, there remained of 400 officers but 44, and of 12,000 men only 2,336.

The performance of the 7th Division during its three weeks at Ypres must be counted one of the most heroic achievements in the history of war. The losses in the entire B.E.F. had, by any standards, been appalling, but in the case of the 1st and 2nd Corps these losses had been sustained over three months; the 7th had been reduced to one fifth of its original strength in three weeks.

The attacks on the 7th Division all followed the same pattern: a furious artillery barrage and, hard behind the shells, a grey mass of infantry, marching shoulder to shoulder as if on a ceremonial parade. Then the deadly fusillade of British musketry cut into them, and German dead piled up before trenches which were often reached but seldom won.

The most eloquent testimony to the vigour and accuracy of the British fire came from a German officer who was firmly convinced that the 7th Division's positions were manned by four Army Corps. And many German prisoners, under interrogation, declared in all seriousness that every British soldier was armed with a machine-gun.

The 7th had been pitchforked into a position of fearful responsibility, for they were all that stood between the Germans and Calais. The Germans had seemingly inexhaustible reserves of men to throw into the assault; the 7th Division had none. The 7th presented few problems to harassed billeting staff when they came out of the line, for not much accommodation was needed for the filthy, bearded and vermin-ridden men who eventually came back into reserve on November 5th: of the three brigades of the division, not one could muster the full strength of a battalion. They were a mere wreck of the fine force which had landed at Zeebrugge just a month before. Their fighting power was all but exhausted, but their fame was secure for all time.

CHAPTER XVIII

I

URIOUS at the continued failure of his soldiers to subdue the
'Contemptible Little Army' and force a way to the Channel
Ports, the Kaiser had come to Flanders to see for himself.
He established himself at La Tache, a few miles from Messines, and
within an hour of his arrival was causing an icy wind of appre-
hension to blow among the German generals.

It was useless for them to protest that they could not break through
the British line, that they were outnumbered and that every British
soldier carried a machine-gun (and some of them two).

'The British soldiers,' declared the Kaiser, contemptuously waving
them aside with a single decisive sweep of his hand, 'are trash and
feeble adversaries, unworthy of the steel of the German soldier.
The break-through will be of decisive importance. *We must and will
conquer.*' He was not concerned about the appalling casualties.
'Take Ypres or die' was the new slogan.

Sir Douglas Haig's 1st Corps, hastily entrained northwards from
the Aisne, had come into the line to the left of Ypres by October
19th—1st Division around Poperinghe, with 2nd Division beyond
it covering Cassel.

Smith-Dorrien's 2nd Corps was a mere shadow of the proud force
which had disembarked just nine weeks earlier; the 2nd Corps had
borne the entire brunt of the early Mons fighting and the Battle of
Le Cateau; it had suffered severely in the Retreat and on the Aisne.
It had sustained a total of 26,505 casualties since the beginning of the
campaign: the 2nd Suffolks, 1st Gordons, 4th Middlesex, 2nd Royal
Irish, 2nd King's Own Yorkshire Light Infantry and 1st Cheshires
had practically ceased to exist; the other battalions had, at best,
half their original numbers. The Corps artillery, after their battering
at Le Cateau, scarcely amounted to more than a token force. They
had nothing, in fact, but rifles, bayonets and guts. On October 16th
they reached a line from Givenchy to Aubers, south-west of Armentières; they could not be expected to do more than hold it against
German pressure.

On October 18th, Pulteney's 3rd Corps took Armentières. The

216

activities of Rawlinson's 4th Corps, which mainly consisted of the 7th Division, have already been described.

Haig's 1st Corps alone remained something like a compact fighting force. But in the course of the next fortnight they were to find themselves in little better case than the skeleton 7th Division.

The British Army, with no reserves and no supports, waited for the final, annihilating attack which they knew must come—the attack by an enemy at least twice their strength and with an overwhelming preponderance of heavy artillery.

To every brigade, battalion, company and platoon commander the order was the same: 'The position will be held to the last man and the last round.'

The Battle of Ypres was a soldier's battle, pure and simple; strategy and tactics went by the board, for there was little or no opportunity to use them. An extended military education at the Staff College was of little practical use when fifty half-starved and sleepless men armed with rifles found themselves opposed by ten times that number, backed by artillery support.

The work of divisional and brigade commanders resembled that of men trying to repair a dam which is undermined by continuous flood; they had to plaster up weak points in the line with a few score of sappers, gunners, A.S.C. men—any man who could fire a rifle; they had to maintain the ammunition and food supply.

One of the early casualties had been Major-General Sir Hubert Hamilton, whose leadership of the 3rd Division at Mons, Le Cateau and on the Aisne had been of the very finest order. Hamilton was essentially a soldiers' general: office work irked him. ('What the hell have I got a staff for?' was one of his frequent complaints when confronted with a mountain of paper work demanding his attention.) Against the advice of his staff, he insisted on visiting the 2nd Royal Scots in the trenches—a daily visit to at least one of his battalions was a 'must' in Hamilton's book—and was killed by a stray shell.

2

The choler of the Kaiser at his armies' failure to break through the British line was understandable enough: a flowing torrent of men, frequently relieved and refreshed by periods of rest and supported by enormous and overwhelming artillery, had been flung repeatedly at the thin-drawn line of defenders; such successes as the Germans obtained were never exploited—using mass attacks against isolated platoons and scattered groups, they often broke into our lines but could never break through; there was always another small force of desperate men to deny them passage into Ypres.

These scattered groups—it may have been a score of guardsmen, a dozen South Staffords and ten lancers, a handful of Queens and Hussars, two dozen remnants of the Royal Welch Fusiliers and South Staffords, fifty men from four different battalions—were withdrawn from one position to another and flung forward into smashing counter-attacks against a force double their number. It was these counter-attacks which amazed the Germans most; by this time they had become accustomed to the stubborn resistance of the out-numbered British soldiers, but that men, in body and mind at their weakest from exhaustion, hunger, and lack of sleep, could *attack* passed their comprehension. It all but passed Sir John French's comprehension as well:

> I felt that they had already done far more than could be expected of any soldiers, and that even if they were driven to the sea, they had earned their country's gratitude for the stand they had made.[1]

The German failure to break through to the Channel Ports is not easy to account for: they had everything in their favour; over-whelming superiority in numbers of men and guns; space in which to manoeuvre these vast forces; the opportunity to replace tired men with fresh ones. To keep up continuous and unremitting attacks against a stubborn enemy requires a crushing preponderance of artillery, followed up by fresh, well-fed and eager battalions of assault infantry; the Germans had all of these things. The British had nothing save guts and the old-fashioned discipline which told them to hold on without support or hope of relief; not the discipline of fear as practised by the German Army, but the discipline of respect for a system; the respect of the *led* for the *leaders*—the high pro-portion of officer casualties in the B.E.F. bore out this hypothesis over and over again.

At Ypres, however, there were certain signs, not quickly noticeable to the private in his hole in the ground, that this discipline was, in its outward forms, being slightly relaxed. Small human incidents here and there bore out this theory, although not a single private soldier of the B.E.F. would have admitted it, and it served only to strengthen the basic discipline which brought victory to the Old Contemptibles at Ypres.

Between officer and man in the pre-1914 army there was a wide

[1] Field-Marshal Lord French in *1914* (Constable, 1919).

social gulf: the officers, according to their financial means, rode, hunted, shot and played polo; the men, again according to their monetary status at the moment, smoked, gambled, pursued women and drank beer—they would not have had it otherwise and felt no envy for the officers. Officers and men met on parade, on man-œuvres and in the company office—the meetings in the last-named venue were invariably of a brief and chastening nature. They met on the field of sport, for an officer who did not play games with the men was immediately suspect and was considered to be spending his off-duty hours unwisely (as he probably was); they met convivially on Christmas Day, when the officers had pressed upon them drinks of at least ninety per cent alcoholic content, thinly disguised as non-intoxicants. They had, however, never got together before in filth, misery and near despair until the First Battle of Ypres.

First Ypres was a great social leveller: Brigadier-General Sidney Lawford, a man accustomed to doing himself well at all times, never enjoyed a drink more than the enamel mug full of issue rum which he shared with a corporal of his headquarters; Lieutenant-Colonel Louis Bols, Commanding Officer of the 1st Dorsets, had a weakness for Oxo and personally prepared hot drinks for all the men in battalion headquarters: 'I don't mind telling you,' said Sergeant 'Titch' Smith, the Dorsets' signal sergeant, 'that if it hadn't been for the old man's Oxo I'd never have got through First Ypres.'

The officers and men of the British Army became more *gentle*, although this was not an adjective normally applicable to the 1914 soldier. It was at First Ypres that the word 'chum'—a word lightly used in 1964, but never among Old Contemptibles—first acquired its real meaning.

The British Army, inspired by the 'chumship' which still survives fifty years later, got ready for their last fight on St. Crispin's Day, October 25th. The positions looked anything but impregnable: barbed wire was in short supply and in many units unobtainable. The better-fortified positions had 'scrounged'—the universal acquisitive British Army adjective—wire from neighbouring farms, and they decorated it with empty tins which set up an unnerving rattle if any enemy reached the wire.

There was little enemy activity during the next three days; on October 28th there were a few half-hearted attacks and a merciful respite from shelling. On this day, all along the line, the German guns were almost silent, but it was like the silence that broods over an Eastern sea before the breaking of a typhoon. The British infantry could only work feverishly at improving their shallow trenches and wait for the attack which they knew must come.

To add to the troubles of the B.E.F., there was a desperate shortage of artillery ammunition; there were no more shells for the howitzers and eighteen-pounders, and the reserve in England was practically exhausted. Every field-gun was placed on a daily allowance of ten shells when ten times that amount was barely sufficient. Nor was the situation improved by a series of 'wild cat' strikes among British munition workers.

At daybreak on October 29th the storm burst. Heralded by a whirlwind of shells of every size, massed infantry attacks were hurled at the British line: in ferocity and weight of numbers, they surpassed anything that had gone before. There was about these attacks a new mood of reckless desperation and disregard for casualties. Clearly, the German generals had paid careful heed to the Kaiser's order that Ypres must be captured by November 1st.

Yet somehow the line still held.

Again and again the German attacks were flung at the slender British line; again and again the British soldier fought back with the grim ardour and fury of battle which has always stood him in good stead when he is desperate beyond thought. Here and there the British line gave back before this fearful onslaught, but no man of the B.E.F. went back until he had to: they rallied, stood firm and charged desperately with bayonets to get back the lost ground. There were still more frantic German charges against these British battalions, now reduced to the strength of companies; but the result was always the same.

The sacrifice of the German Army continued at a rate comparable to the Great Plague: recruits with two months' service were thrown in—men whose military service had so far consisted only of learning to do the goose-step, and had not included more than rudimentary instruction in musketry or trench warfare. The Prussian War Staff were notorious for their disregard for human life, but they must later have regretted that so much of the fine flower of German youth had been frittered away in these futile attacks at Ypres; in another six months they could have been trained to a fine pitch of efficiency and advantageously used in the grim fighting which was to come.

The Germans themselves talk of the battle as *Der Kindermord von Ypern*—the Massacre of the Innocents at Ypres.[1]

Reservists, too, were flung into this holocaust: men nearing

[1] Cyril Falls in *The First World War* (Longmans 1960).

middle-age, whose thoughts were far from war and glory but with their growing families. There were even men in the forty-to-fifty group—men who rightly considered that they had earned a bit of peace and quiet, and longed to be sitting by their firesides with their grandchildren.

The infantrymen of the B.E.F. knew nothing of this: they only knew that fresh waves of infantry were coming at them every day and every night and that they must be shot down. The gunners, with their miserable dole of shells, could only shorten their fuses to burst within three hundred yards. The British Army had no time to think of their own women and children, let alone those of the enemy.

The slaughter of the last three days of October, 1914, seemed to pass human understanding. To Sir John French it seemed that it could not go on for very much longer; however willing the spirit might be, the flesh was fast becoming too weak for much more prolonged resistance.

3

For the British Army, October 31st was a day of practically un-relieved disaster.

The attacks on the 1st and 2nd Divisions, commanded by Major-General Sam Lomax and Major-General Charles Monro respectively, seemed endless; the main weight of these attacks was directed on the village of Gheluvelt. October 31st was the day selected by the Kaiser for his triumphal entry into Ypres. Of all the roads converging on the city of Ypres, the Menin Road was selected as being the best. On this road, denying the advancing Germans passage into Ypres, was Gheluvelt.

The British line, numbering barely one thousand men in all, lay across the road just east of Gheluvelt; it consisted of the remnants of five battalions—the 2nd King's Royal Rifle Corps, the 1st Scots Guards, the 1st Queens, the 1st South Wales Borderers, and the 2nd Welch—and their numbers made up the strength of just a single battalion. Against this meagre force the Germans launched thirteen cheering and singing battalions, and at first sight it seemed that they had plenty to cheer and sing about.

But the skeleton British force did not succumb easily: the con-trolled accuracy of our rifle fire had been beyond all praise ever since the beginning of the war, but it had rarely if ever been so deadly as it was at Gheluvelt: for a full hour the Germans were held at bay.

We were opposed [said a captured German officer afterwards] by automatic rifles . . . over every bush, hedge and fragment of wall floated a film of smoke, betraying a machine-gun rattling out bullets.

As the British force had, at most, two machine-guns, this was a remarkable testimony to British musketry.

Balked of an easy conquest, the German infantry pulled back before this shattering resistance and set about the liquidation of this stubborn force with their artillery. The resultant barrage by two batteries of guns, one firing shrapnel and the other high explosive, came to short range and the defenders were literally blasted from their positions.

The enemy tactics were simple enough: with the defenders dazed into semi-consciousness by the inferno of shelling, they drove a dense mass of infantry into the gap which had been made.

The village of Gheluvelt had become a salient, cut off from the outside world by a curtain of fire. On all sides were tumbling masonry and houses in flames—the village was a smoking ruin; a mess of bricks and rubble; a shambles of dead men, wounded men, dying men and men so shattered and dazed that they were scarcely responsible for their actions.

But as long as there were men left in Gheluvelt who could bring rifles to shoulder and could ram a fresh clip of cartridges into a magazine, the German advance was opposed.

The fate of 'B' Company of the 1st South Wales Borderers was typical of the defenders of Gheluvelt before the village fell. Major William Lawrence, an officer of lengthy service and enormous gallantry, was in command of the right-flank company of the Borderers. Attacked on all sides, he gave an order which seemed to date back to Salamanca (one of the regiment's battle honours): he positioned his men back to back in a hollow square with bayonets fixed. And in this manner, fighting to their very last gasp, did they meet the oncoming tide of Germans.

The nominal roll of the 1st Queens after the battle of Gheluvelt is an appalling document. Of all the units who defended Gheluvelt so valiantly, the 1st Queens were in a very special category of misfortune. They had started the battle with a bare 150 effectives; these included Captain Thomas Aldworth and 95 men, the battalion's sixth detail of reinforcements—all the previous five drafts were dead, wounded or prisoners.

The Commanding Officer, Lieutenant-Colonel Beauchamp Pell, desperately wounded, died in German hands just three days later;

no officer of the rank of major or captain remained; the theory, to be put forward later in the Great War, that the life expectation of a front-line subaltern was a fortnight had, in the case of the 1st Queens, worked out hideously well. It was left to Lieutenant John Boyd to take command of the battalion and he found that the 1st Battalion the Queen's Royal Regiment (West Surrey) was constituted as follows:

Battalion Headquarters: nil (Battalion Headquarters received a direct hit from incendiary shells).
'A' Company: *2 corporals, 2 lance-corporals, 20 privates.*
'B' Company: *4 privates.*
'C' Company: *2 privates.*
'D' Company: *1 lance-corporal, 1 private.*

Of warrant officers and sergeants there were none, and this total of thirty-two included cooks and transport men borrowed from a harassed quartermaster for front-line purposes.

4

October 31st was a disastrous day for Haig's 1st Corps, which now included what was left of the 7th Division. The 1st Division was reeling back; Gheluvelt was lost; it seemed to Sir John French that this must be the end—that the last barrier between the Germans and the Channel seaboard had been broken down.

The 1st Division could no longer stand against an artillery fire which was killing, blinding and maiming men at the rate of something like thirty every five minutes.

The one glimmer of hope in Sir John French's melancholy calculations was for General Lomax, commanding the 1st Division, to rally his division and, in conjunction with Monro's 2nd Division, restore the line. It was, French well knew, a forlorn hope, but the only one which he had to sustain him. French had implicit faith in both generals; it was as well that he had, for it seemed that his own reputation, to say nothing of the Channel Ports, seemed to depend on them.

Although the headquarters of the 1st Division near Hooge was within both sound and range of enemy gunfire, the scene seemed peaceful enough, although great issues were at stake. Generals Lomax and Monro were in conference, formulating a plan to stem the German advance. With the two generals were a dozen anxious-faced, red-tabbed staff officers: General Staff Officers, First and Second Grade; Deputy Assistant Quartermasters-General; Staff Captains; *Aides de Camp.*

Then, disaster struck. Soon after 1 p.m. shells started to fall near the headquarters. Four of these shells straddled the headquarters; the fifth scored a direct hit, bursting among the two generals and their staff. This single shell seemed to make total disaster virtually certain.

It killed six staff officers outright; it wounded four others, one of them fatally; it also wounded both generals—Lomax died three days later; Monro was rendered unconscious. Not only were the 1st and 2nd Divisions shattered; their directing brains had been knocked out.

Sir John French arrived at 1st Corps Headquarters at about 2 p.m. to see Haig:

> I sought to express what I felt to Douglas Haig in order to try and soften the cruel blow I knew this catastrophe would be to him and his command. To me, indeed, it seemed as though our line at last was broken.[1]

The half-hour that followed, until about 3 p.m. on October 31st, was described by Sir John French as 'the worst I have ever spent'. In that half-hour history was made and imperishable glory added to the 2nd Battalion the Worcester Regiment, the old 36th of Foot.

The 2nd Worcesters had not, as yet, been seriously engaged in the Battle of Ypres. Consequently, by Ypres standards, they were comparatively affluent in manpower: they numbered some 500 officers and men, which meant that they could muster half of a full-strength battalion—a most unusual phenomenon in the Ypres area.

The 2nd Worcesters were in reserve in Polygon Wood when Captain Augustus Thorne, Staff Captain of the 4th Guards Brigade, galloped up to Battalion Headquarters with orders from Brigadier-General FitzClarence, V.C., commanding the 4th (Guards) Brigade; FitzClarence had succeeded to the command of the brigade after Brigadier-General Scott-Kerr had been wounded.

The orders were simple enough: the Worcesters would immediately attack and occupy the village of Gheluvelt.

The Commanding Officer of the 2nd Worcesters, Major Edward Hankey, wasted no time in implementing these orders—he at once appreciated their urgency, for Captain Thorne had implied that on

---

[1] Field-Marshal Lord French in *1914* (Constable, 1919).

the Worcesters depended the fate of the entire British Army: this was very near to being the literal truth.

The Worcesters were ready for anything, and this soon became abundantly apparent: extra ammunition was issued and, to help carry it, packs were abandoned; bayonets were fixed. Soon after 2 p.m., while Sir John French and Haig were helplessly watching the retreating 1st Division, the 2nd Worcesters went into the attack.

The Worcesters advanced across open ground and there was not a stick of cover. Everywhere there was evidence of disaster and precipitate retreat: artillery batteries were galloping rearwards; walking wounded were struggling back; the ground over which they advanced was dotted with dead bodies. The 2nd Worcesters alone were moving towards the enemy.

The motto of the Regiment is '*Firm*' and firm they were. As the Worcesters breasted the Palderhoek Ridge and came in sight of Gheluvelt Château, the German artillery rained down a hail of high explosive upon the charging line. In the first ten minutes of the attack, one hundred men fell. But there was no stopping the gallant Worcesters. They tore aside undergrowth to come to grips with the enemy, and they winkled Germans out of hedges and ditches; they fought in the street, on well-kept lawns, in ruined houses and farm buildings—anywhere where a German was to be found. The Germans, thinking that only demoralised and exhausted troops were left to oppose them, recoiled before this violent onslaught—recoiled, broke and finally fled.

The 2nd Worcesters, in truth, had gone fighting mad and it was as well for the rest of Haig's 1st Corps that they had: British and German soldiers swung and swayed across the smooth green lawns of Gheluvelt, driving bayonets through one another or firing point-blank into each other's bodies at a range of six feet or less. Major Edward Hankey, a keen fox-hunting man in happier days, invariably carried a hunting horn; above the crash and clamour of battle its sweet, trilling notes could be plainly heard. The Worcesters, in fact, resembled nothing so much as a pack of hounds, ferociously intent on a kill.

On they went through the village—shouting, cheering, shooting, stabbing. The Germans in Gheluvelt must have thought that they were opposed by devils, and the 2nd Worcesters were no bad substitute. The 242nd Saxons, a redoubtable regiment, fled from them in terror; those Saxons who survived the Worcesters' charge—less than a hundred all told—were happy enough to surrender.

It was said of the 2nd Worcesters this day that every officer and man was a hero; Lieutenant-Colonel Graham Seton Hutchison wrote:

> Nothing in the whole history of the war surpasses the exploit of the Worcestershire at Gheluvelt. It is an immortal story of the tenacity and courage of the British race.

Many officers and men were decorated for this splendid exploit. One of them in particular, Sergeant Frank Sutton, was a one-man wave of destruction throughout. He was awarded the Distinguished Conduct Medal, as were Sergeants George Ell and Arthur Kemp, but there were many Worcesters who swore that Sutton's award should have been the Victoria Cross.

A deadly marksman—he had first qualified as a first-class shot before the outbreak of the Boer War—Sergeant Sutton attacked a German machine-gun post single-handed; he shot three of the crew dead and the fourth man, well nigh crazed with terror, suffered himself to be taken prisoner—he had no wish to put Sutton's prowess at bayonet fighting to the test. Sutton put the machine-gun out of action with a single round from his rifle and a well-timed kick from his size ten ammunition boots. He uttered such a dreadful threat to his prisoner that the man cowered in the mud begging for mercy while Sutton exterminated a section of Germans with six slow and deliberate shots. He then administered a kick to his prisoner's backside, set a match to a lethal-looking clay pipe and shouted: 'Any more for the Worcesters?' It is small wonder that, opposed by Sergeant Sutton and men like him, the Germans fled from Gheluvelt in disorder.

The violent eviction of the Germans from Gheluvelt by the 2nd Worcesters had a galvanic effect on the 1st and 2nd Divisions.

Brigadier-General Herman Landon, who had succeeded to the command of the 1st Division when General Lomax was killed, displayed enormous personal gallantry in rallying the 1st Division; men who had almost begun to assume that the war was lost, found themselves turning about and counter-attacking; Coldstream and Scots Guards, Black Watch, Royal Sussex, Gloucesters, Loyals and Northamptons.

At 3 p.m. on the afternoon of October 31st, a Staff officer galloped headlong to Haig's headquarters where Sir John French, filled with the direst foreboding, waited for news. The 1st Division had rallied, the officer reported, and had advanced again. Gheluvelt had been recaptured.

By late afternoon on October 31st the British had won back all their original positions.

The Germans never again carried their advance past Gheluvelt, by now reduced to a mass of rubble and smoking ruin. The ground they had gained had only been won by the prodigious expenditure of ammunition, followed by a reckless sacrifice of men. Much of this ground had literally to be wrested from the dead.

The cost in human life on both sides was fantastic.

The endless quotation of casualty figures can represent an embarrassment to a commander, an unnecessary application of salt to wounds of the bereaved, a downright bore to a reader fifty years later. The figures make melancholy reading, but they must be set down here as a testimony to Douglas Haig's men in the First Battle of Ypres:

> This record of losses . . . speaks more eloquently than any words of mine of the great role the 1st Corps played in this tremendous struggle.[1]

Killed (including died of wounds and died other causes): 127 officers and 1,666 other ranks; wounded: 316 officers and 7,669 other ranks; missing (including prisoners): 74 officers and 3,663 other ranks; total: 517 officers and 12,998 other ranks. Reduced to their simplest terms these figures mean that the 1st Corps had lost rather more than half their original effectives.

After Gheluvelt the figures in individual units seemed even more terrible: the 1st Loyals mustered one officer and eight men; a company of the 2nd Welch had been reduced from 130 to 16 in half an hour; the Scots Guards numbered 39.

The German casualties at this stage of the war—the best and most practical tribute to our fighting men—were never published in reliable form, but the estimate of 250,000 can be taken as a fair one and, if anything, an understatement. And the B.E.F. had not finished with them yet, very far from it. . . .

5

There was no diminution of the German attacks as October gave way to November, a month which brought with it every conceivable manifestation of vile weather: icy rain, and sleet which soon gave way to swirling snow. Smith-Dorrien's 2nd Corps was

[1] This quotation, and the figures which follow, are from Field-Marshal Lord French's book *1914* (Constable, 1919).

moved up to Ypres to help relieve the weary men of 1st Corps. The men at Ypres stayed in their holes, for now there was nowhere else for them to go. Any further attack was out of the question, for to attack you must have fresh, eager, well-fed infantrymen—there was no such thing at Ypres.

They were not required to hold on until reinforcements could arrive, for there were none to come and they knew it.

Most of the shallow and stinking trenches were dug above natural springs. Consequently, they were undrainable and frequently knee-deep in water. The men were soaking wet and chilled to the bone. Rations and ammunition were fast running out. There was not a man in the trenches who was not disgusted by the dirt which clung to him; by now they all stank so vilely that they had given up telling each other about it. There were—final agony—no fags.

Yet somehow the line still held.

But the Kaiser still had a trump card to play, and a weighty one at that: only one instrument remained which could perhaps cut its way through to the Channel Ports, and that was the Prussian Guard.

The Prussian Guard, equivalent in practically every respect to our own Brigade of Guards, was formidable enough in all conscience. It was commanded by General Winckler, the prototype Prussian general and a fanatical disciple of the Kaiser: like his master, he had fierce upswept moustaches; his face wore the same cruel and imperious expression; he listened to no excuses for failure—if the Prussian Guard were given an objective to capture, then they would capture it.

The men of the Prussian Guard were invincible and indestructible: they were all over six feet tall; they were conditioned by the fiercest possible disciplinary system; they never failed to take an objective in the face of the most desperate resistance (and they had been warned that the B.E.F. would be no push-over); they never surrendered, neither did they take prisoners.

The 9th and 10th of November had been uneventful: only few stray and seemingly casually-aimed shells came over; on the 11th some half-hearted attacks, not in great strength, convinced the depleted Bedfords, Cheshires, Gordons, Royal Irish Rifles and King's Own Scottish Borderers that the Germans were bent on unnecessary and unprofitable suicide. These British battalions, who had proved their mastery of the Germans over and over again, repulsed the assaults of the German 4th Division—West Prussians and Pomeranians—without much trouble. 'All we had to do,' said Sergeant Tom Fish of the 1st Bedfords, 'was work the bolt, the magazine and the trigger. They didn't like it a bit, and never got within a hundred yards of our trenches.'

Winckler's Prussian Guard Division—the 1st, 2nd, 3rd and 4th Foot Guards Regiments and the 2nd and 4th Guard Grenadiers—were a very different and infinitely more formidable proposition.

They advanced north and south of the Menin Road and on the Polygon Wood in serried ranks—'by the right', as the British Brigade of Guards' drill book phrases it. Officers, born of the most illustrious families of the Fatherland, led the way with drawn swords, bellowing '*Vorwarts*' at the full pitch of their lungs; the men, their rifles with bayonets fixed, advanced with giant strides, conscious only of their own invincibility: the Prussian Guard could not and would not fail.

British artillery pieces were few and short of ammunition; machine-guns, in spite of the plaintive cries from German commanders that every British soldier carried one, were in short supply. But there were men with rifles who had already proved that they did not know when they were beaten, and they did not know it now: Scots and Coldstream Guards; Black Watch, Camerons and Royal Scots Fusiliers; Gloucesters, Northamptons, Duke of Wellingtons, Royal Irish, Royal Sussex, Northumberland Fusiliers, Lincolns, Royal Fusiliers and stubborn Liverpudlians of the King's (Liverpool) Regiment.

The Prussian Guard did not waver as the first volleys ripped into their closely packed ranks—they had been warned to expect heavy casualties, and they died as bravely as any soldiers of any race ever have; they still did not waver when only one hundred yards from the British lines. 'Couldn't miss if you tried,' said Private Arthur Dugdale of the 1st King's (Liverpool). Fifty yards . . . forty . . . thirty . . . now it was time for the supreme effort.

The final volleys—the 'mad minute' rifle fire of the British soldier was as effective as it had been three months earlier—halted them and broke them. However, just to the north of the Menin Road, they got through the British line, forcing a way by sheer weight of numbers. There were only a few British gunners between them and success:

At the critical moment the troops who had broken through hesitated. A ragged counter-attack in which cooks and batmen took part closed the breach. As a captured Prussian Guards officer was being taken back past a British battery he asked his escort: 'What have you behind that?' 'Divisional headquarters,' he was answered. 'Almighty God!' was his summing up.[1]

The Prussian Guard rallied once more, advanced again, fell in their hundreds, and finally fell back.

Only two orders were issued by the respective higher commands. The order issued by General Winckler was:

Ypres will be taken at all costs.

That issued by General Sir Douglas Haig was:

No man on any account will leave the trenches.

No British soldier, unless he were dead or desperately wounded, ever did—and not always then. But Major Charles Steavenson, commanding the 1st King's (Liverpool) Regiment, felt constrained to utter a mild reproach to Brigade Headquarters. 'We have no intention of leaving our trenches,' his message read, 'but what about our rations?'

Thus was the line held—with or without rations.

6

On the morning of November 18th the defenders of Ypres stretched their cramped limbs, blew on their numbed fingers and searched morosely and largely fruitlessly for fag ends. Then they made sure that the magazines were charged with ten rounds, speculated bitterly on the non-arrival of tea and waited for the morning hate—the inevitable deluge of shells, which had heralded each dawn since the Battle of Ypres had started. Then would follow the infantry attacks—the Prussian Guard had surely not given up. It was the beginning of another ordinary day at Ypres, a humdrum day of horror.

But something had gone wrong this morning: there was no shelling, only the stench of German corpses which the wind wafted into the trenches. Some of the more pessimistic soldiers theorised that the enemy no longer considered it worth their while to first soften up the defenders with artillery fire; they would shove the infantry straight in and finish the job once and for all.

Yet, amazing to relate, no German infantry attacks materialised

[1] Cyril Falls in *The First World War* (Longmans, 1960).

on that day or the next, although the smell from the bloated and blackened German dead became worse hourly. But the B.E.F. were, by this time, immune to any sort of foul smell and gave themselves up to the blissful knowledge that they were neither being shelled nor attacked. A sullen, brooding silence hung over the entire front.

Soon rumours were circulating among the men that the Jerries had had enough—rumours which were heavily discounted by officers and sergeants, who insisted on a more than ever alert readiness to repel fresh attacks. Of course, it couldn't be true.

But it *was* true, and on the morning of the third day—November 20th, the day which marked the end of the First Battle of Ypres— some men of the 1st Highland Light Infantry (always one of the B.E.F's most optimistic battalions) essayed a cautious cheer; there had been little enough to cheer about in the past month, and two days' freedom from shelling and infantry attacks seemed good and sufficient cause.

The cheering was taken up by other units, and it gradually spread along the entire length of the line in a roaring crescendo of sound.

For now there could no longer be any room for doubt: exhausted, filthy, verminous, but indestructible, the 'Contemptible Little Army' had beaten the flower of the mighty German Army. November 20th saw the relief of the B.E.F. by the French, and two days later the First Battle of Ypres officially came to an end.

With the German failure to penetrate the British line at Ypres, the first chapter of the Great War may be considered closed. The winter of 1914–15—probably the vilest in the memory of man— saw the beginning of four years of trench-bound misery and slaughter.

The First Expeditionary Force had virtually ceased to exist: of the 'First Hundred Thousand' who sailed for France in August, 1914, one-third lay under the soil of France and Flanders. By the end of the First Battle of Ypres the average strength of these original battalions was *one officer and thirty men*.

Of those that survived some had been wounded too badly to take any further active part in the war; some were sent home to train the New Armies; some, in fretful and impatient convalescence, waited for the day when they could be fit to take their place in the fighting line again.

But as the winter of 1914 dragged into 1915, here and there a familiar face could be seen: Lieutenant George Roupell of the East

Surreys (he was to win the Victoria Cross at Loos in 1915); Private Paddy Smythe of the 3rd Coldstream; Sergeant George White of the D.C.L.I.; Private 'Onion' Hill of the West Kents; Lieutenant Robert Churchill-Longman of the Royal Sussex. These were some of the men who had been out there since the very beginning and were still out there at the end. . . .

And so we leave the 'Contemptibles' in their rest billets in Ypres; their numbers by now so very few.

But massive British forces were on the way: firstly, the Territorials —Artist's Rifles, Queen's Westminsters, North and South Irish Horse, the Honourable Artillery Company, Hertfords, Monmouths, Liverpool Scottish, Essex Yeomanry. The London Scottish, the Northumberland and the Oxfordshire Hussars had been out since October, and had proved themselves the equal of any regulars.

More units of the Indian Army, too, were on the way: squat, grinning Gurkhas; grave, bearded Sikhs; hawk-faced Pathans; Punjabis, Baluchis, Dogras, Mahrattas, Garhwalis, to join the Indian troops already engaged.

As the weary 'Contemptibles' staggered into their billets, contingents from Australia, Canada, Newfoundland and South Africa were disembarking at Plymouth, Liverpool and Southampton. And in England Kitchener's New Armies—they had been mastering the intricacies of forming fours at the time of Mons and Le Cateau —were getting ready to take their place in the fighting line.

They were all coming to nourish the seed sown by the original 'Contemptibles': the cheering, laughing, hard-case regular soldiers who embarked for France in August.

Little of that seed remained. But what there was of it was very, very good.

EPILOGUE

This is the end of the story, the end of the year 1914.

Although the events within these pages occurred just seven years before I was born, I can see all these men quite clearly. They are marching before me now, like a long procession of shadowy ghosts. Looking across Berkshire fields—they died so that these fields should remain green and cultivated—I see their grimy faces, hear their grim laughter.

I see them in their finest moments: Private Frank Godley, the lone machine-gunner, pumping bullets into the advancing German hordes; Major 'Cal' Yate, taking his nineteen Yorkshiremen into their last attack; Major Paul Charrier, in his prominent pith helmet, leading the Munsters in their last charge; Colonel David Campbell, galloping hell-for-leather into Moncel; Private George Wilson stumping along with his dripping bayonet; Major Torquil Matheson striding nonchalantly about in the inferno of Landrecies; C.Q.M.S. Thomas Fitzpatrick and his cooks; the dying young private of the West Kents at Wasmes.

Those who still live have little enough to show for it today: three medals—*Pip*, *Squeak* and *Wilfred*.

Across the red, white and blue watered ribbon of *Pip* is a thin silver bar, bearing the inscription '*August 5th–November 22nd, 1914*'. It means that they fought at Mons and Le Cateau; on the Marne and the Aisne; and in the First Battle of Ypres.

These are the only men who can proudly say: 'I was there'. Yet this is not strictly true: every British man, woman and child was there. . . .

BIBLIOGRAPHY

A Full Life by Lt.-Gen. Sir Brian Horrocks, K.C.B., K.B.E., D.S.O., M.C.
How Dear is Life by Henry Williamson.
Three Englishmen by Gilbert Frankau.
Royal Regiment by Gilbert Frankau.
The First Hundred Thousand by Ian Hay.
1914 by Field-Marshal Viscount French of Ypres.
Mons by John Terraine.
The Donkeys by Alan Clark.
From Private to Field-Marshal by Field-Marshal Sir William Robertson.
The Reason Why by Cecil Woodham Smith.
The First Seven Divisions by Ernest Hamilton.
August 1914 by Barbara Tuchman.
The Private Papers of Douglas Haig by Robert Blake.
Mons to Ypres 1914 by Beatrix Brice.
The Battle Book of Ypres by Beatrix Brice.
The Times History of the War.
The Great War by H. W. Wilson and J. A. Hammerton.
Mr. Punch's History of the Great War.
The General by C. S. Forester.
The Retreat from Mons by A. Corbett-Smith.
The Marne—and After by A. Corbett-Smith.
The Old Contemptible—Official Organ of The Old Contemptibles' Association.
Army Diary by Colonel R. Meinertzhagen.
Alarms and Excursions by Lieutenant-General Sir Tom Bridges.
Forty Days in 1914 by Major-General Sir Frederic Maurice.
Liaison, 1914 by Brigadier-General Sir Edward Spears.
The Complete War Stories of 'Sapper' (the late Lt.-Col. H. C. McNeile).
The Official History of the War by Brigadier-General J. E. Edmonds.
Allenby by Sir Archibald Wavell.
The First World War by Cyril Falls
The First Battle of the Marne by Robert Asprey
Histories of every regiment of the British Army (1914–18).

INDEX

B.E.F.—NOMINAL ROLL

235

REGIMENTS OF THE B.E.F.

Cavalry

The Royal Horse Guards, 23, 38, 69, 116, 163, 202, 206
The Life Guards, 23, 69, 116, 202, 206
1st (King's) Dragoon Guards, 61
2nd Dragoon Guards (Queen's Bays), 43, 67, 69, 75, 116, 122, 161, 162
3rd (Prince of Wales's) Dragoon Guards, 202
4th (Royal Irish) Dragoon Guards, 54, 69, 70, 71, 72, 73, 95, 116, 117, 118, 119, 122, 150, 163
5th (Princess Charlotte of Wales's) Dragoon Guards, 43, 69, 75, 116, 161
6th Dragoon Guards, 69, 116
1st (Royal) Dragoons, 202, 205, 206
2nd Dragoons (Royal Scots Greys), 93, 94, 95, 116, 180
3rd Hussars, 69, 116
4th Hussars, 42, 69, 116
5th Lancers, 36, 42, 69, 116, 163
9th Lancers, 32, 33, 53, 54, 55, 69, 75, 116, 117, 118, 119, 120, 121, 122, 163, 170, 171, 172
10th Hussars, 202, 205, 206
11th Hussars, 43, 69, 116, 161, 162
12th Lancers, 69, 116
15th Hussars, 43, 69
16th Lancers, 41, 42, 76, 95, 116
18th Hussars, 54, 69, 116, 172, 173
19th Hussars, 69, 138
20th Hussars, 69, 180

Infantry

Argyll and Sutherland Highlanders, 27, 66, 142, 143
Bedfordshire Regiment, 29, 111, 112, 113, 114, 128, 146, 202, 203, 205, 228
Black Watch, 28, 43, 62, 175, 196, 226, 229
Border Regiment, 28
Cameron Highlanders, 28, 175, 196, 229
Cameronians, 28, 186, 187
Cheshire Regiment, 28, 119, 122, 123, 124, 125, 126, 127, 128, 146, 216, 228
Coldstream Guards, 23, 24, 51, 80, 154, 155, 156, 163, 185, 186, 197, 226, 229, 232
Connaught Rangers, 29, 43, 181
Durham Light Infantry, 28, 56, 190
Devonshire Regiment, 28
Dorsetshire Regiment, 29, 146, 219
Duke of Cornwall's Light Infantry, 28, 37, 57, 58, 109, 124, 146, 232
Duke of Wellington's Regiment, 28, 113, 114, 115, 128, 146, 229

East Kent Regiment (The Buffs), 36, 62, 190
East Lancashire Regiment, 28, 133
East Surrey Regiment, 29, 36, 108, 109, 111, 128, 146, 232
East Yorkshire Regiment, 28, 190
Essex Regiment, 29, 133
Gloucestershire Regiment, 29, 43, 226, 229
Gordon Highlanders, 28, 62, 91, 92, 93, 101, 146, 202, 208, 210, 211, 216, 228
Grenadier Guards, 23, 67, 154, 163, 175, 191, 192, 202, 207, 210, 211, 213
Hampshire Regiment, 29, 147
Highland Light Infantry, 28, 43, 50, 62, 182, 183, 186, 203, 231
Irish Guards, 23, 24, 92, 154
King's Regiment (Liverpool), 28, 43, 62, 229, 230
King's Own Royal Regiment (Lancaster), 28, 133, 140, 141, 147
King's Own Scottish Borderers, 28, 128, 138, 146, 228
King's Own Yorkshire Light Infantry, 28, 49, 111, 112, 113, 114, 128, 138, 144, 145, 146, 203, 216, 233
King's Shropshire Light Infantry, 29
King's Royal Rifle Corps, 27, 188, 221
Lancashire Fusiliers, 28, 62, 133
Leicestershire Regiment, 28, 190
Leinster Regiment, 190
Lincolnshire Regiment, 28, 101, 102, 103, 175, 229
Loyal Regiment (North Lancashire), 28, 43, 226, 227
Manchester Regiment, 28, 124, 128, 138, 142, 143, 146
Middlesex Regiment, 29, 56, 86, 87, 88, 89, 90, 91, 97, 101, 216
North Staffordshire Regiment, 28, 190
Northamptonshire Regiment, 28, 43, 182, 226, 229
Norfolk Regiment, 28, 119, 122, 123, 124, 125, 128, 144, 146
Northumberland Fusiliers, 21, 28, 97, 99, 100, 109, 229
Oxfordshire and Buckinghamshire Light Infantry, 29, 43
Queen's Royal West Surrey Regiment, 29, 36, 39, 43, 60, 161, 197, 202, 203, 205, 213, 218, 221, 222, 223
Rifle Brigade, 27, 133, 189, 190
Royal Berkshire Regiment, 29, 43, 48, 49
Royal Dublin Fusiliers, 29, 133, 147, 149, 150, 151

238